READING THE HOLOCAUST

The events of the Holocaust remain 'unthinkable' to many men and women, as morally and intellectually baffling as they were half a century ago. Inga Clendinnen challenges our bewilderment. She seeks to dispel what she calls the Gorgon effect: the sickening of the imagination and the draining of the will that afflict so many of us when we try to confront the horrors of this history.

Clendinnen explores the experience of the Holocaust from both the victims' and the perpetrators' point of view. She discusses the remarkable survivor testimonies of writers such as Primo Levi and Charlotte Delbo, the vexed issue of 'resistance' in the camps, and strategies for understanding the motivations of the Nazi leadership. She focuses an anthropologist's precise gaze on the actions of the murderers in the police battalions and among the SS in the camps. And she considers how the Holocaust has been portrayed in poetry, fiction, and film.

Searching and eloquent, *Reading the Holocaust* is an uncompromising attempt to extract the comprehensible – the recognizably human – from the unthinkable.

Inga Clendinnen is the author of *Ambivalent Conquests: Spaniard and Maya in Yucatan, 1517–1577* and *Aztecs: An Interpretation,* both published by Cambridge University Press.

READING THE
HOLOCAUST

INGA CLENDINNEN

CAMBRIDGE
UNIVERSITY PRESS

PUBLISHED BY THE PRESS SYNDICATE OF THE UNIVERSITY OF CAMBRIDGE
The Pitt Building, Trumpington Street, Cambridge, United Kingdom

CAMBRIDGE UNIVERSITY PRESS
The Edinburgh Building, Cambridge CB2 2RU, UK
http://www.cup.cam.ac.uk
40 West 20th Street, New York, NY 10011-4211, USA
http://www.cup.org
10 Stamford Road, Oakleigh, Melbourne 3166, Australia

Reprinted 1999

Printed in the United States of America

Typeface Sabon 10.25/13.5 pt.   *System* Penta [BV]

*A catalog record for this book is available from
the British Library.*

Library of Congress Cataloging-in-Publication Data

Clendinnen, Inga.
Reading the Holocaust / Inga Clendinnen.
p. cm.
Includes bibliographical references and index.
1. Holocaust, Jewish (1939–1945) – Historiography. 2. Holocaust,
Jewish (1939–1945) – Personal narratives – History and criticism.
3. Holocaust, Jewish (1939–1945), in literature. I. Title.
D804.348.C54 1999
940.53'18'072 – dc21   98-53636
                                                          CIP
ISBN 0 521 64174 8 hardback
ISBN 0 521 64597 2 paperback

ACKNOWLEDGMENTS
Photographs: Courtesy Jewish Holocaust Museum and Research Centre, Melbourne,
Yad Vashem, Israel, and the Auschwitz Museum, Auschwitz.
The chapter titled 'Representing the Holocaust' was published in the *Michigan Quarterly Review*, Winter, 1998.
The author and publisher wish to thank the following authors and publishers for
permission to reprint copyright material: p. 164, 'Daddy' by Sylvia Plath from *Ariel:
Poems by Sylvia Plath*, Faber and Faber Ltd, London, 1968; p. 165, 'Written in Pencil
in the Sealed Railway-Car' by Dan Pagis from *Points of Departure*, trans. Stephen
Mitchell, Jewish Publication Society, Philadelphia, 1981; p. 167, 'Todesfuge' by Paul
Celan from *Paul Celan: Poet, Survivor, Jew,* John Felstiner, Yale University Press, New
Haven, Conn., 1996; p. 184, 'Could Have' by Wislawa Szymborska from *View with a
Grain of Sand: Selected Poems,* trans. Stanislaw Baranczak and Clare Cavanagh,
Harcourt Brace and Company, New York, 1996.

The hero Perseus undertook to cut off the head of the Gorgon Medusa, half human, half monster, and so hideous that all living creatures turned to stone at the sight of her.

Athene lent the hero her shining bronze shield, and Hermes his winged sandals and curved sword.

Perseus sought out the Gorgon, and found her sleeping.

Holding her reflected image steady in the shield he carried on his left arm, he struck her head from her shoulders.

Even in death the head retained its power to petrify.

Ovid, *Metamorphoses*, Book IV

Alas, to our great grief, we now know all. I spoke to an eyewitness who escaped. He told me everything. They're exterminated in Chelmno, near Dombie, and they are all buried in the Rzuszow forest. The Jews are killed in two ways: by shooting or gas. It's just happened to thousands of Lódz Jews.

Do not think this is being written by a madman.

> Letter from Jacob Schulmann, Rabbi of Grabow Synagogue, to Lódz, 19 January 1942

When all is said and done, a single word, 'understanding', is the beacon light of our studies.

> Marc Bloch, *The Historian's Craft* 1944

ACKNOWLEDGMENTS

I owe thanks to Tony Barta, Betty Burstall, John Cashmere, Colleen Isaac, Sandra Lauderdale Graham, Margaret Holding and Bill Taylor for reading early drafts of the text, to Scarlett Freund for her generous expenditure of moral, intellectual and emotional energy on a later version, and to Alan Frost for rescue at a critical juncture. Much of the text was written on a small island off the coast of North Queensland, remote from metropolitan libraries. Emily Booth, my Woman on the Mainland, met every bibliographic request, however enigmatic, with insight, energy, wit and grace. Frank Smith, editor and friend, made rough places plain.

There are new friends to thank at the Jewish Holocaust Museum and Research Centre in Elsternwick, Melbourne: Ms Saba Feniger, Honorary Curator, for her expert advice and assistance with the photographs, Mr Abraham Goldberg for his help on a related matter, and the ladies of the volunteer staff at the museum, especially Sonia and Marta, for their wisdom, and for the warmth with which they embraced an outsider.

This has been a taxing book both to read for and to write, and I have been a bad companion for its whole duration. Fortunately my husband John's patience, like his good will, seems inexhaustible. I am deeply grateful for both.

Inga Clendinnen, March 1998

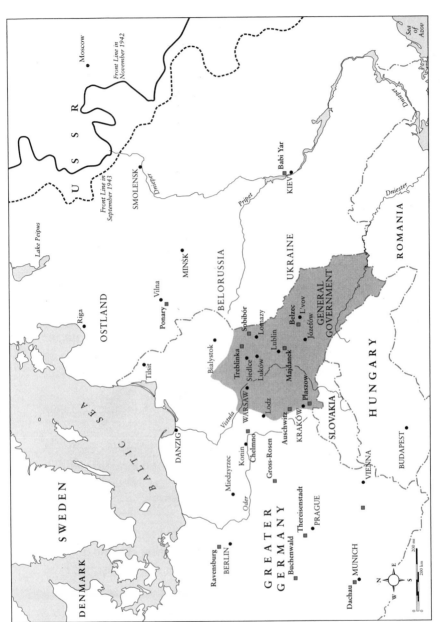

Northeastern Europe under the Nazis, 1942.

BEGINNINGS

I have known about Nazis for as long as I can remember. The outbreak of World War II very nearly coincided with my fifth birthday, and for the next few years I lived in the uneasy dread that the two events were obscurely, fatally, connected: that it was, in an intimate sense, my war. I was especially terrified of Germans, because they clearly gloried in their wickedness: they wore black uniforms, flaunted an insignia of a human skull couched on human bones and unabashedly proclaimed themselves 'Nasties'. At a time when Australia stood in real and present danger from the Japanese, my dreams were full of the stolid minions of the men in black, in their grey uniforms and pudding-bowl hats, invading across the back paddock, through the back gate and into the kitchen to kill us all.

As it turned out, I was not far wrong in my reading of the Nazis. By the time I was twelve I knew that my child's nightmare of the early 1940s had been reality for thousands of people not much more formidable than I, although as a gentile household mine might have been spared. Later, at university, I had friends whose families had been killed by the Nazis, and a few who had survived Nazi concentration camps. I learnt the basic alphabet of those camps: that there were work camps, where the labour of 'enemies of the state' was exploited until they could work no more and were killed; and death camps, where bulging trains arrived to discharge their human cargo directly into the gas chambers. For the first time I heard the word 'ghetto', and understood that the Nazis had re-invented the enclosed Jewish sections of some medieval towns as holding camps for Jews en route to death. I learnt no more from my friends, because they chose to speak no further about these things, and I did not like to ask because I felt myself a child in their company.

Like many of my generation I continued to be attentive to the Holocaust, reading the better-publicised scholarly contributions and witness testimonies as they appeared in translation, watching the better-publicised films and television documentaries. I did this for much the same reasons that I read the memoirs and poems which came out of the trenches of World War I, as a matter of moral and social duty: attention ought be paid to extreme human suffering and we must do what we can to make some human sense out of it.

There was also an element of guilt. These great events brushed my own privileged, uneventful personal history only lightly. While my father fought in the France of the trenches, my brothers were too young for World War II, as were my sons for the small wars which followed it. In this, as in many things, I have been unduly fortunate. I have lived through interesting times, but I have not had to suffer them.

Despite a similarity of motive, the two reading experiences had very different outcomes. In both wars suffering was acute and prolonged, and the deaths counted in millions. The scale of the killings in what was properly named The Great War, along with the use of gas and machines to inflict death and injury at a distance, made nonsense of whatever threadbare military conventions had survived into the twentieth century. There were, nonetheless, vast differences between the piled corpses of World War I and the mass killing of civilians which accompanied its successor.

In 1914–18 the primary victims were soldiers. The German and Allied troops trapped in the trenches were equally victims, with the agents of their predicament partially unwitting and largely elsewhere. While it was made possible by war, the Holocaust was not a war. The harm was done, directly and deliberately, to unarmed, unresisting civilians of all ages and conditions, who had offered their persecutors no injury. One was a bungle, the other a crime.

There was another difference. A lesson was learnt from World War I. A generation of young men learnt to despise old men who told them it was a sweet and fitting thing to die for their country. Through the words of Wilfred Owen and other soldiers, complemented by those of scholars like Paul Fussell and John Keegan, we have come to a reasonably good understanding of life and death in the trenches: how that lethal attrition had come about, how it was for those who survived it, how it might have been for those who died.[1] The Great War is adequately mapped and held in the collective memory.

With the Holocaust I had none of that sense of accumulating comprehension. I read dutifully – and remained unenlightened. And every time I read I would be invaded by a paralysis, a chilled inertia in the face of what seemed an impenetrable monotony of suffering, an impenetrable monotony of cruelties. My childhood nightmare was made real, but no more comprehensible. A classic history like Raul Hilberg's *The Destruction of the European Jews* provided the bony structure of the Holocaust – the events, the main actors, the main decisions – set out with clarity and precision. I could learn who ordered what, how many died in what region, by what method. Forceful interpretations of motives were offered. But I still could not comprehend it. I could not frame the kinds of questions that would let me make the human connections – connections with both perpetrators and victims – which lie at the root of all purposeful inquiry. The repetitive cruelties, the blank anguish of pain and despair, remained indecipherable. And this for events of little more than fifty years ago.

I felt guilt about my bafflement because I suspected its origins: that it arose because my reading of the Holocaust had been no more than dutiful; that I had refused full imaginative engagement. I had felt a similar repugnance before. I had circled the Aztecs of Mexico for years before I decided to write about them, because I was unwilling to commit myself to the full pursuit of a people for whom the ritualised killing of humans was, in some seasons, a daily event. A decade of reading and thinking later, I thought I at least understood what the Aztecs had been up to.[2] The horror roused by the Holocaust was more intimate, more inchoate, and more comprehensively disabling. I suspected a failure of nerve. And when illness forced me to abandon university employment and a long-term research project, I knew I had been given the opportunity, rare among academics, to do some concentrated reading and thinking in an area not my own.

Therefore these essays. I am nervous about them. Like most historians, I prefer to stay snug inside my own field, a familiar territory populated by Aztec priests and warriors, Mayan peasant-sages, Spanish clerics and conquerors. Encroaching onto unfamiliar territory – especially this territory, so jealously guarded – is an anxious business, lacking as I do the local languages, local connections and local knowledge of the terrain.

Reading as an outsider, I am writing for outsiders. While I will discuss films, photographs and documentaries, my main focus is on books. Over the last decades the Yad Vashem Research Institute in Israel and the Fortunoff Archive at Yale University have been collecting filmed interviews from Holocaust survivors. As I write, more interviews are being recorded by the Shoah Foundation in my home city of Melbourne. That material will surely expand our understanding when we find ways to exploit it, but for the moment books remain our chief source of information and our surest, most accessible and most democratic medium of communication.

Writing as a reader and not as a scholar, I have read only a fraction of the Holocaust literature available in English, which is itself only a fraction of the literature available in Yiddish, Hebrew, German, Polish, Hungarian, Dutch and other languages. The books I discuss are those which proved their value by providing me with the system of ladders I needed to scramble out over the abyss. They are also accessible to the general reader and likely to be available in any good library. I have sampled current scholarly opinion by way of two recent collections of conference papers, each wide-ranging, each sophisticated, each pivoting around the question of understanding the Holocaust, and each confirming that fifty years after their occurrence, the events of the Holocaust remain for some of their most dedicated students as morally and intellectually baffling, as 'unthinkable', as they were at their first rumouring.[3]

The primary aim of these essays is to challenge that bafflement, and the demoralisation which attends it. I want to dispel the 'Gorgon effect' – the sickening of imagination and curiosity and the draining of the will which afflicts so many of us when we try to look squarely at the persons and processes implicated in the Holocaust. I want to arrive at a clearer understanding of at least some of those persons and processes to be confident that the whole is potentially understandable. This is not a matter of arriving at some 'Aha! now I comprehend everything!' theory or moment. The understanding I seek comes from framing sufficiently precise questions to be able to see exactly what is before us, whether persons or processes. It is both cumulative, and never complete.

I write as a general reader who also happens to be a historian (the historian is to blame for the footnotes). I have not tried to keep the voices separate. They have been too long married for easy divorce. These are essays in the strict sense of the word – personal explorations along self-made paths, not progressions down the well-signed highways of academic scholarship. I have written neither for specialists nor for those for whom the Holocaust was a lived actuality, but for perplexed outsiders like myself, who believe with me that such perplexity is dangerous. In the face of a catastrophe on this scale so deliberately inflicted, perplexity is an indulgence we cannot afford.

2

IMPEDIMENTS

By the spring of 1942, when the 'Final Solution' in Europe was just getting underway, two million Russian prisoners of war were already dead, some by shooting, most from exposure and starvation.[1] Of the estimated five and a half million Russian soldiers who lived long enough to reach German prisoner-of-war camps, just over a million survived the war. The struggle with Germany cost the Soviet Union more than twenty millions of its people, a figure far too huge to be comprehended.[2] Poland lost nearly as many Gentiles as it did Jews, although almost all its Jews were destroyed.

It remains true that the Holocaust was a peculiarly Jewish tragedy. In the immediate aftermath of conquest Germans killed Russian and Polish civilians casually, and their leaders very deliberately. These killings were carried out for pragmatic political motives – to be rid of the burden of prisoners, to destroy a future generation of enemies, to increase German living space. The victims' compatriots were permitted to live, if only as potential slaves for the Thousand Year Reich. In the Nazi hierarchy these were indubitably inferior peoples, but they were not by definition enemies of humankind. It was the Jewish Question to which the death camps were the Final Solution.

THE GYPSIES: FORGETTING

Only one other group was nominated for extinction. The Nazis began their attack on the Gypsies before their attack on the Jews. In 1933 Gypsies were defined as natural-born criminals, and therefore subject to laws against 'social deviants', while some were being involuntarily sterilised under the Law for the Prevention of Hereditarily Diseased figured; part of the long argument they were conducting with their god. They took comfort from the promise that while individuals and groups might suffer persecution or even death, the Jews as a people would surely survive. As the intensity and ambition of Nazi actions were revealed, these beliefs became untenable. It was clear that present horror dwarfed ancient myth, and the archetype was being forged within our own time: Apocalypse Now. Yet the theological struggle to comprehend the Holocaust as an episode in an enigmatic deity's intentions regarding his chosen people continues to shadow putatively secular debate. For as long as the Holocaust resists integration into a Jewish mythic framework, the key questions for many people, not all of them Jews, will lie in the zones of the theological and the metaphysical.[6]

One consequence is that it is a constant task for the secular reader to distinguish speculations about metaphysical significances from this-earthly issues. That is not always an easy matter, given the seductive power of elevated language. What is certain is that language matters. Elie Cohen, a Dutch survivor, argues that all these victim-oriented terms blur responsibility, and insists on the German *Endlösung der Judenfrage*, on the excellent grounds that 'Germans planned and carried out the murder of the Jews, [that] the correspondence and the orders were written in the German language, [that] in every other language they lose their aim and sharpness'.[7]

IMPLICATIONS OF PERSONAL CONNECTION

There is another more delicate influence which works to discourage the outside investigator. The newcomer to Holocaust studies will notice how often books and articles declare the writer's personal relationship with people who died in the camps. This is a natural and moving declaration of a particular tender interest. Some analysts are themselves survivors, which not only lends a peculiar poignancy to their writings, but quite properly increases their authority as commentators: 'being there' matters. They know the taste and texture of daily experience which no one working from records can ever know. They also know how they endured the camps – and will then face the vast problem of communicating that experiential knowledge. It is also true that writing history is always a personal business: for better or worse we can only speak in our own voice. Standards of evidence and inference, however, do not depend on point of view. It is therefore imperative that the roles of witness and of analyst be held separate; that there be no slide from potentially demonstrable intellectual to ascribed, untestable moral authority.[8]

The Holocaust was a Jewish tragedy. Every Jew, however slight their attachment to Jewish religion and tradition, must be powerfully impressed and threatened by it. It is nonetheless the Gentiles' crime and the Gentiles' problem, because Gentiles conceived it, and Gentiles carried it out.

'Good' history depends on the commitment to seek to understand human action in the past by the critical evaluation of sources and the disciplined procedures of the analyst, whoever she or he may be, or at least as close as we can manage it. Any other criterion – right gender, right ethnicity, right skin-colour, right class, right personal history – risks locking us into a tribalism that destroys (along with a lot of other things) even the possibility of comprehending the movement of the past.

The greatest difficulty for any reader is to keep one's critical balance in face of this material. Even reduced to marks on paper it is profoundly disturbing, exacting sleepless nights, darkening days. Powerful responses of guilt, anger, fear and remorse should and do attend its reading. Among the handful of photographs rescued from the murderers there is one in which a small girl of perhaps seven walks a little behind the remnants of a family group: a burdened woman, bundle under her arm, two smaller children in hand. The girl may or may not be attached to them. She walks alone, head slightly bent, shoulders hunched against the cold. Above too-large shoes her bare legs look thin and fragile, but she is walking resolutely, with a slight air of independence. Girls of that age value independence. I cannot easily bear to look at that photograph. Had she lived, she would be an old woman by now. As it is, she is forever my grand-daughter, trudging towards death in shoes too big for her.

THE ISSUE OF UNIQUENESS

It must be cruel work for those who read and reflect with known and loved faces before them, and I respect their courage. It is the more puzzling that scholars sometimes seem to enmesh themselves in abstract issues, and so deflect attention away from individual experience. The continuing argument between scholars both secular and religious as to whether the Holocaust constitutes an event unique in European (even in world) history usefully focuses attention on particular characteristics of the events, but the discussion easily leaks in one of two directions; either tempting us to regard the Holocaust as no more than the worst pogrom in Jewish history, or to declare it unique in human history because it is unique in Jewish history. Elie Wiesel, perhaps the most widely read writer on the Holocaust, assumes the natural dominance of the metaphysical over the historical: 'The universality of the Holocaust must be realised in its uniqueness. Remove the Jews from the Holocaust, and the Event loses its mystery.'[9]

Eberhard Jäckel has devised what is probably the most satisfying summary definition of Holocaust uniqueness: 'The Nazi extermination of the Jews was unique because never before had a state, under the responsible authority of its leader, decided and announced that a specific group of human beings, including the old, the women, the children, and the infants, would be killed to the very last one, and implemented this decision with all the means at its disposal.'[10] Hannah Arendt extends Jäckel with her splendidly stabilising judgment that 'the supreme crime [of] the physical extermination of the Jewish people was a crime against humanity, perpetrated on the body of the Jewish people, and that only the choice of victims, not the nature of the crime, could be derived from the long history of Jew-hatred and anti-Semitism'. Here Arendt is challenging the assumption of Eichmann's Israeli prosecutors that the Nazi attack on the Jews was 'not the most recent of crimes, the unprecedented crime of genocide, but, on the contrary, the oldest crime they knew and remembered' – the crime of pogrom.[11]

Saul Friedländer gallantly attempts to further refine the singularity of the Holocaust:

What turns the 'Final Solution' into an event at the limits [of understanding and of representation] is the very fact that it is the most radical form of genocide encountered in history: the wilful, systematic, industrially organised, largely successful attempt totally to exterminate an entire human group within twentieth-century Western society. In Jürgen Habermas' words:

'There [in Auschwitz] something happened, that up to now nobody considered even possible. There one touched on something which represents the deep layer of solidarity among all that wears a human face; notwithstanding all the usual acts of beastliness in human history, the integrity of this common layer had been taken for granted . . . Auschwitz has changed the basis for the continuity of the conditions of life within history.'[12]

A devastating assessment, if agreed to. The words have been carefully chosen: these issues are protean, as the protagonists well know. The claim is that during those years something had happened of a kind which had never before happened; that those events were unprecedented. And we are immediately uncomfortable. Surely all situations are unprecedented? We remember, vaguely, with guilt for our vagueness, long-ago torturings and sackings, slaughters and annihilations; small scale, perhaps, but terrible for those engulfed by them, and as systematic and comprehensive as contemporary technology allowed. Or is the tacit assumption that both the 'historical continuities' we most care about, and that 'deep layer of [human] solidarity', are the peculiar properties of 'twentieth-century Western society'?

COMPARISONS

Either way, the position is an awkward one. To claim the durability of such solidarity until the fourth decade of the twentieth century is to take a large way with earlier times. Human history being what it is, there has been a lot of beastliness about. Consider the Aztecs of Mexico, a people in whom I take a special interest. The Aztec state forced men, women and children from subject settlements out of their homes, away from their familiar territories and along unfamiliar roads, to parade them through jubilant, jeering crowds into holding camps within the Aztec imperial city. There a chosen few were decked in gorgeous regalias, fed mind-dazzling drugs and forced to dance as gods before they died under the knives of blood-drenched priests. Most of the prisoners – thousands annually – were stripped to slave dress and chivvied in shuffling queues up the stone stairways of the Great Pyramid to the killing stones which crowned it. So great was the slaughter that the last victims had to take their last steps through a slow tide of congealing blood.

The processing, while not 'industrialised', was technically as sleek as Aztec ingenuity could devise. On such occasions men, women and children died; families were broken up; infants were strangled as they were carried wailing though the streets. These victims were also innocent, or guilty only of being non-Aztec. They also were terrorised by gruesome rumour and jeeringly told their fate before they suffered it. And for them, too, there was no hope of escape. These herdings and stabbings and stranglings occurred five hundred years ago, before America felt the withering touch of Europe. Does that exclude them from our concern?

It is true that the Aztec enterprise could not properly be labelled 'genocide'. They had no desire to extirpate their subjugated peoples, but only to crop them. We know that many of the Jewish families and communities seized and murdered by the Nazis had no opportunity to comprehend the generality of their fate: in this assault, all Jews would die. How many of the millions of murdered Jews understood that they were murdered because they were Jews? Did the Gypsies know they were the victims of genocide? 'Genocide' defines the perpetrators' intentions and is highly relevant to understanding their motives and assessing their guilt – but is it of much moment to the victims as they face their own deaths and the deaths of all those they love?

The Aztecs' victims did not die because they were considered to be less than human, but precisely because the Aztecs believed in that 'deep layer of solidarity among all that wears a human face'. It was this belief that led them to offer the blood and hearts and lives of non-Aztec humans as pledges against their own and humanity's common debt to the gods.[13] It is possible that the recognition of underlying fellowship made some difference, at some level of experience, including the victims' own – but how much? And how are we to tell?

There had been scant indication of 'human solidarity' in Europe's energetic claiming and clearing of non-European lands for European occupation, or in the repopulation and working of those lands with variously labelled but universally brutal forms of slave labour.[14] When Vasco da Gama returned to Indian Calicut with a great force in 1502 he had his men board the ships in the harbour and mutilate the sailors they managed to capture by cutting off their noses, ears and hands, which were sent to the local ruler 'suggesting he might like to make curry with the pieces'.[15] This is the kind of exercise which appears in textbook shorthand as 'establishing European authority'. It seems eccentric, not to say ethnocentric, to cancel from consideration other notorious Western doings unto largely non-Western others which preceded, accompanied and have succeeded the Holocaust, and which were and are certainly systematic, if not much talked about. Did any of these concerted actions amount to genocide? Surely some did, as do some in process now?[16] Surely now, as I write, we continue to bear with tolerable equanimity not only the prospect but the actuality of the wanton killing of neighbour by neighbour, for no crime beyond ethnic affiliation?

There have been too many recent horrors, in Rwanda, in Burundi, in one-time Yugoslavia, with victims equally innocent, killers and torturers equally devoted, to ascribe uniqueness to any one set of atrocities on the grounds of their exemplary cruelty. I find the near-random terror practised by the Argentinian military, especially their penchant for torturing children before their parents, to be as horrible, as 'unimaginable', as the horrible and unimaginable things done by Germans to their Jewish compatriots. Certainly the scale is different – but how much does scale matter to the individual perpetrator or the individual victim? Again, the wilful obliteration of long-enduring communities is surely a vast offence, but for three years we watched the carpet-bombings of Cambodia, when the bombs fell on villagers who could not have had the least understanding of the nature of their offence. When we think of innocence afflicted, we see those unforgettable children of the Holocaust staring wide-eyed into the cameras of their killers, but we also see the image of the little Vietnamese girl, naked, screaming, running down a dusty road, her back aflame with American napalm. If we grant that 'Holocaust', the total consumption of offerings by fire, is sinisterly appropriate for the murder of those millions who found their only graves in the air, it is equally appropriate for the victims of Hiroshima, Nagasaki and Dresden. Picasso's *Guernica*, with its horses and humans screaming under attack from untouchable murderers in the sky, could astonish and outrage when it was unveiled in 1937. By 1945 – by 1995 – it had lost its power to shock.

The notion of 'genocide' – to me, thinking most easily in terms of individuals – is a difficult one to grasp. Is the guilt attaching to the intention to destroy a whole people, regardless of the variables of local culture and circumstance, even of subjective identification (some died who did not believe themselves to be Jews), different in kind from the intention to kill an equal number of individuals? Does the crime of 'genocide' inhabit a moral category of its own? Perhaps it does. And while the scope of the intention of the murderers may not directly affect the experience of the victims, its emotional content may well express itself in the infliction of phobic cruelties and humiliations before death, as was so often done to Jews.

Perhaps what most distinguished the perpetrators of the Holocaust was not their weirdly archaic ambition – the annihilation of whole peoples and the systematic enslavement of others for the greater glory of a third – but their very modern capacity to fulfil that ambition, a capacity demonstrated by the terrifying speed and scope of their success. In a wave of 'secret' mass murders, the population profile of central Europe was permanently altered in less than a year. Centuries-old communities were obliterated. While transfers and annihilations of populations were not new (consider only the devastations of Greek and Turkish populations during the long death agony of the Turkish empire), devastation effected on such a scale must carry a special awe.

It is also true that the idea of the gas chambers outrages our feelings in a way which the mass shootings, with all their brutality, do not. I confess I am puzzled to understand the sentiment, even as I share it. The Nazis also recognised this repulsiveness: while the shootings in the east were something of an open secret, much energy was expended on keeping the extermination centres and the gas chambers hidden from outsiders, and then, when their use was past, on destroying all physical evidence of their existence. Gitta Sereny comments:

... among [Hitler's] murders of millions – Orthodox, Catholic and Lutheran Christians, Gypsies and Jews – it was the killing of the Jews in the gas chambers of occupied Poland which struck deepest into the conscience and remained in the consciousness of the world. It is the one action which those who admired Hitler fifty years ago, and those whose nationalist and racist aims today resemble and indeed are modelled on his, are desperate to deny.[17]

Our revulsion does not rest on the quantum of anguish suffered by the victims of the gas. Some of the people delivered to Treblinka or to Auschwitz-Birkenau realised their fate only in the 'undressing rooms', while others entered the killing chambers apparently still deceived.

From the evidence of their corpses, we know that their last moments in the gas were terrible. But was the manner of their dying more terrible than that of the men, women and children routed from their dwellings, beaten, abused and humiliated, made to wait through long hours in the knowledge of imminent death, and then forced to walk naked to the pits, and to the guns? It is difficult to measure their suffering, especially when they had children whom they were helpless to protect. I think it is rather the revelation, implicit in the existence of the gas chambers, of the premeditation, the ruthlessness of intention, the 'cold-bloodedness' of those who conceived, organised and built the death factories which confounds us. It is one thing to read the speeches expounding such policies. It is quite another to see those policies realised in railway timetables, in concrete, wood and metal, in guards with whips and clubs. The gas chambers force us to recognise what we are looking at: factories designed by humans solely to produce human death swiftly, on a grand scale, and with all the material by-products frugally, efficiently, exploited.

What most disquiets about a too-shrill insistence on the uniqueness of the Holocaust is the danger that, if the Holocaust were indeed to be accepted as unique, it would risk falling out of history – the consultable record of the actions of our species, and the active interrogation of that record – altogether. That is something we cannot afford. We need to know both ourselves and the worlds we are capable of making if we can hope to change any part of either.

UNDERSTANDING LARGE EVENTS

There remains another issue, at once larger and deeper. In a melancholy essay Saul Friedländer records a melancholy fact. While 'the reconstruction of the most detailed sequences of events related to the extermination of the Jews is progressing apace . . . an opaqueness remains at the very core of the historical understanding and interpretation of what happened'. This sense of bafflement afflicts some of the ablest analysts who will admit to a 'feeling of incomprehension', an 'unease in historical understanding', in the face of this great matter.

Friedländer's analysis of the reasons behind this uncomfortable condition is at once ambitious, complex, compacted and tentative, which makes its reduction to propositions difficult, but these are important matters, so I must test the reader's patience for a time.

For Friedländer the how of the Final Solution – those reconstructions of 'detailed sequences of events' – is already sufficiently clear. The problems lie with the why. One is the lack of agreement on an appropriate 'global historical interpretation' under which these events could be subsumed. For instance, we may choose to represent the events located under the heading 'The Industrial Revolution' as exemplifications of and as episodes within a grand narrative like 'The History of the Class Struggle', or 'The March towards Social Enlightenment'. The 'Final Solution' finds no place within such larger narratives. Friedländer asks, 'Does an event like the "Final Solution" allow for *any kind* of narrative, or does it foreclose certain narrative modalities? Does it perhaps escape the grasp of a plausible narrative altogether?'[18]

My own view is that the quest for global interpretations and grand narratives is always a mistaken one, assuming a shapeliness in human affairs and a simplicity of human motivation never encountered in muddy actuality. Nowadays no one much hankers for the panoramic view of where we all were and where we are all going once offered by Marxism or Whiggism, or the more obscure and even less testable stories and metaphors psychoanalysts offer to explain our darker private obsessions. Large theories may generate good questions, but they produce poor answers. The historian's task is to discover what happened in some actual past situation – what conflicting or confused intentions produced what outcomes – not to produce large truths. The most enlightening historical generalisations tend to be those that hover sufficiently close to the ground to illuminate the contours and dynamics of intention and action in circumscribed circumstances.

In place of consensus we have a prolonged, uneasy debate around the question: is the Holocaust unique? Or is it an extravagant example of some established category of deliberate mass killings? It is clear that there is an unusually good case for labelling The Final Solution – the Holocaust viewed not from the victims' but from the perpetrators' perspective – as a unitary phenomenon, an Event. The Industrial Revolution may have happened without its many protagonists having much grasp of what was going on, and even World War I, with apublicly acknowledged beginning and end, was for much of its duration a makeshift affair of opportunistic tactics and shifting, failed or stalled strategies. By contrast, the Final Solution was a program slowly formulated in the minds of those who were to direct it before its implementation – and then implemented with terrifying single-mindedness. It was also larger than its parts, in that we must be aware of the scope and speed of its events to measure the immensity of the killers' malice, and to comprehend the bewilderment and terror of its victims, helpless before the juggernaut.

However, as Peter Haidu has reminded us, 'a historical event, though we speak of it in the singular, consists of a configuration of traits which together make up the event's uniqueness. Its components . . . could not be recognised were they not available in the remaining repertoire of human existence'.[19] My own conviction is that our sense of Holocaust uniqueness (and we do have that sense) resides in the fact that these ferocious, largely secret killings were perpetrated within 'twentieth-century Western society', and that both our sense of portent and of the peculiar intransigence of these actions before puny human interpretation find their ground in the knowledge that they were conceived, executed and endured by people very like ourselves.

It is not that this material stands too far from us. It stands too near. We do not easily imagine ourselves Aztecs or Rwandans or, for that matter, Serbian or Croatian farmers. We do recognise ourselves as very like urban Europeans of five or six decades ago: people who looked like us, lived like us, who had like us come to assume the reliability of physical and emotional comfort, with death tamed to a distant prospect. Add to this our indebtedness to individual Jewish thinkers, musicians and artists whose features and whose minds are known to us, who have become precious to us, and their jeopardy becomes our own. Gypsies are absent from our imaginings of the Holocaust, and absent from 'the vivid photo library of Nazi imagery that we helplessly house in our heads', because they are too obviously 'other'.[20] We feel pity and guilt for them, as we do for the rest of the Holocaust's great dark mass of victims, but the persecutor-victim images caught on the page which most transfix us, which make our hearts shrivel, are those that represent ourselves become not ourselves. It is this most direct threat to our confidence in our own personal integrity which lies at the heart of the Gorgon effect.

The point is economically signalled in the Costa Gavras film, *The*

Music Box. The film's action centres on the trial in the United States in the late 1980s of a man accused of having perpetrated atrocities in Hungary in 1944–45. A quietly dressed woman, reserved in manner as middle-class European women tend to be, is in the witness box. She is saying incredible things, things she seems to find incredible herself even as she is saying them, about the vile and most carnal connection there had been, one dreadful day, between herself and the impassive old man seated opposite her.

Her listeners are outraged by what they are hearing; they are angry, or they weep. But they are also bewildered. They know that what they are hearing is true. It remains, nonetheless, incredible. Imagination makes its accustomed leap – and falls. The difficulty does not lie in the representation: the woman's words are all too graphic. It is we, the listeners, who recoil, who are baffled, who are at both an imaginative and a cognitive loss. The condition is not induced by the distancing effect of film, or by our baulking at manipulation by fabricators. We are persuaded of the truth of her words. It is just that we cannot believe them.

Existential incredulity persists into ordinary life. One sunstruck summer day a small tanned woman in shirt and shorts gathered apples for me in her orchard. She was worrying about caterpillar holes in the apples, worrying because it was hot and I had forgotten my hat. For me the silence behind the talk was deafening. I knew that she had survived Auschwitz, that she had conceived a child just before she was taken there, that her pregnancy had been noticed, but that she had been able to scramble aboard a truck taking female prisoners to work in a flax factory, where a baby was born to her just before the war's end. I knew it, but I could not comprehend it, of this small kind woman in her orchard, worrying about caterpillars. I was discovering that the recognition of 'likeness' in face of different and dissonant knowledge paralyses rather than liberates imagination.

There is a major mystery about understanding. It must begin with sympathy – the recognition of a shareable human condition. But sympathy is inadequate for me to understand the past experience of my friend, and even less adequate to understand those who tormented her. Intuitive flashes of 'empathy', possible only when experience is closely shared, are no less dubious, because they are untestable and may simply be wrong. (Consider, for example, the variability of response within an apparently homogenous group of women to the experience of giving birth.)

In my view understanding can best be advanced by unglamorous techniques we use every day for the evaluation of gossip. These are the same techniques used by biographers and historians: the piecing together of contexts, the establishing of sequences of actions, the inferring of the likely intentions behind those actions from our knowledge of the individuals involved and our general stock of knowledge about human motivations. What distinguishes this laborious and inherently contestable process from the lightning flash of intuition is that it is at all points open to scrutiny, criticism and correction.

If Perseus in his winged sandals could hover in the air, we must keep our feet on the ground. But as even the light-footed Perseus discovered, the only way to destroy the Gorgon is to begin by holding her reflected image squarely in one's shield – and then to stare steadily back.

As usual, prescription is easy and execution difficult. There can be no naive documentation coming out of the Holocaust: none of the detritus of the everyday which provides much of the historian's usual meat. For the perpetrators, these were actions swiftly conceived, furiously executed – and designated secret. In that context, each document must be squeezed for everything it can yield. Consider, for example, Raul Hilberg's brilliant reconstruction from commonplace and apparently innocent railway timetables, with their scrupulously aseptic language, of the map and the temporal process of mass murder.

The most immediate block to a practised, professional scepticism is not cognitive but emotional, and manifests itself as a sense of trespass. Already precious by virtue of their rarity, the witness testimonies can seem imbued with an air of unchallengeable authority. They appear as immutable as icons – but icons opening not onto heaven, but to hell. We who would learn from them are therefore faced with what I shall call the problem of transcendence.

TRESPASS AND TRANSCENDENCE

Elie Wiesel has famously asserted that 'the truth of Auschwitz remains hidden in its ashes. Only those who lived it in their flesh and in their minds can possibly transform their experience into knowledge. Others, despite their best intentions, can never do so.' For Wiesel only the survivors may speak, because 'no one who has not experienced the event will ever be able to understand it'.[21] A similar warning is signalled by the subtitle given the Yad Vashem Holocaust memorial in Jerusalem, with its great collection of witness testimonies, the 'Heroes and Martyrs Remembrance Authority'. The implication is that the only possible and proper stance for the observer is one of awed incomprehension.

If that is true it is a threat to us all, as abominations seem to multiply, as our reservoirs of shared metaphors for the systematic and serious discussion of human affairs beyond the narrowly personal are running dry. It is a particular threat to historians, who are committed to the quixotic notion that the human actions of the past are sufficiently amenable to retrieval, analysis and interpretation to generate useable truths for the present, and that no part of the human record can be declared off-limits. Therefore, while we respect the sentiment and recognise the grounds for Wiesel's position, we must deny the conclusion, because the doing of history, our ongoing conversation with the dead, rests on the critical evaluation of all the voices coming from the past, on our reconstruction of the circumstances of their speaking, and on our critical evaluation of our own 'natural' unexamined responses to those voices. We know that the words of survivors of the Holocaust have come to us through a formidable act of will, written by those fortunate enough to be able to write of their experiences, and gallant enough to do so. The poignancy is real – as is our duty to analyse both the poignancy, and the writings.

ASSESSING WITNESS TESTIMONY: FILIP MÜLLER

As an example of the difficulties in assessing witness testimony, consider Filip Müller's account of his time of service in the Auschwitz *Sonderkommando*, or 'Special Squad'. Müller had come to Auschwitz with the first Slovak convoy on 20 April 1942 (his camp number was 29136). He survived the camp and the disruptions of liberation to become 'the oldest member of the Auschwitz and Birkenau *Sonderkommando* and the only one to have lived through everything'.[22]

The *Sonderkommando* was the name given the team of prisoners, nearly all of them Jews, who supplied the labour to keep the Auschwitz-Birkenau gas chambers and the crematoria running – shepherding victims into the chambers or manhandling them to the execution pits, and disposing of the corpses afterwards. There were no volunteers in the *Sonderkommando*. Men were picked out from the camp or the arrival platform for their brawn or (as in Müller's case) some small infraction of discipline, and put to their loathsome work. They were also under sentence of death, it being SS practice to kill and replace all members of a squad every few months in the interest of secrecy. For the same reason they were allowed no contact with the rest of the camp.

Müller wrote his story in two stages. In 1945 or 1946 he set down a brief account for two ex-prisoners who devoted their first years of freedom to compiling an archive of detailed information on the camps, collecting maps and drawings from ex-inmates, as well as names and places in the prisoner hierarchy and all the personal information they could garner, as if they were out to reverse the whole clanking Nazi machinery designed to depersonalise their victims. They also had their contributors sign their work both with their name and their camp number, so reclaiming their whole past as constitutive of their identity.

Twenty years later this rough-hewn, magnificent work was translated from Czech into English and published under the title *The Death Factory: Document on Auschwitz*. Later Müller explored his memory again as he prepared his testimony for the 'Auschwitz Trial' at Frankfurt in 1964. It was only after that experience – and in the knowledge of a rising tide of popular interest in matters relating to the Holocaust – that he sought out not only a translator but a 'literary collaborator' to assist him in preparing a manuscript for publication in English and German in 1979.[23] That work was *Auschwitz Inferno: The Testimony of a Sonderkommando*, or, in the United States, *Eyewitness Auschwitz: Three Years in the Gas Chambers*.

Vivid, vigorous, the memoir documents the closed world of the undressing rooms, the gas chambers, the crematoria and the burning pits. Müller's position made him the custodian of crucial information: he knew how the Jews murdered at Auschwitz had met their deaths. That knowledge was of immeasurable importance to many, especially to those whose closest kin had died there. In his foreword to the 1979 English translation Yehuda Bauer, a distinguished Holocaust scholar, wrote: 'Filip Müller's book is a unique document indeed: it is the testimony of the only man who saw the Jewish people die and lived to tell what he saw . . . He saw a civilisation being destroyed by devils in ordinary, human form. He not only saw the martyrs, but also spoke to Satan.' Bauer concluded: 'this unembellished telling is a terrible accusation against God and humanity'.[24]

Historians are made restless by metaphysical talk of devils, martyrs and Satan. They would certainly prick their ears at the assertion that Müller's was an 'unembellished telling'. Even honest eyewitnesses can sometimes get things wrong, and not all eyewitnesses are honest, or not all the time. Müller, who wrote vividly and well without assistance, had taken the trouble to seek the services of a literary collaborator. He was clearly interested in a market. His potential readership was of grieving people. Might not that influence his telling? I suspect the collaborator's hand in the use of the convention of dramatic direct-speech reportage for long public speeches from the SS and, more remarkably and rather less plausibly, for the responses from their victims. The collaborator may also be responsible for the book's expert structuring, from the high-impact drama of the opening scene to the skillful placement of 'uplifting' episodes through a grim and otherwise unrelenting narrative of atrocities. Time and again, after gruelling descriptions of gas-chamber killings – descriptions which can be broadly authenticated from other sources – the reader is comforted by notably less well-authenticated scenes of defiance and/or faith.

On the night of 8 March 1944 the members of the 'Czech family camp' were gassed. We know that the Czechs displayed extraordinary dignity – that they sang their national anthem and the Jewish 'Hatikva' before they entered the chamber – because several witnesses have told us so. Scepticism stirs when Müller goes on to tell of his own frustrated attempt to die in the gas along with his compatriots. He claims he was dissuaded by the intervention of 'a few girls, naked and in the full bloom of youth', who begged him to live so that he might memorialise their deaths. One of the girls is Yana, who sends a tender message to her lover and arranges for Müller to take a necklace from her corpse to give to him. Müller fulfils the mission, claiming he finds her body without difficulty because it lay just where he had left her.

Yana's story is, in Bauer's words, 'perhaps the most poignant story of any Holocaust testimony'. But is it believable? We know what typically happened when Zyklon B gas was released – the rush and clamber for air, the packing and piling of bodies, all in total darkness. Would she have died where he left her? It may be true. Extraordinary things happened in Auschwitz, as in every camp. But it is also true that in any other context I would challenge Müller and some of his death-chamber stories on the ground of implausibility. I would do this the more readily because he also provides a version of another story which was a ubiquitous myth in the camps about the heroic defiance of a young dancer, whose defiance he implies he witnessed.

The core narrative of the dancer myth tells of a beautiful young woman (on the unloading platform or in the undressing room – the location varies) ordered by an SS man to dance. In some accounts she is first made to strip. She dances up to her persecutor, snatches his gun and shoots him. This story, with minor variations – the girl's nationality, the venue, the precise sequence of action – was told in many of the camps, and became a cherished legend, bringing hope and comfort to thousands who found small hope elsewhere: one of their number had defied their oppressors.[25] The Yana story is in that tradition. I do not think that Müller was 'lying', but rather that the story slowly flowered in his mind, growing out of smaller actual moments in the undressing room, and his own terrible inability to intervene.

This is also the difficulty of accurately recalling desperate situations long after the event. The problem is succinctly presented by Philip Roth in his account of John 'Ivan the Terrible' Demjanjuk's trial in Israel in 1988. Eliahu Rosenberg, the key prosecution witness – key because he had confidently identified the man in the dock as 'Ivan' – was unexpectedly recalled by the defence to be confronted with his own written testimony of 1945 in which he related the events of the Treblinka uprising of 2 August 1943. There he had given what appeared to be an eyewitness account of Ivan's death. Ivan, he wrote, had been struck on the head by a shovel by one of the rebels and killed.

An abashed Rosenberg tried to explain that 'this is how it was told to me in the forest', where he and his panicky, triumphant comrades had taken brief refuge after the revolt. Desperately wanting and need-ing the story to be true, visualising it, exulting in it, they made it true, and took necessary courage from it. Later, they knew they had de-ceived themselves. But how to explain how it had been for them in the forest outside Treblinka in the August heat of 1943 to a court in Israel in 1988?[26]

Am I making too much of the possibility that a few harmless fantasies which could bring comfort to thousands might lurk in Müller's text? No, because the critical evaluation of texts ('may I accept this? must I reject that?') stands at the heart of the historical enterprise. Some of Müller's stories of death bravely, gravely or defiantly met are confirmed by others. The whole memoir remains indispensable because he provides the most detailed account we have of the Auschwitz *Sonderkommando* at work. We judge we can rely on his account of that work because it is both plausible and internally coherent, and because many of its details are corroborated from elsewhere. On some matters it provides our only illumination into the darker corners in that dark place, the working life of the Auschwitz *Sonderkommando*. Nonetheless, all sections of this rare and precious text must be assayed against the standard measures of evidence.

The Müller example brings into focus a major difficulty in reading witness testimony: how to assess it without piety.[27] Something of the same transcendental effect envelops the handful of photographs saved from destruction at the end of the war. The best known are those taken after the opening of the German camps like Belsen and Buchenwald, which received the human wreckage from camps within and beyond Germany who were then left to rot. The photographs taken by the appalled liberators present gaunt creatures never before imagined; creatures who seem more animated anatomical exhibits than human – until we look into their eyes. There we see humanity distilled. Usually we can stare at pictured eyes with impunity as they gaze from the frame as if through a window. These eyes are different. They lock on ours. They accuse us of living ignorantly, comfortably, while they were dying.

There is a decent and natural tendency to drop our glance and to defer to those eyes, as there is to defer to any words that might come from those dry lips. We know as we look that our experience cannot encompass theirs. We know that we cannot pretend to 'understand' with the intimacy of familiar experience either these ghosts or the people who brought them to their condition. The experiences of Holocaust victims and the actions of their persecutors stand at one extreme of the continuum which begins with the familiar and extends to the profoundly strange. It is, however, a continuum, and understanding is always difficult. After all, we cannot fully understand even intimates, although in moments of self-delusion we may like to think we do.

There are other lesser difficulties. We cannot easily compare across testimonies, because every survivor testimony, however similar to others it may appear, is unique. While generically similar, every camp changed through time, and every prisoner's situation and station within the camp was both distinctive and always changing. To the outsider 'Auschwitz' is a single, monstrous reality. The actual Auschwitz was a sprawling complex of hundreds of acres containing many separate camps. In the barracks and huts of that vast conglomerate each prisoner, as Primo Levi tells us, 'both objectively and subjectively, lived the Lager in his own way'.[28] The time of incarceration mattered. Levi congratulated himself on having been arrested and imprisoned in 1944 rather than in 1943, because by 1944 labour shortages had forced even the most brutal *Kapos*, the work-squad foremen, to be careful with the lives of their Jewish slaves. Even the brutal Auschwitz of 1943 was not as brutal as the Auschwitz of 1941–42, when, as another prisoner tells us, 'each man, really each one, who lived longer than two weeks, lived at the cost of other victims, at the cost of lives of other people or on what he had taken'.[29] Hermann Langbein sums up the variety of prisoners' experiences in that grim place: 'Each of us carries within him his own personally coloured memory, each has experienced "his" own Auschwitz. The perspective of someone who was always hungry is different from the perspective of a prison functionary . . . every single sub-camp was a world of its own'.[30]

Finally there is the issue of sparsity. Out of thousands of victims only a few survived. Of these few fewer still were able or willing to record their experiences. We therefore cannot follow the historian's standard procedure of piecing together a context and sequences of action from surviving fragments. For accounts of camp organisation we have to turn to survivors who by virtue of their German blood or their facility in the language (they were usually political prisoners) were assigned administrative or technical tasks. Although they were at risk of execution for offences, they were not, like the Jews, under automatic sentence of death. Lifted above the general squalor, physical labour and the worst hunger, their living standards were adequate. They also enjoyed a cognitive advantage: the opportunity to develop an overview of camp life. Some among them had the coolness and the dedication to record what they could discover.[31] Their writings are invaluable for the administrative workings of the camp. But for life as it was lived by the mass of prisoners, for its bitter taste and its texture, we need different informants, willing to convey their subjective experience, and capable of doing so.

We have to train our ignorant ears to hear those communiqués from the underworld. The voices we will hear find their context within a vast silence: the multitude of the dead. It is almost imposssible to fathom the depth of that silence, to remember that behind the shoulder of every individual who survived the camps stand a thousand who did not.

We must also remember the silence of those who lived, but who did not speak.

3

WITNESSING

Nothing belongs to us any more; they have taken away our clothes, our shoes, even our hair; if we speak, they will not listen to us, and if they listen, they will not understand. They will even take away our name: and if we want to keep it, we will have to find in ourselves the strength to do so, to manage somehow so that behind the name something of us, of us as we were, still remains.

    – Primo Levi, *If This Is a Man* 1947

He that keepeth his mouth keepeth his life: but he that openeth wide his lips shall have destruction.

    – Proverbs, Chapter 13, Verse 3

Historians have to think hard about how the documents and artefacts before them relate to the actuality they are trying to retrieve and to understand. Preservation of the record is a central duty. Now, more than fifty years after the extinction of the Nazi state, there is a renewed determination to record everything we can from the survivors of Nazi persecution, typically by audiovisual interview. This is a relatively recent phenomenon, in part for technical reasons, but also I suspect because it is only now as their lives are drawing to a close that many survivors find themselves able to speak about the terrible events of their youth. But while the audiovisual archives developed over the last years will in time constitute a remarkable resource for historians, they are not my concern here. As a separate genre they require their own critique, and they are not yet accessible to the general public.[1] For most of us, whatever understanding we develop of the experience of the Nazis' victims will come from the published written testimonies.

The majority of those victims were hustled unceremoniously to their deaths, leaving few material traces of their passing. Some were killed as they were driven out of their homes, or rounded up and shot in fields or forest. Others, packed into trains for hours or days of acute physical and mental distress, were thrust through the dazzle of lights of the unloading platform straight to the gas chamber or the execution pit. We glimpse their circumstances and condition from some who saw their passing, and from some who were with them until the final separation, so it is possible to reconstruct a bare outline of their experience – although we may well lack the moral stamina to do so.

The more prolonged anguish of those held for months, even years, in starving, shrinking, stinking ghettos stretches imaginative capabilities further. From them we have a handful of diaries and records (the writings surviving when often the writers did not), some survivors' reports, and some remarkable sequences of photographs. However, the bulk of the written testimonies we have come from survivors of the concentration camps, those minimally viable social worlds in which some individuals were able to endure for a month, or a year, and a few even until liberation.

Of those few fewer still have chosen to record what they endured. If we are to learn from their words we have to remember the silences which supply the context: the silence of the mute dead, the silence of those who chose not to speak, the silence of those unable to speak.[2]

On the face of it the obligation to testify might appear overwhelming, whether to commemorate those who were murdered or to defy their murderers, who had promised they would die without memorial or trace.[3] Many of those who spoke thought themselves bound by sacred duty to testify to this abomination before God and man. Others, not all of them believers, knew they had witnessed unspeakable crimes, and felt themselves obliged to speak. Nonetheless, for the first decades after the war most survivors remained silent. Much of that silence arose from the bitter fact that there were few who cared to listen; some testified to the effort of rebuilding lives and communities devastated by the events of the war. Some spoke only within their home communities. A friend born into a Brooklyn neighbourhood of Orthodox Jews from Eastern Europe tells of a conversation between two elderly men in the office of a Jewish scribe: 'Their conversation, in Yiddish, was interspersed with the usual formulaic comments in

Hebrew ("May God bless his, or her, memory"), but the exchange of information (of wives and young children lost in the camps, of lives started over) was very "normal", even colloquial, in the manner of people meeting for the first time and asking each other about jobs, families, mutual histories, although of course, with much more poignancy'. She concludes, 'the Holocaust for some survivors has become so enmeshed in everyday social practices and social rituals that it remains a living reality, a daily presence . . . [it] has become, not only a marker of trauma, but an existential compass of sorts'.[4]

The same friend reminds me that for some individuals the trauma remains so raw that they cannot speak of it even to their own children, who nonetheless see the wounds, and too often suffer from them. It may also be that we need to think in terms of different levels of memory. In everyday life it may be possible to speak out of what Charlotte Delbo, a Frenchwoman who endured the concentration camp experience, calls 'external, intellectual memory', where sensation has been tamed by conventional expression, but any attempt to call up 'deep memory [which] preserves sensations, physical imprints' will renew trauma and throttle speech.[5] Or it may be that memory lives silently, without speech, in the quiet recesses of the day. On the last page of *The Bellarosa Connection* Saul Bellow has his haunted Jewish narrator trying to converse with a very young, very American American, who mocks him for his burdened past. The narrator reflects:

Suppose I were to talk to him about the roots of memory in feeling – about themes that collect and hold the memory: if I were to tell him what retention of the past really means. Things like: 'If sleep is forgetting, forgetting is also sleep, and sleep is to consciousness what death is to life. So that Jews ask even God to remember, "Yiskor Elohim" '.

God doesn't forget, but your prayer requests him particularly to remember your dead.

While we can never be sure what lies behind silence, I will begin to map the silences behind the words we have by exploring the circumstances under which people might feel the compulsion to speak, but find themselves unable to do so: situations, that is, when words fail.

WHEN WORDS FAIL

One of the ambiguous blessings of television is that it opens a door into other people's nightmares. Nowadays we are privileged observers of refugees in all conditions and stages of terror and despair. We watch as survivors of horrors – houses pillaged and burnt, families devastated, individuals brutalised by a drunken, vengeful soldiery – try to speak of what has just been done to them. There is no problem of memory here: eyes still wide with astonishment, still breathless with shock, they are desperate to communicate the enormities they have witnessed and suffered. A woman from what was once a peaceful village in what was once Yugoslavia begins to speak: 'We were all there, the soldiers came and ordered us outside, they were hitting people, they took the men, told them to stand over there, then the lorries came'. The voice ceases. She looks down, takes a long breath, speaks again, 'The men, they told the men to get in'. The lips close, and curve downwards. She shakes her head. She flaps a hand, stares into memory. And is silent. This thing that was done cannot be spoken of. We watch as she learns that words fail.

Some do speak, at some length, in a monotone, and very flatly. The eleven-year-old who says levelly that yes, she was raped, the first night there were five men, she knew some of them, her dentist was one of them, yes she was sure, he'd said 'open wide now', and laughed. The second night perhaps eight; she didn't know how many on the third night, because she fainted. Then they let her out, and told her to go back to the others. She recites steadily, without apparent affect. Can it be true? Yes, it is true. But words have failed her, too.

Or have exposed their limits. She recites the 'facts' as sparely as she is able, because words cannot catch the chaos of emotions which enveloped the events. I suspect this is the psychological origin of the affectless 'witness style', now so familiar that it has become a standard rhetoric apt for imitation. Her experience defies verbalisation. How could she express it? How could a professional writer, however skilled in language, expand her words to comprehend what has been done to her? Whose art could represent her flinching child's body, her flinching child's heart, under those multiple blows?

It is reasonable to ask if we have ever known how to communicate the experience of deliberately inflicted violence in words, beyond comic-book 'ughs' and 'oofs'. Film, with its astonishing illusions of freedom and velocity, can convey at least the look of violence. Martin Scorcese's *Raging Bull* makes us watch in close-up as a fist splays human flesh, as its impact effects a parodic grin. But the inner experience? We do not know what lies behind that mashed, involuntary grimace. Indeed, most of us 'can't begin to imagine it', never having received a blow of a force to stun us, much less to induce an eruption of blood. At most we may have fallen down stairs and had the sickening sensation of the self being sent sprawling too. And this is accident. We have no notion of what it would be like to suffer a single blow deliberately dealt, much less a prolonged, deliberate beating. That experience is, quite precisely, 'unimaginable', and 'unspeakable' because it is 'unsayable'.

The people incarcerated by the Nazis lived through a monotony of physical and psychological assaults inflicted in conditions of complete helplessness, where their voices were neither heard nor heeded. Silence was enjoined upon them. It was after the experience of these coercive circumstances that 'ordinary' individuals, rendered extraordinary only by what had been done to them and by their largely accidental survival of it, were confronted by the problem of communicating previously unimaginable experience by way of the written word.

For most of us the abyss between language and experience yawns briefly in times of excessive joy, or terror, or engulfing anguish. On such occasions language loses its modest competence to figure and convey experience. For those who thought to speak their Holocaust experience the gap must have been close to disabling. Many felt themselves to be disabled, and remained silent. Others, despite the silence around them, despite the difficulties, decided to speak. To better understand their difficulties, I want to explore the normal social uses of catastrophe-tales.

CATASTROPHE TALES

Extreme trauma may strike us dumb, but what we typically do after catastrophes – after bushfires, car accidents, funerals, divorces – is talk. Elizabeth Bowen recalled the curious group responses during the worst days of the blitz in wartime London under the 'hammer-like chops' of reality. When 'what was happening was quite out of proportion to our faculties for knowing, thinking, and checking up, [when] the violent destruction of solid things, the explosion of the illusion that prestige, power and permanence attach to bulk and weight, left all of us, equally, heady and disembodied'. In that destabilised world individuals tried to reassemble themselves through dreams: 'strange deep intense dreams . . . we have never dreamed like this before; and I suppose we shall never dream like this again', and through objects: 'People whose homes had been blown up went to infinite lengths to assemble bits of themselves – broken ornaments, odd shoes, torn scraps of the curtains that had hung in a room – from the wreckage.' But they also talked: 'They assembled and checked themselves from stories and poems, from their memories, from one another's talk'.[6]

In blitzed London, dreams by night, storytelling and reminiscences by day. In devastated Europe Italo Calvino remembers that the first weeks of peace produced a 'curious narrative compulsion', as 'every traveller told strangers about the things which had happened to him . . . the greyness of daily lives seemed to belong to another era; we circulated in a multicoloured universe of stories'.[7]

As humans we seem to feel the need to talk: to find words and images, to organise shaking experience into narrative, to bring the extra-ordinary back to the ordinary, the 'unspeakable' to the spoken. Typically, we do this spontaneously, naturally, and in company. (Some schedule it, and do it privately and expensively, but then it is called therapy.) Thus, easily, socially, and of course always retrospectively, we contrive to bridge the gulf between language and experience.

Communal and personal healing through talk is effected at some cost, not least to individual memory. Václav Havel, thinking back over his own wartime experiences, recalls:

Twenty or thirty years ago, in the army, we had a lot of obscure adventures, and years later we tell them at parties, and suddenly we realise that those two very difficult years of our lives have become lumped together into a few episodes that have lodged in our memory in a standardised form, and are always told in a standardised way, in the same words. But in fact that lump of memories has nothing whatsoever to do with our experience of those two years in the army and what it has made of us.[8]

Here again we have narrative as social glue, as collective myth-making, but also narrative as the road to personal forgetting. Havel's and Calvino's stories became currency. Traded between strangers, they lost their bright edge. But they made those strangers kin.

WITNESSING THE HOLOCAUST: PRIMO LEVI

Released from Auschwitz, returned to Turin, Primo Levi was bursting with stories.[9] He had already begun telling them, at least to himself, scribbling notes secretly over the last months of his imprisonment when discovery could have meant death. In Turin he found family and friends waiting to embrace him. (While Italy had implemented some racial laws, it contrived to yield up very few of its Jews to the Nazis. Caught as a partisan, Levi had been sent to Auschwitz as a Jew.) And in Turin he found himself among innocents, so the stories swelling in his throat could not be told. Their war had been harsh, but it had not approached the horror of Auschwitz. He recognised himself as an Ancient Mariner button-holing the wedding guests on their way to the feast, darkening their unshadowed celebrations with his doleful tales: an importunate, isolated revenant from an irrelevant, macabre Elsewhere.[10]

Levi was to find both personal peace and a way back to society not through the social activity of talking but the private one of writing: 'By writing I found peace for a while and felt myself become a man again, a person like everyone else, neither debased nor a saint: one of those people who form a family and look to the future rather than the past.'[11] Within three months of his homecoming, and having learnt the impossibility of speech, he was writing his first book, *If This Is a Man* (published in the USA as *Survival in Auschwitz*), at breakneck speed. *The Truce* was written nearly as quickly after the earlier book, exhumed from near-oblivion in 1957, found an enthusiastic and expanding readership. That readership continues to expand. *If This Is a Man* has been acknowledged as a classic, one of those books we cannot do without. Most of us have learnt most of what we know of the camps from Levi.

Levi, initially silenced for want of an audience, found he could write the stories he wanted to tell. Other survivors, returned to a distracted or indifferent world, found no recourse save silence.

SURVIVING

To begin with that apparently simple word, 'survivor'. Most people who came out of the camps would agree that the word is altogether too smug in its assumption of the 'natural' continuity of the individual persona, regardless of circumstance. Their experience taught them otherwise. Those flung into the work camps found themselves abruptly reduced from a unique 'someone', comfortably located within a web of work, place, family, friends and associates, to a shorn and naked biped marked by a tattooed number. Simultaneously, they suffered the rupture of that interior narrative – 'the rough and perpetually changing draft of our autobiography that we carry in our minds' – which gives meaning and direction to our hourly living.[12]

We are powerfully committed to continuity. We will admit the possibility of change over time – 'did I really wear that, think that, do that?' We can be flexible in our accounts of our autobiographies – 'I thought I was a wife; I'm really an artist', 'once I was a sinner, now I am saved'. But we also know that such changes, if they are real, take painful time. In the camps there was no time: only the initial, brutal and total insult to the old conception of self – and then the eternal *nunc* of blows, labour, hunger, squalor, fear. Levi writes, 'Do you know how one says "never" in camp slang? "*Morgen früh*" "tomorrow morning".'[13]

Many of those so assaulted relinquished the struggle and became *Muselmänner*, 'Muslims', men and women reduced to staring, listless creatures, no longer responding even to beatings, who for a few days or weeks existed, barely – and who then collapsed and were sent to the gas. We can guess that the term *Muselmänner* refers to the docile acceptance of one's destiny popularly ascribed to Islam and 'the East'. The term, like the condition, was current in many camps among prisoners and guards: a small linguistic indicator of the coherence of the *univers concentrationnaire*.

Of Levi's own contingent of ninety-six healthy Italian men selected for labour on their entry into the camp, more than half were dead within two months. Why did these men die so quickly? Because, Levi tells us, 'they are overcome before they can adapt themselves; they are beaten by time, they do not begin to learn German, to disentangle the infernal knot of laws and prohibitions until their bodies are already in decay'. And then it was too late.[14]

The discipline of the camps – the discipline which destroyed these men as sentient beings – was largely in the hands of prisoners, most especially the block leaders and the *Kapos*, the bosses of the work teams. It was the SS who decreed that Jews should be tattooed and reduced to a number, that Jews be labelled as inferior by their yellow star, but Jewish and Gentile survivors alike have testified it was the immediate, gratuitous assaults by fellow-prisoners that most destroyed hope and fortitude. Some among the newcomers might find the energy to scramble for the tiny, life-giving privileges of a petty job in the camp hierarchy – jobs which became increasingly available to Jews as the war consumed more and more men – but here physical survival came at a high cost to their moral being, for it required them to become part of the system of their subjection.

Only a few of the few who survived the camp believed they had remained 'themselves' throughout their ordeal.* Nearly all of those who have spoken or written about the camps acknowledge a scarring disruption: the dissolution of the old sense of self under the impact of the camp, the shame of that dissolution, and the guilt of the memory of moments when the passion to survive swamped every other senti-ment. How could they tell the joyful relatives who embraced them at the war's end that the person they were embracing had been part of a world where fathers stole bread from sons, and sons from fathers – and who had, damningly, survived in that world?

Those who emerged from the camps had lost more than members of their families and their camp companions. Childhood is our only certain homeland. The sense that it is forever lost has caused every one of us pain. Most of those who survived the camps, like those who had escaped them by emigration, knew that the physical place of their childhood, along with the whole nexus of persons and affections which had made them home, had been obliterated. Such a loss is

---

* If Primo Levi was one, Kitty Hart, the physically and morally tough teenager, was a very different other. Caught after a year on the run from the Germans, from her first day in the camp she used her teenage recalcitrance against her camp bosses. She remained very much herself throughout the war, and (as her later experiences in England make clear) afterwards. Kitty Hart, *Return to Auschwitz*, Panther, Granada Publishing Ltd., London, 1983. Hart's *I Am Alive* is the same book in an earlier (1961) printing, which lacks the prefatory chapter describing her triumphant acclimitisation to genteel Birmingham.

chronically disabling. After the liberation their surviving comrades had dispersed to their separate desolations. When those who will understand are dead or lost or scattered, why speak?

Under such conditions to choose to speak requires rare courage, especially as honesty might be unwelcome. Lawrence Langer, working out of the great Yale Fortunoff Video Archive, has analysed the filmed interviews archived there with acuity and sensitivity.[15] He demonstrates how often interviewers trained in 'non-intervention' will intervene ruthlessly, if unconsciously, to preserve their own comfortable confidence in the continuity of the individual moral being, the rewards accorded to virtue, and the full redemptive effect of 'liberation'. Survivor testimony places all these notions under threat. Langer gives a memorable account of one man who, in face of the growing panic of his audience (which included members of his family), insisted on revealing something they emphatically did not wish to hear. In the last desperate days of war, when the concentration camp at Mauthausen had been bombed by the British, he and a few fellow prisoners rooting around in the mud had found a human hand churned to the surface – and had eaten it. He was proceeding to tell of another episode of cannibalism when the interview was abruptly terminated.[16]

There are many other examples of the discruption of 'normal' moral codes. When German soldiers broke into the children's hospital of the Warsaw ghetto to seize the children for deportation to Treblinka – meaning to terror, pain and inevitable death – a woman doctor quickly administered poison to all the children in her charge. The survivor who recorded her action also recorded other survivors' response to it: 'People thought she was a hero'.[17] Indeed she was. But could she be confident that men and women who knew nothing of the ghetto or the history of anti-Jewish actions by the German army would have the moral imagination to recognise her action as the heroic act of compassion it was?

Perhaps the sure knowledge that luck is the great determinant in life was even more subversive of 'civilian' expectations of security, continuity, and the virtues of the disciplined, forward-looking will. We all have the habit of optimism. The Jews who climbed out of the cattle trucks and trudged along the road towards the tall chimneys were blinded by a decent incredulity. The Jews dumped into the work camps had to learn that the whole elaborate madhouse – the gaunt buildings, the walkways and open spaces, the guards with their guns, whips and truncheons, the bizarrely garbed people moving about, most of them 'on the double' – was organised around one purpose: the prisoners should be humiliated and brutalised daily, and then made to vanish from the earth.

In that setting the significance of a moral rule or restriction of one's own choosing – never to steal bread from a fellow-prisoner; to struggle to keep clean in the midst of filth – could be extinguished in a moment of irritation, while other actions, however innocently taken, could swell to monstrous consequence. Olga Lengyel had been deeply relieved when an SS officer on the disembarking platform at Auschwitz consented to her request that her eleven-year-old son, who had been placed with her, be allowed to join his little brother in the children's group. She was confident that not even Germans would put children to work. She was even more relieved when the officer agreed to her mother leaving her to join her sons, to 'take care of them'.[18] Days later, she learnt that her loving interventions had sent her mother and her boys direct to the gas.

In such a world, exigency is absolute. Langer lets us hear the voices of survivors desperate to make us understand that their survival was not a matter of moral strength, but of pure, blind luck. This is not what we want to hear, because it affronts what Langer calls 'one of the deepest instincts in the civilised mind: the need to establish a principle of causality in human experience'.[19]

From Langer's work it seems that many of those interviewed on camera were ready to speak about experiences they would never have recorded in writing. They were right to be daunted. Writing is a difficult medium. To write of what happened in the camps requires honesty, tough-mindedness, unusual self-knowledge, and unusual moral stamina. To write of the camps lucidly and illuminatingly requires something even more rare: developed writing skills. There are hundreds of survivor testimonies in print and thousands more manuscripts in museums and repositories throughout the world which will remain largely unread, or if read will fail to inform as their writers hoped. This is bitterly unfair. It is also how it is. In what follows I want to examine the ways in which Primo Levi, accidental survivor, gifted writer, has contrived to instruct so many of us as to what life was like in his part of Auschwitz.

Levi, who came to write only because of his Auschwitz experience, who for years thought his writing career had ended with the publication of his first two books, is a natural stylist, lucid, flexible, elegant even in translation, and capable of the most poignant simplicity ('When it rains we would like to cry'. 'I had never seen old men naked.' 'Alberto is my best friend'.). Consider the scope, precision and economy of the two sentences I chose as an epigraph for this section. A few sentences more, and he can sketch an individual so vividly that the figure levitates from the page to join the select group of ink-wrought characters who take up permanent lodgings in our minds.

Preternaturally alert to language, aware how profoundly 'normal' communication depends on agreement as to what is normal, Levi also has the insight to help us grasp the jarring incommensurability between the language the prisoners brought with them into the camps, and their experience 'inside':

Just as our hunger is not that of missing a meal, so our way of being cold needs a new word. We say 'hunger', we say 'tiredness', 'fear', 'pain', we say 'winter' and they are different things. They are free words, created and used by free men who live in comfort and suffering in their homes. If the Lagers had lasted longer a new, harsh language would have been born; and only this language could express what it means to toil the whole day in the wind, with the temperature below freezing, wearing only a shirt, underpants, cloth jacket and trousers, and in one's body nothing but weakness, hunger and knowledge of the end drawing near.[20]

That 'new harsh language' was being born in blood. Entering the camp, Levi had been catapulted into a brutal cacophony where information that could prevent a blow, even save a life, was not heard or misheard or heard as an animal bawl. Camp slang for the *Kapo's* club was 'the interpreter'.[21] We normally associate speech with sociability, but in that artificial society a raised human voice signalled the prospect of immediate physical assault. From the moment of entry men and women were severed from their mother tongue as surely as from their hair and their old identities – unless that tongue was German. The Nazis were intent on building a new Babel, in which only a new and barbarous language would be heard, a language that began from gutter German, but added its own brutal idioms.

Inmates were never to be called 'men' but *Haftlinge*, Prisoners, and when they ate the verb was *fressen*, the word for animals eating. The human corpses which were the camps' main product were not corpses but *Figuren*, Figures, mere things, or even rags.

In contradiction to the conscientious barbarisation of everyday speech official written language was euphemised to a surreal gentility: *Sonderbehandlung*, Special Treatment, for immediate killing; *Säuberung*, Cleansing, for the destruction of all Jews in an area. Proclamations had to be puzzled over before their venom was released. This deliberate pulping of language seems not only a Nazi strategy to discourage inquiry, but a Nazi habit of mind, facilitating the self-protective lie and the magical transformation of a vile act into a wholesome one.*

For the prisoners inside the camps who could read the signs the wordplay was cruel: the exhortations to hygiene in the midst of filth where basins, soap and clean water were lacking; the slogan 'Work Makes Free' when they knew that work would end only with their death. Levi had his own pure and uncontaminated tongue to go home to, but the language of the camp, evolved out of the actuality of Auschwitz, continued to shackle the tongues of many who at last escaped its physical boundaries.[22]

If camp German was the official tongue, the dominant unofficial languages of the camp changed through time – at first Yiddish and Polish, then by 1944, Polish, and for a time Hungarian. But until its last days the camp remained a mosaic of languages. With all other bonds systematically broken, loyalty poured into groups formed out of shared speech. Levi was awed by the 'admirable and terrible Jews from Salonika', who, despite speaking neither German nor Polish nor Yiddish, for a time 'conquered in the kitchens and in the yards'. He shows them squatting in the black-market centre of the Monowitz camp, trading their thick soups, 'the fruits of their labour, of their cooperation and of their national solidarity', or, singing and circling,

---

* For a list of the coded terms used to mask murder, see Raul Hilberg, *The Destruction of the European Jews*, Quadrangle Books, Chicago, 1961, p. 216. Raul Hilberg reflected that a 'Special Train' order was not marked secret because it may have raised questions. 'The key to the entire operation from the psychological standpoint was never to utter the words that would be appropriate to the action. Say nothing; do these things; do not describe them . . . ' Raul Hilberg, quoted in Lanzmann, *Shoah: An Oral History of the Holocaust*, p. 139. For a brilliant, brief and contentious discussion of the role of the lie in Nazism, see Arendt, *Eichmann in Jerusalem*, pp. 51–4, and for the psychological consequences when the lie fails, pp. 85–6.

shoulder to shoulder, stamping out the dances of their homeland.[23] We see them again, this time through the eyes of Filip Müller, stamping and singing in the ashpits of the Birkenau crematoria as members of the *Sonderkommando*, and later, 'selected' for death and abandoned by their fellows, launching a desperate last-ditch attack on their overlords.[24] Levi's own share-everything alliance with fellow Italian Alberto, and his friendship with the civilian worker Lorenzo – relationships which sustained him both physically and emotionally over his last six months of servitude – began with shared language, although they were to deepen into love.*

These friendships were formed in face of the systematic denial of all the ordinary reciprocities of social life. The historian Hermann Langbein, assigned a job in the Auschwitz adminstration because he was *Reichsdeutsch*, a German from the Homeland, and a 'political', can tell us a great deal about the official organisation of the camp, but we need a Primo Levi to tell us about its internal dynamics. Levi is the Erving Goffman of the camps, with Goffman's uncanny flair for selecting the detail which actualises the whole.† He presents the vicious dwarf Elias, manic, violent, bellowing, as the embodied metaphor for Auschwitz, its evolved 'natural man'.[25] And he can take the smallest and most trivial moment and render it revelatory. Soon after admission he plucks an icicle from a window frame to quench his desperate thirst – a natural human use of a gratuitous natural object. A guard snatches it from him. Levi, still capable of innocence, asks why: why should this trivial thing be denied him? The guard replies: *'Hier ist kein Warum'*. 'There is no Why here'.[26]

I labour these points because the very simplicity of Levi's prose can

---

* Yiddish, that yeasty brew of Hebrew, German, Romance and Slavonic, which for the Jews of Eastern Europe had been their only homeland, was very nearly destroyed by the Holocaust. Many Yiddish-speaking survivors found the language too painful to speak, with so few left to speak it with them. Rejected in Israel as the language of the Diaspora, Yiddish survives now largely among the Orthodox or in the universities, where there is growing student enthusiasm for it. Before the war there had been twelve million Yiddish speakers in Europe. Now there are perhaps one million.

† Erving Goffman was a sociologist whose eye for uncovering the social import and pattern of apparently trivial encounters won him admirers far beyond his field. See his *The Presentation of Self in Everyday Life* [1959], Penguin Books, Harmondsworth, England, 1990, and (for students of the Holocaust) his *Asylums: Essays on the Social Situation of Mental Patients and Other Inmates*, Penguin Books, Harmondsworth, England, 1961, now, shamefully, out of print.

blind us both to its beauty and its intellectual penetration, as the shining surface of clear water dazzles our sight and hides the depths beneath. Levi had trained as a chemist, and he was in love with his trade. That love was no impediment to his writing. Anton Chekhov, who trained and for a time practised as a doctor, once compared the serious writer to a chemist, because 'to chemists there is nothing unclean in the world. A man of letters should be as objective as a chemist; he has to renounce ordinary subjectivity and realise that manure piles play a very respectable role in a landscape and that evil passions are as inherent in life as good ones'.[27]

The manure pile in which Levi found himself played no role in any decent society, but it was still a human product, and he set himself to analyse it. He thought there had been a decisive moment in his writing when he returned to his trade after the war. The three months after his return had been painful: 'I felt closer to the dead than to the living, and felt guilty at being a man, because men had built Auschwitz, and Auschwitz had gulped down millions of human beings, including a woman dear to my heart'. But then he met another woman, 'young and made of flesh of blood', and 'in a few hours I felt reborn and replete with new powers, washed clean and cured of a long illness'. He thought his revived sense of self revealed itself in a change in his writing: 'no longer the dolorous itinerary of a convalescent, no longer a begging for compassion and friendly faces, but a lucid building, which now was no longer solitary: the work of a chemist who weighs and divides, measures and judges on the basis of assured proofs, and strives to answer questions'.[28] He realised that with the renewal of love and hope his old passion for objective analysis had been rekindled.

We who read him see this flowering as the end of a longer, more continuous process. In Auschwitz Levi was able to sustain his integrity, his sense of a coherent and enduring self, because of his training and his habit of watching, analysing, identifying – by being a good and faithful chemist. He acknowledged that his scientific training had given him not only 'the baggage of practical notions' he brought with him into the camp, but also an 'ill-defined patrimony of mental habits': 'Can I anticipate what will happen around me in one minute or tomorrow or in a month? If so, what are the signs that matter? . . . Can I foresee the blow, know from what side it will come, elude it?' And more specifically: 'from my trade I contracted a habit that can be variously judged, and defined at will as human or inhuman – the habit of never remaining indifferent to the individuals that chance brings before me'.[29] Levi the chemist may lack Dr Chekhov's delicacy of nuance and high comic spirit, but he shares his self-irony, his tolerance, his cool observant eye and his unshakeable moral poise.

Levi also has the Chekhovian eye for what he calls the 'eloquent episode': the apparently trivial moment which illuminates a world. We have seen one such moment in the 'icicle' interchange. That incident establishes the crucial characteristic of Auschwitz, that of a systematically deranged society. Maniacally ordered, the order is not designed to regulate the exercise of power but to maximise its capacity to injure and to render its victims abject. Their submission must not be allowed to appear as voluntary: it must be exacted, and exacted brutally. Nazi racism, which can so easily seem a demented abstraction, reaches its perfect realisation in Auschwitz in slaps and blows, colours and symbols, prohibitions and privileges, ladles of soup, floggings, deaths.

And Levi is there to name, describe and analyse the process. Whether in the thick of those blows and curses and the rush to comply with multiple contradictory rules, or deep in the labyrinthine calculations and tiny exchanges on which survival could depend, he continues to seek the pattern behind the chaos. A hut companion disappears, 'perhaps into the hut next door, perhaps cancelled from this world'. He recognises that the arbitrariness is not accidental but designed to destroy the social and the private being, which both require some small predictability to endure. Even trivial malice, like the spreading of false rumour, is designed to deepen anguish and to exhaust those minds still capable of hope. Levi makes us see that while in the 'normal' world we are protected from the existential terror of enveloping madness by our capacity to isolate its victims physically, in Auschwitz it is the sane individual who must relinquish sanity and any expectation of rationality, justice and reciprocity if he is to survive within a crazed society that exists in order to destroy him.

The German delight in manipulating their victims psychologically while denying their humanity was for Levi the most unnerving feature of that supremely unnerving system. He requires only one episode to expose the icy splinter at its core. Summoned for a 'state examination in Chemistry' – bizarrely, it appears that some of these abject creatures may be permitted some access to their past selves through work in a laboratory – he is to be assessed by a Dr Pannwitz. Pannwitz raises his eyes from his desk and looks at the creature before him, once Primo Levi, honours graduate in Chemistry, now *Häftling* 174517. The look, Levi remembers, 'was not one between two men': rather, it came 'as if across the glass window of an aquarium between two beings who live in different worlds'.[30]

The examination proceeds. They discuss abstruse chemical matters and compare notes on training. Levi is given the job. But he never forgave Pannwitz that glance. He believed that had he known how to explain that tranquil repudiation of shared humanity he may have been able to lay bare 'the essence of the great insanity of the Third Germany'. He could not explain it. But he could isolate it and display it for our attention.

Too much detachment, like too much anger, can exacerbate the inquirer's sense of helplessness before what can easily seem to be an undifferentiated sequence of horrors. In face of those horrors we can be brought to believe that indeed 'there is no Why here'; to suffer at a remove the paralysis of mind and emotion that afflicted the Muslims, and delivered them to death. In such circumstances it is essential to have a friend: someone to trust, someone to help us look sufficiently closely to see. Levi had Alberto, and the majestically reliable Lorenzo.[31] We have Primo Levi.

Readers may be puzzled at my emphasis on Levi's Auschwitz account rather than on Eli Wiesel's *Night*, which effectively created the genre of Holocaust memoir in Europe and the USA when it appeared in 1958, and which explored the status of the testifying voice heard from the abyss. For me Wiesel's story remains an essentially theological drama, as if he were looking for an obstinately absent God rather than at the humans all around him.[32] The human experience he describes becomes abstract and remote in the telling. Contrast Levi: 'There is Auschwitz, so there cannot be God'.[33] Levi's concern is exclusively with the human. At the close of his life he reminded his readers that through all his endeavours to describe 'the tragic world of Auschwitz' he had assumed 'neither the lamenting tones of the victim nor the irate voice of someone who seeks revenge', but 'the calm, sober language of the witness', but his voice is more flavourful than that.[34] He is incapable of dismissing any individual, however brutal, from life-bestowing awareness. When his thuggish German *Kapo*, readying him for his Chemistry examination, tugs down Levi's jacket and resettles his cap while he mutters 'what a messy recruit', we have so pleasant a parody of the fussy German papa that we are tempted to forget that this is a father out of nightmare, with the will and the power to obliterate his offspring.

Levi had intended *If This Is a Man* to be a memorial to the Muslims, that tragic mass of silent victims who under the insult of sustained brutality first ceased to be sentient, and then ceased to live.* It is not. It is, like all his writings out of Monowitz/Auschwitz, a celebration of individuals who remained individuals despite dehumanising circumstance: ex-Sergeant Steinlauf of the Austro-Hungarian army, grimly washing in icy water, refusing his consent to degradation by living under his own harsher discipline; the builder Lorenzo, with his 'silent courage, not innate, not religious, not transcendent, but deliberate and willed hour by hour'; the gay, alert, resourceful Alberto who 'understood before any of us that this life is war', who 'entered the battle from the beginning', and yet who remained uncorrupted.[35] *If This Is a Man* is also a celebration of human encounters contrived within that anti-human milieu. Levi was later to name such episodes 'moments of reprieve', and declared them to be gifts. As we read, we know something he does not – that he played an essential part in their making.

Having come to know him – having come to love him – we want to believe that he survived because of his remarkable qualities: the curiosity which kept him ever alert and the humour and compassion which, we intuit, inspired steady devotion in Alberto and Lorenzo and deflected the malice of others. Through the darkest days he continued to insist on recognising his companions and himself as 'men, not things . . . thus to avoid that total humiliation and demoralization which led so many to spiritual shipwreck'.[36] Demurring from Jean Améry's recollection of the death-centred nature of thought and talk in Auschwitz, he remembers: 'I almost never had time to devote to death; I had many other things to keep me busy – find a bit of bread, avoid exhausting work, patch my shoes, steal a broom, or interpret the signs or faces around me'.[37]

---

* 'If I could enclose all the evil of our time in one image, I would choose this image which is familiar to me; an emaciated man, with head dropped and shoulders curved, on whose face and in whose eyes not a trace of thought is to be seen'. Levi, If *This Is a Man*, p. 96.

'Interpret the signs or faces around me'. That last phrase encapsulates his genius. It is only because of his refusal to accept demotion to a creature, his tenacity in 'being a man', that we have the beginnings of an answer to that most human and enduring of questions: Why?

Nonetheless Levi knew, as profoundly as anyone who had survived Auschwitz could know, that he had survived by luck. He had the 'good fortune' to have been deported to Auschwitz in 1944, when even slave labour was valuable. A Jew, and therefore a member of the most despised and brutalized class in camp society, Levi was young and fortunate enough to be selected for work at Monowitz, and not sent directly to the crematoria of Birkenau. Most of the other young Italians selected for labour were dead within fifteen days of arrival, seemingly from 'hunger, cold, fatigue and disease', but 'after a more attentive examination' (we see him, attentive) 'due to insufficient information: from their inability to comprehend the nature of the life around them. Meanwhile Levi had been building on his chemist's German, paying for his lessons in bread.[38] During the final six months of his imprisonment, when hunger and hard labour were exacting a bitter toll, he was preserved by his share-everything partnership with Alberto and the steady benevolence of the civilian worker Lorenzo, who through all those months smuggled his compatriots a daily supplement of soup.

Levi believed that he would have died were it not for the friendship of those two men.[39] There was also the luck of winning the privilege of work in the sedentary warmth of a laboratory through the worst months of the winter of 1944–45, and of contracting scarlet fever and being in the camp hospital when 24,000 'healthy' prisoners embarked before the Russian advance on what was to be their death walk through the snow. Alberto, for all his energy and ingenuity, died somewhere along those bitter roads.[40] Of the 800 sick abandoned in the camp hospital perhaps a hundred were still alive ten days later, when the Russians arrived. Of the eleven men in Levi's room – a good room to be in, as it turned out, and well organised because it contained two Frenchmen newly imprisoned and not yet debilitated – only one man died during the interregnum, though five more were to die in the coming weeks. Through that time Levi took wild risks to preserve himself and his companions, later boasting his ownership of 'a first-rate eiderdown', one of four he had looted from the SS camp just beyond the perimeter, and 'today in my house in Turin'. Of the 650 men, women and children who had arrived at Auschwitz with Levi, only three lived to return to Italy.[41]

That bitter calculus leaves no space for quirks of individual personality or personal history. It was indeed 'blind luck' that Levi, this man we cannot do without, did not fall victim to a selection, the boredom of a guard, the bite of an infected louse – any one of the 'accidents' which obliterated so many other irreplaceable individuals in that artificial world, slung as it was between the twin poles of arbitrariness, and utter contempt for the value of human life.[42]

Given that calculus any survivor, however rational, must feel a burden of guilt. Levi diagnosed the emotion as 'the shame of survival'.[43] No prisoner in Auschwitz exercised significant choice. For most, the immediate and brutal denial of autonomy which marked their initiation into the camp established their permanent condition: they were programmed for death, by starvation if nothing else, because their daily ration was calculated to be too meagre to sustain life. In that contrived 'state of nature', life could be maintained only at the cost of others. In 1986, writing what was to be his last book, the shame of that helpless implication in the deaths of others was still raw: 'nestled deeply like a woodworm; it is not seen from the outside but it gnaws and rasps'. Levi 'knew' himself to be innocent; that even on the rack of hunger he had never stolen bread from his fellows. It was the damning fact of survival that enrolled him among 'the selfish, the violent, the insensitive, the collaborators'. Thus Levi did penance for his own will to live. The arch-humanist who survived the camp with reserves of honour, grace and affection for his fellows, died haunted by that cruellest of cruel stories, that 'everyone is his brother's Cain', that 'I might be alive in the place of another, at the expense of another; I might have usurped, that is, in fact, killed'.[44]

'In fact', nothing of the kind. But we are speaking here of visceral dread, not reason. Levi had wanted to memorialize the *sommersi*, the 'submerged' or the 'drowned ones', the multitude of prisoners who could not withstand the assaults on body and spirit. That was the proper task of the *salvati*, the 'saved'. But after all his years of dedicated reading, writing and witnessing, Levi decided that the saved could not speak for the drowned, that they could not be 'true witnesses' precisely because they had survived. 'We are those who by their prevarications or abilities or good luck did not touch bottom. Those who did, those who saw the Gorgon, have not returned to tell about it, or have returned mute'.[45]

He is, of course, right. Only the dead know the full bitterness of their victimhood, and they are silent – except for a few voices, like that of Anne Frank, miraculously preserved in all its eagerness and bright promise; a single voice which forces recognition of the incalculable cost to us all of those years of systematic Nazi killings.[46] Levi was a Jew in Auschwitz, the lowest level of the camp hierarchy, distinguished in the eyes of his masters by nothing save his expertise in chemistry. What he can tell us is how corrosive that experience was even for a man of singular grace, who happened to stay alive, who was capable of bearing the guilt of that fortuitous survival, and who had the rare skills required to speak the past clearly. Levi gave a voice to the voiceless.

It is true that he ended his own life. Those who knew him best say that ill-health and personal griefs, including sorrow at the decline of his aged and much-loved mother, were bearing heavily upon him at that time; that strong medications rendered his moods unstable; that when he stepped into air at the head of the stairwell of his family home he did so on impulse. I hope it was like that. It fits the man. And I would not like to think that he had chosen, finally, to abandon us.

Levi was not only a fine writer but a fine historian. He measured the spans of his generalisations, and fretted over how differently men behave as individuals and as members of a group. He reflected on the vast authority and debonair irresponsibility of memory, devoting a full chapter of his last book, *The Drowned and the Saved*, to a discussion of 'the factors which may obliterate or deform memories'. He knew that too frequent handling can lend a false lustre while dulling precision. Nonetheless, he insisted that his own memories of Auschwitz were sharp, accurate and clear. 'I conserve pathologically precise memories of my encounters in that now remote world.'[47]

His confidence in the clarity of his memory is justified. His reputation as a truth-teller remains unsullied. But I suspect the detailed freshness of his recollections is rarer than he thinks, and that we are looking at an unusual phenomenon, a compulsive thought-and-experience-into-words formulator – a 'natural', not to say compulsive, writer. Levi claims he would have remained a happy chemist were it not for

Auschwitz. That may be true, but during what were to be his last months in the camp we see him scribbling notes to himself – notes he cannot keep, notes which put him in mortal danger – in odd corners of the laboratory at every unsupervised minute. Most of us have never been sufficiently physically or psychologically reduced to discover the near-autistic tenacity of certain habits of mind even in extremity – habits in which the essential self seems to be vested. But remember the limpid prose in that first book, 'written at breakneck speed', he tells us, with 'no thought given to questions of style'. How much inchoate experience had already been selected and formulated into as-yet-unwritten words, sculpted into as-yet-unwritten sentences?

Levi could tame painful emotion by its precise inscription. Some other men and women who stumbled out of the camps were able to find the words to tell their stories, and to record them. Most did not. Their release was into a chaotic solitude that gave them only the leisure to count their losses: homes and countries gone, kin dead without record, grace or grave. After the war, returned to society, they moved among ordinary people again, and in time sampled the luxuries they had dreamed of – warm baths, good food, soft beds – an abundance of everything, except the everything they had lost.

It is on issues like the incurable nature of grief that Primo Levi, reliable witness though he is, inadvertently misleads. He could see and report so much of his first days in Auschwitz because he was not distracted by terror regarding the fate of family members. He was also a partisan, and therefore understood something of the viciousness of Nazi ideology. In that sense he was prepared for Auschwitz. Later he was to contrast his situation with 'poor unfortunates who had five years of continuous persecution behind them . . . who had been overtaken by the Nazi tide, or else poor devils from the Ukraine, Byelorussia, or eastern Poland, with no contact with Western civilization, suddenly hurled into a situation they didn't understand'.[48] He suffered personal losses: the woman he had loved, his three-year-old niece Emilia, a 'curious, ambitious, cheerful child' until the Germans killed her. But at the end of the war Levi was still young, relatively sturdy, and returning both to a family and to a family home. That was not the condition of the great majority of survivors. In his account of that return Levi refers only glancingly to the desolation at the breaking open of the camps, when the world seemed filled with 'defective, abnormal human specimens' blindly searching for a place in the chaos. He notes only in passing the 'indeterminate illness' which felled even the formidable and apparently indestructible Greek, Mordo Nahum, for weeks. *The Truce*, his second book, is largely a celebration of the rare fellows he meets on his wobbly odyssey back to Turin. Even as he recounts catastrophes we are reassured, because Levi is Levi still: responsive, ironic, gravely gay.[49]

The celebration of a remarkable witness-source like Primo Levi exposes a core paradox of history writing: our most significant insights into how it was for the many will usually depend on the words of the remarkable few. It is because Levi is the man he is that he can tell us so much, so movingly. It is also because he is that man that there are some things he cannot tell us. He cannot communicate dour endurance, or what it feels like to retreat into autism. He tells us that while in Auschwitz he became an animal, but we do not believe him. No animal could observe or respond as he does, no animal could have framed such memories. And he cannot communicate despair.

If we are to understand despair, and fortitude in despair, we need the words of a woman who became a writer in Auschwitz when she harnessed the magic of remembered stories to build small dream worlds for her companions in a desert of deprivation and humiliation. And then, when the deprivations and the humiliations were ended, she wrote to make them real again.

Writing is a transcendence of experience, not a replication of it. How then can the experience of abjection of the self be communicated through writing, that most conscious demonstration of self-possession? As we will see, by supreme and conscious art.

WITNESSING THE HOLOCAUST: CHARLOTTE DELBO

In 1941 Charlotte Delbo, a young Frenchwoman touring in South America with a theatrical company, learnt that her country had been invaded and occupied by the Germans. She chose to return home, joining her husband late in 1941 and working with him for the Resistance. In March 1942 they were arrested by the Gestapo. Her husband was executed in May. Delbo was permitted a brief meeting with him the night before he was shot.

For the rest of 1942 she was to remain in French prisons. In January

1943 she and other French women, most of them 'politicals', were deported to Auschwitz. In January 1944 Delbo and the handful of others still alive were sent to Ravensbrück, from where they were released to the Red Cross in the last days of the war. While (as Delbo scrupulously makes clear) she and her companions were not subjected to the ferocious maltreatment visited on Jewish women, out of the original convoy of 230 only forty-nine returned to France.[50]

Like Primo Levi, Delbo spent much of her life 'after Auschwitz' writing about her experiences there. She too was moved to write soon after release, although she chose to delay publication of her writings for twenty years.[51] Like Levi, she tried to use her writing as kind of exorcism: to turn memories into meaning. Like Levi, she wrote to educate her readers: to confront the ignorant and the amnesiac with what had been done in those apparently forgotten times. Like Levi, she saw her role as that of moral witness.

Unlike Levi, she was eager to enter her deepest subjective experience as part of the evidence: to recall on paper her interior monologue as she strove to remain upright during an interminable, snow-swamped rollcall, or as she ran with her frantic comrades through a storm of blows, their aprons filled with earth to make an SS garden. Unlike Levi, she wrote to mend a fractured life: to describe her own incapacitation when confronted once more by an ordinary world; to trace the ways a common past continued to disable her own and her comrades' separate lonely presents, living among innocents still persuaded of the durability of the individual and of the stable moral structure of the social world.[52] In the face of such sanguine convictions the ex-prisoners' knowledge that the self is a fragile creature had to become a guilty secret.

After his release, Levi achieved blessed ordinariness. 'I became a man again, a person like everyone else, neither debased nor a saint: one of those people who form a family and look to the future rather than the past.'[53] The miracle was not immediate. In 1946 he still was still aware of a radical disjunction: 'Today, at this very moment as I sit writing at a table, I myself am not convinced that these things really happened.'[54] Years later, he was still troubled by a dream-within-a-dream. Dreaming, he lies 'embedded in the fond routines of family, nature in flower, my home'. And then, suddenly, he is 'alone, and afraid, in the centre of a grey and turbid nothing . . . I am in the Lager once more, and nothing is true outside the Lager. All the rest was a brief pause, a deception of the senses'. He lies quiet, desolate, waiting a single word, 'not imperious, but brief and subdued', 'Get up. *"Wstawach"* ' – the dawn command of Auschwitz.[55]

For Levi these are dreams, fleeting interruptions in the flow of ordinary days. For Delbo even the act of remembering is perilous. It was not that she has forgotten: 'Auschwitz is so deeply etched in my memory that I cannot forget one moment of it.' It is rather that she 'remembers' out of two very different kinds of memory. First there is *'mémoire profonde,'* 'deep memory', almost physical, saturated with emotion and sensation: 'Auschwitz is there, unalterable, precise, but enveloped in the skin of memory, an impermeable skin that isolates it from my present self.' In daylight hours that terrible reality is sealed away, and she lives by what she calls *'mémoire ordinaire'*: memory grounded in the everyday, and in ordinary narrative sequences. The words she speaks in daily life come from that 'external memory . . . from intellectual memory'. But in dreams, *and when she writes*, that 'deep memory [which] preserves sensations and physical imprints' erupts, and she is famished, stinking, exhausted, in the grip of death again.[56] With reckless, astonishing courage Delbo stares into the black crystal and tells us what she sees.

She sees her terror, and her despair. She sees her comrades suffering. She sees them murdered or scattered, and her own unassuageable loneliness. She had felt that loneliness from her first moments of liberation, in the thick of the flurries of goodwill which swirled around her; she continues to feel it. In Auschwitz her old self was stripped from her as surely as her clothing and her hair. She was forced to make herself anew. But the experiences-become-memories out of which that new self had been forged are alien to the people who surround her now. Now she is alone, as she had never been in the camp.

Freedom hands her the necessities she once had to fight for, the luxuries she dreamed of, but the abundance leaves her derelict. She experiences herself as an empty creature, devoid of purpose, devoid of desire, incompetent to carry out the simplest acts of living.[57]

Reading Delbo, we are reminded of Levi's friend, Lorenzo, whose life, crammed with purpose and meaning within the camp as he strove to keep his two compatriots alive, lost all significance once 'outside'.[58] We might call this state, haunted by extreme depression and dissociation, 'madness', but it is terrifyingly sane. Life in the universe of the concentration camp for all its terror, because of its terror, had to be lived at a pitch of intensity unknown in the ordinary world. Untested general kindliness is thin gruel after the bone-harsh intimacy Delbo had shared with her fellow-prisoners. Months after her return to civil society she is still scanning the faces of family members, of strangers casually encountered, to answer a question she knows to be irrelevant but which remains the only question that matters:

I peruse their lips, eyes, hands . . . Facing people I meet I wonder, Would he have helped me walk, that one? Would he have given me a little bit of his water? . . . I tell myself I'm stupid. I no longer need to be held up, given a drink of water, I no longer need someone to share her bread ration with me. This is no longer the way we ought to look at people we meet in life . . . I tell myself it's of no importance today. So what's important today? I'm left with the fact that I know many more human beings than I require to continue living among them, and there will always be between them and me this useless knowledge.[59]

'Useless knowledge'. Inapplicable, even destructive knowledge, when society shrugs at such questions, when survival does not depend on such assessments. Jean Améry, as the Austrian philosopher Hans Mayer renamed himself after his release from Auschwitz, had been seized and tortured by the Gestapo because of his political activities, and then sent to Auschwitz because he was a Jew. Améry believed the knowledge he gained was useful. He wrote of what had been done to him so that all who read his words would know that the damage was irremediable; that 'anyone who has been tortured remains tortured . . . Anyone who has suffered torture never again will be able to be at ease in the world . . . Faith in humanity, already cracked by the first slap in the face, then demolished by torture, is never acquired again.'[60]

That is bleak knowledge indeed. Nonetheless, it is to be treasured, not least because it might increase our determination to stop the torturers who in the course of our century have come to be such respectable fellows. In such a world none of us can afford to be at ease.

Delbo found herself obliged, as Levi was obliged, to keep on communicating her 'useless knowledge': to continue to write about the camps and what was done to humans there. Like Levi, she believes there is a mystery at the core of these sufferings. She begins her final work with the words: '*Expliquer l'inexplicable*'. 'To explain the inexplicable'. She cannot do that. But she tells what she has seen and experienced.

She is also a devoted clerk of record in her inscription of the tortures to which she and her comrades were subjected. She insists that we must know them in their excruciating detail. Her litany is: '*Il faut donner à voir*', 'we must show it as it was'. Some of the passages are long, as when she makes us see what it is to experience true thirst, when she can think of nothing, care for nothing save to snatch a cup of water from a brook – breaking ranks, scrambling out (the SS man and the dog coming fast) scrambling back into the safety of the column – and then, in face of a weaker woman's parched, beseeching gaze, swallowing the tiny cupful herself. Other passages are short, glimpses only, cinematic in their visual intensity:

A woman dragged by two others, holding on to her arms. A Jewish woman. She does not want to be taken to Block 25. [Block 25 was the holding barrack for women condemned to the gas.] She resists. Her knees scrape on the ground. Her clothing, pulled up by the tug of her sleeves, is wound around her neck. Her trousers – men's trousers – are undone and drag inside out behind her, fastened to her ankles. A flayed frog. Her loins are exposed, her emaciated buttocks, soiled by blood and pus, are dotted with hollows.

She is howling. Her knees are lacerated by the gravel.

Try to look. Just try and see.[61]

'Try to look. Just try and see', because for Delbo to look and see is to draw close to the lost actuality. But why should we look, how dare we look, at such degradation? What are we meant to learn from this viewing of a fellow human *in extremis*?

There are a number of answers to that question. One is prudential: this knowledge is not useless but essential. Two women are dragging the one we have been made to see. Who are they? Why do they do what they are doing? Such things were done because men and women willed them and were able to implement their will. We would be fools not to try to understand as precisely as we are able how that situation came about.

There is also, for me (as well as I am able to decipher it) a deeper moral imperative. These things were done – some survived to tell what had been done. We, to whom such things have not been done, have an obligation to be attentive. In another context the English critic Michael Wood has written of the 'unusual but not impossible demands' the dead make upon the living.[62] This is one of those demands – unusual, close to unendurable, but surely, not impossible?

4

RESISTING

It's not honest in life to ask from a man such things. I'm not optimistic
about my own behaviour, you see. And still I am not a bad man. Really
not. But life asks me, 'You or me?' and I say 'Me.'
> – Auschwitz prisoner-doctor [Lifton, *The Nazi Doctors*,
> p. 223]

Those survivors of the camps who chose to speak were faced not only
with the deliberate amnesia of the guilty and the self-protective amnesia of 'bystanders', but the incredulity of the ignorant. Primo Levi had
initially written to memorialize the anonymous dead and exorcize grim
experience. Later, in *Moments of Reprieve*, he wrote to celebrate the
remarkable men who had contrived to live freely in servitude, whether
by stoical inwardness or a marvellous lightness of being. Later again
he wrote to confront Germans with what they had done, to try to
force some answer to that unendurable question: Why? However, as
the years passed he became involved in a different project: combating
the ignorance and complacency of a deaf and increasingly distracted
world. At the close of his life he was still responding to the provoca-
tion of a reiterated question: why no resistance?[1]

Bruno Bettelheim is perhaps only the most famously fatuous of the
many who take this cruel and silly question to be serious when he
declares:

'Strange as it may sound, the unique feature of the extermination camps
is not that the Germans exterminated millions of people . . . What was new,
unique, terrifying, was that millions, like lemmings, marched themselves to
their own deaths. This is what is incredible; this we must come to understand.'

Bettelheim 'came to understand' by invoking the ghostly shade of Freud: those who died, he said, died 'because they failed to resist, and they failed to resist because they yielded to the death instinct'.[2]

'Millions of Jews of Europe who did not or could not escape in time or go underground as many thousands did, could at least have marched as free men against the SS, rather than first grovel, and then to be rounded up for their own extermination, and finally walk themselves to the gas chambers.'[3]

Bettelheim may have been unduly influenced by personal experience. He had endured ten months incarceration in the camps of Dachau and Buchenwald before his release late in 1939. These camps were terrible enough, *Knochenmühlen* or 'bonecrushers' devised to destroy the resistance of political opponents of the regime by savage discipline, forced labour and acute physical deprivation. But they were not Auschwitz. The inmates spoke the same tongue as their guards and they knew why they were there. They could receive parcels. They could look forward to release. They did not live under sentence of death, as did every Jew incarcerated after 1941. Bettelheim's attitude, which seems to spring from a defective capacity for comparison and a gross failure of imagination, is unfortunately widespread. It is a painful fact that this same question was asked of witness after witness by the prosecution during the Eichmann trial in Jerusalem in 1961: 'Why did you not protest? rebel? attack?'[4]

Some survivors, sensitive to the derogation implicit in the question, resort to a form of word-magic, as with Olga Lengyel:

> Our entire existence in the camp was marked by [resistance]. When the employees of 'Canada' detoured items destined for Germany to the benefit of their fellow internees, it was resistance.* When labourers at the spinning mills dared to slacken their working pace, it was resistance. When at Christmas we organised a little festival' under the noses of our masters it was resistance . . .[5]

One understands what she means and why she says it, but smuggling a can of meat from 'Canada' into the main camp for sale to a fellow-internee is not obviously 'resistance', although it may be an essential survival strategy both for its material advantage and its reinforcement of an individual's sense of potency.

---

* 'Canada' was the name given the warehouse of goods collected from incoming victims, to be sorted, packed and sent to Germany.

It is a simple failure of imagination to expect overt acts of defiance or resistance under concentration camp conditions. Levi has told us of the eerie calm interspersed with sudden random violence which enveloped the victims from their first moments in the camp. Anxiety, exhaustion and confusion, together with a 'natural' confidence in an imaginable future and the rationality of one's fellow humans, must have vitiated any impulse to question or to hesitate, especially as questions and hesitations were brutally dealt with. There can no puzzle in the 'lack of resistance' from distracted men and women brusquely separated from beloved kin. The woman who walked away from her fifteen-year-old daughter in the group selected for labour and life, choosing instead to keep fast hold of the hand of a four-year-old girl separated from her parents, was not only a hero – she was clearly that – but unusually prescient, intuiting the meaning of the selections, realizing that she was deciding to die rather than allow a child to go to her death alone.[6]

Outside the camps the killings were done by armed, trained, organized men. By early 1942 the Germans had killed half a million Jews behind the Russian front, usually by shooting them at the lips of mass graves. These people did not die because of some collective death wish but because soldiers with guns decided to kill them. It is not difficult for soldiers to kill unarmed civilians. During the same period the Germans killed even more Russians by similar methods. Inside the ghettos, when Nazi lies had been exposed as lies, some Jews began an unrelenting resistance. More did not, in the reasonable, tragically mistaken belief that not even the Nazis could mean to kill them all.[7]

Occupied Poland, with its terrorized population, its many Jews and its admirable railway network was perfect for the Nazi's next project: the systematic destruction of Europe's Jews by gassing. Factories were constructed for that sole purpose: at Chelmno, where techniques were being tested by December 1941, at Belzec by March 1942, Sobibor by May the same year and Treblinka by June. In the summer of 1942 Commandant Hoess began to build his own death factory at Auschwitz-Birkenau to supplement Auschwitz I, already with its own small crematorium. By late summer the first makeshift premises in two converted farmhouses were in action. The five new gas chambers came into operation in the winter of 1943. The two largest of Birkenau's gas chambers or *Leichenkeller*, 'corpse-cellars', were capable of accommodating up to two thousand persons at a time.

For most of the exhausted, famished and parched thousands funnelled into the extermination camps – almost a million in Auschwitz-Birkenau alone – oblivion came within a few hours of their arrival. Only the younger men and fewer young women were selected to be used for a term as work-Jews.[8] It was from among the doomed men of the *Sonderkommandos*, or Special Squads, that revolt came: first in Treblinka, later in Sobibor, last in Birkenau. As the Russians advanced, as the Nazis faced the task of obliterating all evidence of what had been done in the extermination camps, the death-workers knew that their time had run out. Revolt was their last chance for life.

Even then they knew the most likely outcome would be a swifter, crueller death. Richard Glazar, one of a handful to escape during the Treblinka revolt, was adamant that its brief success depended on men who, accepting their own deaths as inevitable, fought to cover the escape of others. 'No one at all could have got out of Treblinka if it hadn't been for the real heroes: those who, having lost their wives and children there, elected to fight it out so as to give the others a chance.'[9] At Sobibor the spirit of insurrection arrived with a contingent of Jewish-Soviet prisoners of war from Minsk, men accustomed to guns and strategic planning, though leadership fell to a flour-mill worker from eastern Poland. On 14 October 1943 the plan was brilliantly implemented, with seven SS killed before the alarm was raised. Nonetheless, few prisoners survived. Out of 550 prisoners more than half initially escaped, but approximately eighty died in the perimeter minefields, and 170 more were caught in a dragnet of more than four hundred men and shot in the forest. Of the 150 who got clear away ninety-seven were killed in hiding, most by 'hostile local elements', and five died fighting the Germans. Only forty-eight survived to be liberated by the Allies.[10]

If even those rebellions of young, strong, relatively well-fed men promised little beyond a more ferocious death, an individual escape guaranteed savage reprisal against one's fellows. In Treblinka the price was officially set at ten lives. For those sealed inside the labour camps overt resistance was, simply, suicide. We sometimes glimpse an individual resenting a blow or questioning an order. Typically, we see that individual die on the instant. Even under these conditions there were some heroic, artfully planned escape attempts. Few succeeded, and the camp authorities made sure that those they captured died horribly and in public.

As witnesses like Primo Levi and Charlotte Delbo have shown us, the most viable and effective 'resistance' occurred within the mind, with the determination not to yield to despair but to survive, whether by obdurate stoicism or sinuous adaptability. And any and all of these strategies, if they were conscious enough to be called strategies, could be extinguished in a moment by a *Kapo's* club or the whim of a guard. Even suicide, that ultimate act of self-assertion, could be negated. Guards were ordered to shoot any prisoners who ran for the electrified fence before they could touch the wire.

There was an organized resistance in Auschwitz, as in every camp, a shadowy group engaged in the secret and risky business of gathering information, liaising with the Polish Resistance, and confounding at least some of their masters' intentions. Its leaders were typically German 'politicals' assigned to the adminstration offices by virtue of language and race, and so having access to information. As Germans and Gentiles they were also exempt from the death sentence imposed on every Jew in the camp. We have an extraordinary account of the Auschwitz Resistance from the young Pole Wieslaw Kielar, who survived five years 'inside'.[11] At inordinate risk the Auschwitz Resistance managed to smuggle small amounts of arms and explosives into the camp, but the most essential role of Kielar and others like him was the breaking of the Nazi monopoly over information about what was happening both inside the camp, and at the front. It is impossible to measure the psychological importance of the network.

Engagement in the camp Resistance transformed the morale of the prisoners admitted to it. Olga Lengyel, who knew her parents and her two young sons had died in the gas and who had glimpsed her husband only once through the wire, regained purpose and pride when she was recruited. 'In the beginning I did not know much of the enterprise in which I was participating. But I knew I was doing something useful. That was enough to give me strength. I was no longer prey to crises of depression . . . that, too, was a way to resist.'[12] Her curiosity was reawakened and vitality with it: she was now avid for every shred of information so she could preserve it for the future and the outside world. Comrades within the camp Resistance, like Dr Paske, the physician to the *Sonderkommando* who had given her crucial information on the secret killings and was himself killed long before the liberation, became the dear companions of her solitary thoughts. She titles the chapter which tells of her recruitment 'A New Reason for Living'.

Lengyel discharged her duty to her comrades. Her account of Auschwitz-Birkenau was published within two years of the war's end. The larger story of the internal resistance has been told by Hermann Langbein, one of the key members of the Auschwitz Resistance and now historian to his own past.[13]

During the *Sonderkommando* revolt in Auschwitz the official Auschwitz Resistance had maintained its commitment to information-gathering, developing its contacts with the Polish Resistance and waiting for the Russians. It played no part in the Special Squad action, judging, correctly, that a general outbreak would lead to a general massacre. Nonetheless, the explosives which destroyed one of the crematoria had come by way of the Resistance, and Olga Lenyel played her part in moving some of those little packages along the human chain. The risks were extravagant but easy to accept, she said, because:

the danger of death had a different meaning for us who lived in Auschwitz-Birkenau. Death was always with us, because we were always eligible for the daily selection. One nod could mean the end for any of us. To be late for roll call might mean only a slap in the face, or it might mean, if the SS man became enraged, that he took out his Luger and shot you . . . We would die, whatever happened. We would be gassed, we would be burned, we would be hanged, or we would be shot. The members of the underground at least knew that if they died, they would die for something . . .

We lived to resist and we resisted to live.

To survive inside the camps was heroism enough. To resist was heroism indeed, when for all prisoners exigency could eclipse intention at any moment. Under such circumstances any systematic attempt to measure the force of moral principle in face of hostile pressures, either generally or individually, must fail.[14]

5

INSIDE THE GREY ZONE

The Auschwitz *Sonderkommando*

I experienced a great deal at the crematorium and I saw sights that the world ought never to have to hear about. It was not intended that an eyewitness should survive, nor did I myself suppose that I should ever be at liberty again. I do not want, nor would I be able to describe everything in detail. There is too much of it and it is so horrible that many would not believe it. And even today I cannot grasp all that I witnessed . . .

What I went through seems incredible to me today, like some sort of evil dream. It was much more terrible than could ever be described.

– Filip Müller, *Häftling* 29136, *Sonderkommando* Auschwitz-Birkenau, May 1942 – November 1944[1]

Who ought be declared a perpetrator of the Holocaust? Daniel Goldhagen offers this definition:

A perpetrator is anyone who knowingly contributed in some intimate way to the mass slaughter of Jews, generally anyone who worked in an institution of genocidal killings. This includes all people who themselves took the lives of Jews, and all those who set the scene for the final lethal act, whose help was instrumental in bringing about the deaths of Jews.[2]

On the face of it this is a good working definition, demonstrating Goldhagen's determination to snare all the guilty, from the bureaucratic 'desk-murderers' like Adolf Eichmann and the churchmen who drew up lists of Jewish converts for the Gestapo, through the men who rounded up their quotas of Jews and packed them into the trains, down to the camp guard with his bloodied truncheon and the SS man with his whip. Goldhagen casts a wide net because he is determined to catch every significant fish.

As always with definitions, difficulties thicken around the edges. The contributions must be made with 'knowledge'. Were the railway men who serviced those closed trains, who heard the cries from behind the sealed doors, complicit in what was happening behind the doors, in what would happen after the doors were opened? What of the men who drove the trains, who threw the brake at stations called Auschwitz, Sobibor, Treblinka? Goldhagen's net also scoops up the frantic small fishes trapped inside 'institutions of genocidal killing': the inmates who competed for jobs because those jobs carried tiny, life-giving privileges – along with the obligation to beat and bully their comrades, and to push them towards gas. Most of the work of Auschwitz, including the coercion and punishment of prisoners, and the doling out or withholding of pitiful starvation rations, was carried out by prisoners. At Treblinka, a camp whose only function was the production of death, the work was done by a thousand Jews of various nationalities under the direction of eighty Ukrainian guards and forty SS, of whom only twenty were on duty at any one time.

The recipe for 'co-operation' was simple. Pen groups of humans for one, five or ten or more days' travel in squalid and demoralizing conditions, supplying neither water nor food nor sanitary facilities. Then separate individuals from families and friends, thrust them among strangers and strip them of their possessions, clothing, hair – every trace of their previous social identities. Plunge them in a Babel of unintelligible commands and extreme random violence. Make hunger their daily companion. Then make a double-dip out of the communal soup pot, access to goods looted from incoming victims, or the chance of a few weeks or months of life the reward for 'co-operation'. What will be the outcome? What requires explanation is not that some complied but that any found the strength to resist.

Ought those who co-operated, the 'Prominents', as they were called, be counted among the perpetrators? Their labour was as essential for the running of the camps as was the labour of the Jewish councils and the Jewish police to the running of the ghettos – which included the smooth delivery of manufactured goods to the German war machine and the delivery of batches of Jews to die in the gas. Every one of these 'officials' gained some advantage from their services. All knew or soon came to know the lethal consequences of their actions. May we therefore judge them to be culpable? Did any individual fully in the power of the Nazis and their agents, where the penalty for non-co-operation could be death, enjoy sufficient freedom of choice to be judged responsible for what he or she did? Some of the men chosen to direct affairs inside the ghettos, those sealed warehouses of the doomed, believed that through their actions some remnant of their community might be permitted to survive. They were wrong. Raul Hilberg estimates that more than half a million Polish Jews died inside the ghettos, most from starvation, because food supplies were murderously inadequate, and because food distribution was in the hands of internal hierarchies and systematically inequable.[3] When I read the writings of two men who died inside a ghetto, one excluded from any privilege and dying at nineteen from starvation, the other a policeman who had struggled to preserve himself, his wife and his daughter at the cost of every other person, and who failed, what I understand most clearly is that I lack any footing from which to judge them. Under such chronically abnormal conditions the pressures on individuals were so urgent, so disparate and so irreconcilable as to vitiate the possibility of judgment.[4]

Once inside the concentration camps all office was initially a reflex of race. Whatever their personal qualities, their inclinations or their crimes, men and women of German blood were given power over those not of that blood. Given the nature of the camps the power was close to absolute, and commonly expressed by whip, club or fist. Most German block-leaders and *Kapos* exercised their power savagely. Some did not. By 1944, the year Primo Levi was incarcerated in Auschwitz, the decreasing supply of labour meant that some Jews were promoted to overseers' jobs: Filip Müller reports that 'when the work teams marched out there were, now and then, kapos and foremen wearing the Star of David, something which would have been impossible in 1942'.[5] These men, self-selected in the sense that they had to prove their hardness before their blockleaders, knew they had to keep demonstrating that hardness to keep their precarious grip on privilege.

Many survivors have testified to their peculiar viciousness. The usually compassionate Levi dismisses such men as defective social beings who had betrayed the 'natural solidarity' they owed to their comrades. He also believed them to be crueller than their Gentile counterparts. He explained that 'present, past and atavistic sufferings' combined with 'the tradition of hostility to the stranger' to 'make them monsters', whose 'capacity for hatred, unfulfilled in the direction of the oppressors, will double back, beyond all reason, on the oppressed'.[6]

For a man of Levi's insight this is facile psychologizing. It is also, of course, completely understandable, coming as it does from a helpless victim of their malice. Levi says, and I believe him, that he would never have accepted a position which separated him from his comrades. But how are we to judge those other men, knowing nothing of their histories? The coerciveness of those circumstances makes confident moral judgment impossible.

Another implication attaches to the Goldhagen definition. If camp inmates are to be exculpated for carrying out their superiors' orders, and – more subtly and more perniciously – for fulfilling the intention to degrade behind those orders because they would suffer penalties for non-compliance, might we not be forced to exculpate their SS guards as well, who would later claim that they had acted against inclination, and under duress?

This is a difficult matter, and readers must make their own judgments. My own view is that there is a great distance between those who do what they must to survive in an imposed situation, and those who design or participate in the imposition of that situation. It follows that prisoners or ghetto-dwellers forced to live within artificially demoralized worlds cannot be judged culpable for any action they took or failed to take to survive in that world, or to help those dear to them to survive, even if by so doing they jeopardized or directly damaged others – although I will of course celebrate those individuals like Levi who steadfastly refused to be corrupted. The moral responsibility for the evil done in the camps and ghettos, including the evil done by inmates, lies squarely with those Germans, whether dedicated to Nazi ideals or to their own advancement, who filled, sealed and starved the ghettos, and who organized and directed the camps.

As for the guards – as every prisoner knew, and as later judicial investigations were to discover, a few guards, even some SS officers, conducted themselves with reasonable decency and humanity within the general degradation of the camps. In post-war trials SS defendants often cited their fear of transfer to a fighting zone, especially the Eastern front, as justification for their obedience to inhuman orders. Punitive transfer was certainly a risk, and a risk which could not be measured: not only prisoners suffered the arbitrariness of their masters. It was, however, also a risk which some individuals were prepared to take: a few SS men refused camp or killing duties, and some were indeed sent to the front. Most guards and officers discharged their duties efficiently, and some with gleeful, inventive cruelty. Again, given the variability of both circumstance and conduct, each case must be assessed individually, but in view of the demonstrated existence of choice, each individual must be regarded as responsible for the choice he or she made.

The *Sonderkommando*, the men, nearly all of them Jews, whose labour kept the crematoria working, who were involved consistently and most intimately in the killing of Jews, and who lived high on the pickings of their doomed fellows, require separate consideration.

These men are rarely talked about in the literature. These are the men from whom the humanist Levi recoils. He calls them 'crematorium ravens'. He believed that their moral being had been extinguished from their first moment of co-operation with their masters, however savagely that co-operation had been won, and that their submission represented the foulest and most complete triumph of the Nazi system by the full implication of the victims in the crime being committed against them: 'it must be the Jews who put the Jews into the ovens, it must be shown that the Jews, the sub-race, the sub-men, bow to any and all humiliation, even to destroying themselves.'[7]

I want to explore the situation of the men of the *Sonderkommandos* in the man-made infernos of the death camps, so that we may retrieve some part of their experience.

IN THE ZONE OF FIRE: THE AUSCHWITZ *SONDERKOMMANDO*

Primo Levi had spent his year as a prisoner at Monowitz, part of the Auschwitz complex seven kilometres from the Birkenau extermination plant. While he usually wrote only of people and situations he had experienced directly, he broke that rule for the *Sonderkommando* because he considered the squads to have a peculiar significance: they were, he said, 'National Socialism's most demonic crime'. While he pitied the prisoners 'flung inside the walls of an indecipherable inferno', he believed that their acceptance of their filthy work fully enmeshed them in the crimes of their tormentors. For Levi the 'crematorium ravens' had become as evil as their masters. Knowing the *Sonderkommando* to be lavishly supplied with alcohol, he imagined them as being 'in a permanent state of complete prostration and debasement'.[8] They, along with their controllers, fall outside the wide embrace of his compassion and curiosity.

I think Levi's characterization is mistaken. However terrible their circumstances, the men of the Auschwitz *Sonderkommando* did not live in a state of 'prostration'. Both the demands of their work and substantial evidence from the men themselves preclude that interpretation. Of necessity they were physically tough. Whether selected on the ramp or from within the camp population, they had already endured the traumas of arrival. They were then projected into a world of Boschian horrors; where the air was not air but a choking, reeking vapour, where vision was clouded by smoke, where naked human bodies, tangled, contorted, smeared with blood and excrement lay all around them.*

In that place of nightmare they enjoyed none of the dreamer's physical immunity. From the first moment blows thudded on backs, arms and heads as they were forced to grapple with fouled, slithering corpses. One of them remembered:

We were running under the threat of the clubs of the SS men who supervised us. We lost ourselves to such a degree that none of us knew what he was doing, and how, and whatever was happening to him. Driven on we ran like automatons, not knowing whither we were running, what for and what we were doing . . . I know that not one of us was fully conscious, did not think, did not reflect. They reduced us to such a state that we became like [illegible] when we came to our senses somewhat [we saw] who was being dragged to be burnt and what was going on around us.

The beaten men ran and tugged and heaved, because even in that world 'the truth is one wants to live at any cost, one wants to live because one lives, because the whole world lives'.[9]

---

* Compare Hell – a place restricted to wilful sinners – as described in the 'retreat' sermon in James Joyce's *A Portrait of the Artist as a Young Man*: 'Hell is a strait and dark and foulsmelling prison, an abode of demons and lost souls, filled with fire and smoke . . . The prisoners are heaped together in their awful prison . . . the fire of hell is a neverending storm of darkness . . . amidst which the bodies are heaped one upon the other without even a glimpse of air . . . The horror of this strait and dark prison is increased by its awful stench . . . [Imagine this sickening stench] from the fetid carcasses massed together in the reeking darkness, a huge and rotting human fungus.'

This is the voice of Salmen Lewenthal. It is also a voice from the grave. It was SS policy to execute the men of the Special Squad every few months, presumably because they learnt too much of officially secret matters. The men knew that they were doomed. But even in that place some secretly wrote of what was being done there. Few of the thousands who worked in the special squads survived: from Belzec two, Chelmno four, Sobibor fifty, and from Treblinka perhaps sixty out of the thousand working there.[10] Lewenthal's diary was unearthed almost twenty years after he had buried it near the crematoria at Auschwitz-Birkenau. This man, bereft of a personal past and all personal ties, immersed in daily horrors, in the knowledge of his own imminent death, still retained sufficient faith in his fellow humans to record what was being done in that place in the hope that one day we would read his words.

The ferocious breaking-in was standard policy. The SS men knew that new recruits had to be driven like beasts through their first hours because if allowed time to 'collect themselves' they would baulk, and the whole weary business would have to be done again. A few managed to withstand panic long enough to refuse and to be rewarded with death. Others collapsed, and if beatings failed to move them were shot where they lay. Most stumbled on, worked and lived. Can we blame them for that?

At first the men worked exclusively with the bodies of the dead. In times of peace the tender handling of corpses is taken as a sure measure of respect for the living, and so of 'civility'. For religious Jews respect for the cadaver is of particular importance, both by tradition and Jewish theology's hope for a corporal resurrection. The Nazis must have relished the infliction of that additional insult. (In the Auschwitz *Sonderkommando* the processing of murdered womens' hair was malevolently assigned to a group of ultra-Orthodox Jews.) It was also during those first days that recruits were most likely to find the bodies of wives, children, parents or friends among the tangled dead, and to know themselves alone in their desolation – a knowledge others would have to endure only at liberation.

We all know how quickly habituation breeds callousness. Operating theatres, where bodies no more than mimic death, are notorious for gallows humour. And some of those thrust into these duties were already hardened. Young Simon Srebnik was unmoved by what he saw at Chelmno extermination camp because he was already a graduate of the starving ghetto at Lodz: 'When I saw all this, it didn't affect me . . . I was only thirteen, and all I'd ever seen until then were dead bodies . . . In the ghetto at Lodz I saw that as soon as anyone took a step, he fell dead . . . I thought that's the way things had to be, that it was normal.'[11]

Reward was inextricably implicated in the horror. Filip Müller of the Auschwitz *Sonderkommando* recalls how on his first day, still dazed, still nauseated, he was struggling to strip a corpse when he saw a half-opened suitcase. In it was bread and poppy-seed cake. In an instant he had them: 'With my filthy, blood-stained fingers I broke off pieces of cake and devoured them ravenously.'[12] The unholy compact was struck: food and a cessation of beating in exchange for back-breaking, degrading labour.

Saul Friedländer has urged that attention given the 'political decisions and administrative decisions' of the perpetrators should not blind us to the 'concreteness of despair and death' of the victims, reminding us that 'the *Alltagsgeschichte* [the 'everyday life'] of German society had as its necessary shadow 'the *Alltagsgeschichte* of its victims'.[13] This is a useful reminder, especially when Germany and the victim societies they were systematically draining of life were geographically distant.

Understanding the relationship between the two becomes a major challenge when the societies of perpetrators and of victims are brought face to face, as occurred in confrontations between local Jewish communities and the German Order Police in Poland, subsequently analysed by Christopher Browning and Daniel Goldhagen. The work of these scholars has vastly extended our understanding of the *Alltagsgeschichte* of the Order Police abroad, yet the intensity of their inquiries into the actions of the perpetrators preclude more than a gesture towards the experience of the victims, despite transparent concern for their sufferings. Interaction between police and victims was also typically brief, and violent. The concentration camps present a different situation, because there we find an *Alltagsgeschichte* of near-continuous contact within a society at once highly artificial and highly interactive. As we will be shown, camp authorities evolved a number of strategies to minimize any softening effects of that enforced proximity.

There was, however, one situation in which the two groups met and mingled in intimate interaction: the weird *Alltagsgeschichte* of the crematoria and the killing facilities, where the strong male prisoners of the *Sonderkommando* worked alongside their SS directors at one demanding job: the creation and destruction of corpses.

The work in the crematoria was physically tough: tugging, lugging, heaving, shoving, in choking heat, always at a furious pace, with the pace quickening whenever the trains banked up. Joshua Rosenblum, a member of the Auschwitz *Sonderkommando* from March 1944 to the closing of the killing centres in October of that year, remembered how during those months the squads had to deal with so many bodies that, even though squad numbers had increased to 180 or more men, each squad with four SS supervisors, they were still working twelve to sixteen hours at a stretch.[14] Four hundred thousand Hungarian Jews died in the course of that long summer.

The selection of workers to handle living victims was more cautious. Only seasoned men were allowed to work in the ante-chambers, easing each new intake through the business of preparing for the 'showers'; leading them, like Judas sheep, into the gas chambers.[15] They were instructed to keep the people reassured and docile, and by and large they followed their instructions. Ought they have done otherwise? On the few documented occasions when victims were warned and comprehended the warning, the scene ended as planned, but with far more blood and terror.

Filip Müller sometimes played that Judas role, but most of the time he worked as a stoker: a stoker of bodies. Once the furnaces were kindled the main fuel relied on was human fat, so an effective burn depended on intelligent selection as well as artful stacking. Müller had been transferred to Birkenau from the Auschwitz I crematorium in April 1943, and what he later remembered about his first Birkenau year was its relative easiness. In those early days there were only about 200 men in the *Sonderkommando* divided in four squads of fifty, each division with its four regular SS overseers. For the prisoners this was an enclosed community, and scarcely less so for the SS, given their long working hours. While there were some Russians, Salonika Greeks and a few Czechs, most of the workers were Polish or German Jews, and nearly all could converse with their fellows.[16]

Fifty is a good number for a work group, large enough to accommodate individual quirks, small enough for the development of *ésprit de corps*, especially if the teams are male, the work physical, the bosses reasonably benevolent, and there are other teams with whom to compete. After his experiences in the Auschwitz squad, where savage beatings and abuse had been commonplace, Müller was amazed by the easygoing ways of his first Birkenau *Kapo*, a young Pole 'leaning on his stick without either goading or beating us', who would talk about news from the front – until the arrival of an SS officer sent him leaping into a flurry of pantomimed activity. Another Polish *Kapo* notorious in Auschwitz I for his 'uncontrollable' temper (he had killed several men in his rages) after transferral to Birkenau was transformed into an image of remote calm.[17]

The *Kapo*'s actorish composure was presumably modelled on the local SS style, which was notably 'cool'. Relations between supervisors and workers were commonly easy, and once the frenetic initiations were over, beatings were rare. They happened. Müller reports that his block senior was given twenty-five strokes on the buttocks for allowing too many of his subordinates to report sick. The senior in turn pummelled the French-trained doctor in charge of the infirmary and abused him: 'Listen, you bloody academic idiot,' he yelled, 'you're not at the Sorbonne now, you bastard.'[18] Twenty-five strokes is no trifle, but compared to the arbitrariness, the viciousness and the mechanical impersonality of the punishments inflicted in Auschwitz I, these exchanges are at least recognizably human.

Outside working hours the living was easy. Unlike ordinary prisoners, the men of the *Sonderkommando* were not in competition with each other for necessities. For most of the time food, clothing and bedding, some of the finest quality, were in abundant supply. A doctor attached to the unit remembers silk coverlets and cushions on the individual wooden bunks, a tiled shower room for the two compulsory showers daily, and the men as being in prime physical condition – although suffering from 'acute nervous depression, and often neurasthenia'.[19]

Easy access to goods allowed trade with the rest of the camp. That trade could only occur with the co-operation of the *Kapos* and the guards outside the extermination sector, and the indulgence of at least some of the *Sonderkommando*'s SS bosses. Forbidden even to touch the bodies themselves, the SS had to rely on their underlings for access to the gold and jewels hidden in the luggage, or sometimes inside the bodies themselves. These riches were exchanged for goods from 'outside', most commonly alcohol and cigarettes, which under Auschwitz living conditions were necessities.[20] The two sets of parasites lived best when they lived in comfortable symbiosis. Müller lets us glimpse an unbuttoned moment of corrupt exchange when he describes Voss, the *Sonderkommando*'s first and most amiable commander, slipping off his jacket for 'mending' before departing on home leave, so that jewels pilfered from the dead could be stitched into the seams.

Preposterous as it must sound Müller's account suggests that until the general reorganisation of May 1944 the majority of SS men working with the *Sonderkommando* at Birkenau did not conduct themselves as virulent anti-Semites to the Jews who worked with them. I do not want to exaggerate the ease of relations, to deny the vileness of the men's tasks, or to minimize their absolute vulnerability before their masters. Mengele doubtless enjoyed the joke when he called on the platform for medically trained volunteers for delicate dental work, and then set those who stepped forward to levering open the contracted jaws of naked corpses to wrench out any gold-work with pliers.[21] The anti-Semitism enacted inside most of Auschwitz was pathological. It bore not the least resemblance to the pallid antagonisms, the weary jokes and unwearying condescension we might associate with the term. Rather it was the active expression of the conviction that Jews were not human at all, but *Untermenschen*, vile creatures whose one aim was to contaminate anyone in their proximity.

Inside the *Sonderkommando* relations were different. Müller offers many moments of 'natural' co-operation between their own SS and the workers against outside intruders. When camp superiors up to and including the commandant made an appearance, the whole team, like work-teams everywhere, would spontaneously 'put on a show'. Both men and officers would scrupulously conform to the regulation mode of corpse destruction to an accompaniment of appropriate abuse: 'Can't you watch what you are doing, you bloody Jewish bastard?', 'Watch it, or you will end up inside the oven too.'[22] Then the outsiders would leave, the abuse would stop, and they could go back to their comfortable ways again, cutting corners, bending rules, the very nature of the work, with its production-line structure, encouraging a shared rhythm.

The Hungarian doctor Myklos Nyiszli, pathologist to Dr Mengele's researches and medical officer to all the men of the *Sonderkommando*, reports a particularly eerie example of comradely fun: an impromptu twilight football match between scratch teams from the 'SS' and the 'SK', with much shouting and laughter from players and onlookers alike.[23]

When Primo Levi read Nyiszli's account he was utterly repelled, precisely for what it indicated about the comradeship between the SS and the veterans of the *Sonderkommando*. He heard the echo of 'Satanic laughter' in this game played 'as if on a village green and not at the gates of hell', seeing in it Nazism's final triumph over the Jew: 'You are like us, you proud people, dirtied with your own blood, as we are. You too, like us and like Cain, have killed the brother. Come, we can play together.'[24]

We can see what he means, and why he feels it. It is possible, however, to read the game differently – as men being allowed to recognize each other, however briefly, as fellow humans. Both teams knew that at some unspecified time in the future one would eliminate the other, but in Auschwitz the future had little reality.[25] Even when that unreal future at last came, with the camp abandoned and its people dispersed, we glimpse a moment of non-ideological affection when SS *Unterscharführer* Gorges came across his old workmate Müller at Mauthausen in April 1945. The SS had been combing the camps seeking out and killing every member of any *Sonderkommando* they could lay their hands on. Gorges chose not to betray Müller. Instead he arranged to meet him the next day, and handed over some illicit bread and tobacco he had 'organized' for him.[26]

I do not know what these fugitive softenings might suggest about the effect of daily experience on ideological obsession. The SS were men who had been trained to kill and to hate, and when ordered or challenged they killed their erstwhile workmates without recorded remorse. Yet the reduction of the artificial distancing maintained in the larger camp clearly had some effect. The men of the *Sonderkommando* were exempt from the visual dehumanization inflicted upon the ordinary inmates of the camps. With their tiled showers, clothes looted from rich Jews brought in from the West, and plentiful food, they could always appear as men.

Hannah Arendt noted that even the 'hard' Nazis sent to Denmark to control that small, tough country came in the course of time to be almost as unwilling as their Danish subjects to yield up Denmark's Jews, effectively refusing to co-operate when required to do so. Arendt believes that when these men met with the principled and open opposition of the Danes, 'their "toughness" had melted like butter in the sun'.* I would claim much less for the *Sonderkommando* at Birkenau: only that some small sense of community and some recognition of the other as a comrade seems to have bloomed in that unlikely place, and in that blooming lightened one corner of the darkness that was Auschwitz.

When *Hauptscharführer* Moll replaced the easygoing Voss early in May 1944, everything changed.[27] Moll, a highly efficient technician, an earnest worker, and even among Nazis a passionate anti-Semite, brought with him a squad of like-minded officers who wrought an immediate transformation in the rules, tempo and mood of work. Skilled workers were used as laborers digging the great cremation pits to receive the Hungarian dead, and knew themselves to be despised Jews again, beaten and cursed and abused.[28] New killing and disposal methods were introduced. Behind the converted farmhouse beyond the birch grove the workers now dragged terrified victims from the 'undressing room' straight to the guns of the SS and to the burning pits.[29] Old alliances shredded as the *Sonderkommando* nearly doubled in size, and swelled again as the trains kept rolling in.[30]

The uprising in October 1944 as the crematoria were being closed was occasioned by the revolt of 250 or so *Sonderkommando*, most of them Greeks and Hungarians who knew they had been 'selected' to die. The rebellion became a radical, unplanned 'selection' as the SS shot down the rebels, leaving 450 dead.[31] That savage culling secured an extension of life for the rest, who were required to man the single crematorium kept in working order to deal with 'natural' deaths, casual murders, and the human results of Dr Mengele's experiments. Few survived the enforced exodus away from the camp in January 1945 as the Russians advanced.

* Arendt expands the observation with her usual sanguine daring, claiming their tentative change of heart demonstrates that 'the ideal of "toughness," except, perhaps, for a few half-demented brutes, was nothing but a myth of self-deception, concealing a ruthless desire for conformity at any price', with the inference that if more people had 'stood up to' Nazism, it too would have melted. Arendt, *Eichmann in Jerusalem*, p. 175.

At Treblinka, solely a death camp, where those who handled the dead were sealed away from those who pushed the living into the gas, where there were no competing groups to stimulate a sense of solidarity, matters were different again. Richard Glazar, a German-speaking Czech transported to Treblinka in October 1942, was put to work in the clothes-sorting team in the lower camp. He was one of the handful of men who escaped in the course of a long planned, long dreamed-of revolt which erupted on 2 August 1943, and who then contrived to survive until liberation.

You have probably seen Glazar's face and heard his voice in Claude Lanzmann's film *Shoah*, or in one or another of the documentaries on the Holocaust. His is a notably attractive presence: direct, unaffected, warm, ironic. This 'crematorium raven' reminds me of Primo Levi in his stable humanism, but with a warmer wit.

When the first rich transports from Warsaw and the West were rolling in, Glazar tells us that he and his Czech comrades from the sorting room, who were treated by SS and prisoners alike as a kind of natural elite, dressed as dandies: they wore 'black boots made from highly polished fine leather, jodhpurs, belts around our short jackets, silk scarves around our necks, and the caps on our heads worn at a rakish angle', and when their clothes were soiled they threw them away: they were, he says wryly, 'fashionable young men from the realm of death and decay'.

This was not vanity but strategy. Officially the *Sonderkommando* was permitted only to take blankets from the sorting shed. All other clothing had to be filched from the piles of goods they sorted and packed to send to Germany. The punishment for theft was severe, but the evidence of theft could be flaunted daily: a classic case of SS doubleness. Given the risk, why the dandyism? On advice from their own veterans: SS whips cut the faces and bodies of well-dressed, well-shaven Czechs far less than the faces and bodies of Polish Jews, because the SS saw the husky 'boys from Bohemia' as racially superior to Slavs and Poles – indeed, as close to themselves. It was therefore advisable to signal one's human status by way of well-shaven skin, dapper dress and erect posture, so that even in the heat of anger (some SS were chronically angry) the distinction would be remembered. By contrast, nightwear could be selected on purely pragmatic grounds, women's nightgowns, preferably long silk ones in pastel shades, being the first choice as they were found to discourage fleas and bugs.[32]

Distance between the SS and work-Jews inside Treblinka was also increased by the presence of Ukrainian guards. Nonetheless, trade flourished at and between every level, excluding only the most austere SS – who were also, interestingly, the most vicious. In Treblinka as in Auschwitz sorters stole not only food and clothes but whatever gold, jewels and currency they could, some to add to an escape fund, some for themselves. They also set aside choice items – fur coats, leather goods – to fill personal orders for the SS. Beyond the wire the Ukrainians and their work-teams ran a furtive market, brokering local deals in ham, sausages, vodka and loaves of bread for money from 'good' SS and the wealthier prisoners. The 'Gold Jews', official collectors of the jewellery, gold and notes discovered at any stage of the processing, also took their cut. The trade network stretched as far as Warsaw and Lublin, but its beating heart was Treblinka. 'The entire region, near and far, sucks blood out of this greedy slaughterhouse. It is in their direct interest to keep Treblinka going, to keep its valuable by-products flowing-money, gold, diamonds.'[33]

The death factories cultivated minor differences. They used different gassing agents: at Auschwitz-Birkenau Zyklon B, at Treblinka carbon monoxide generated by a diesel engine, at Chelmno gas vans. At Treblinka women's hair was cut before they were killed, at Auschwitz afterwards. At Auschwitz bodies burnt inside ovens or in pits, at Treblinka on 'roasts' – great grids over wood-stoked fire-pits. They also divided their slave labour differently. At Auschwitz the men who cleared the gas chambers and manned the crematoria and burning pits also processed the baggage of their victims, and so had easy access to profits. At Treblinka incoming victims were received, reduced to shorn nakedness and forced along the 'Tube' into the gas chambers in Camp I (the lower camp), while Camp II (the upper camp), retrieved the dead bodies from the chambers, removed the gold from the mouths of the naked corpses, and then disposed of them. There was no whipping post in the upper camp – infractions were punished by a pistol shot – but the upper camp was dreaded, because there was only death there: 'It is all they will have in their hands – death, but in thousands of forms composed of naked flesh.'

Of the forty SS who rotated in and out of Treblinka four were particularly dreaded: Kurt Franz, 'the Doll', young, handsome, an artist with the whip; Fritz Küttner, or 'Kiewe', a frenetic tyrant given to lethal rages; Willi Mentz, the tireless executioner in the 'Infirmary', where those too weak for ordinary processing were shot; and softfooted Willi Miete, 'in Czech the Good Hunter, in Yiddish Crooked Mug, and, most fittingly, the biblical Malchamoves, the Angel of Death'. Miete specialised in sniffing out weakening men and awarding them 'special treatment' in the Infirmary.

The rest were less savage and more equable. There were even occasional acts of kindness. When one of the formidable Czechs – in fact the military brains of the prisoners' revolt committee – fell ill with typhus, genial Sergeant Suchomel, head of both the 'Gold Jews' and the tailoring shop, sent him a fresh orange and soup from the German mess. Later, when the same man had been sent to the upper camp for some minor infraction, another SS sergeant visited the sorting warehouse to have his prisoner friends make up a parcel of clothing for him.[34] And one day an SS master-sergeant marched into the little office of the prisoner in charge of the sorters' barracks to announce he would not be returning after his Christmas leave because what was being done at Treblinka outraged his sense of military honour, and he was volunteering for the front.[35]

The master-sergeant was a rare case. The rest of the SS, however casually indulgent, were sworn to 'hardness' and to murder. Richard Glazar, as fine an observer as Levi, emphasises the 'incredible rivalry' between individual SS and the terrifying consequences for prisoners at risk of being shot to spite a rival. He allows that from early in 1943, with the development of some stability in work relations, there came to be 'a terrible kind of communality of basic purpose between the murderers and the victims – the purpose of staying alive'. Both cheered when rich convoys were due. But he does not confuse this temporary communality with warmth of feeling. He is always mistrustful: 'Perhaps some SS men developed a kind of "loyalty" to one prisoner or another – though one hesitates to call it that; there really was almost invariably another, and usually nefarious, reason for any act of kindness or charity. One must always measure whatever they did against the deep fundamental indifference they felt to all of us'.[36]

'Fundamental indifference'. At Chelmno the boy Simon Srebnik sang Polish folk songs for the pleasure of his SS bosses, and in return they taught him German marching songs. He would sing to them as he rowed up the river to fetch lucerne for the officers' rabbits. We hear those songs when he sings, grey-haired now but the voice still beautiful, for Claude Lanzmann and the *Shoah* film crew. Neither his youth nor his songs saved him from the SS: when they were leaving Chelmo they shot him in the head and left him to die in a pile of corpses, where a Pole found him and hid him in a pig sty.

Ought the men of the *Sonderkommandos* be judged morally defective because, surviving long enough to become habituated to the iron circumstances of their existence, they strove to make a kind of life in the midst of the horror? My own inclination is to admire their toughness of spirit. Adaptability is a human virtue, requiring its own brand of courage. And surely it is absurd to evaluate moral performance in a setting studiously designed to deny the autonomy, indeed the moral existence, of the majority of its members? Within so grotesque a social architecture we cannot look to the victims, oppressed in every direction, for enlightenment as to the capacities of humankind for cruelty. For that we must look to the men and women who devised, directed and administered the system.

6

LEADERS

The lighting [in the gas vans] must be better protected than now. The lamps must be enclosed in a steel grid to prevent their being damaged. Lights could be eliminated since they are never used. However, it has been observed that even when the doors are shut, the load always presses hard against them as soon as darkness sets in which makes closing the doors difficult. Also, because of the alarming nature of darkness, screaming always occurs when the doors are closed. It would therefore be useful to light the lamp before and during the first moments of the operation . . . [1]

– Secret Reich Business, Berlin, 5 June 1942

Aharon Appelfeld, the Israeli writer, lost his family and his childhood to the Nazis. At eight he was trying to survive alone in the Ukrainian forests. His novels memorialize the slow erosion of innocence among ordinary Jewish men and women approaching the brink of the Holocaust. He refuses to concern himself with the motives of the perpetrators because he considers them to be so irrational, so atavistic, as to be beyond human understanding:

The Jewish experience in the Second World War was not 'historical'. We came into contact with archaic mythical forces, a kind of dark subconscious the meaning of which we did not know, nor do we know it to this day. This world appears to be rational (with trains, departure times, stations, and engineers), but in fact these were journeys of the imagination, lies and ruses which only deep, irrational drives could have invented. I didn't understand, nor do I yet understand, the motives of the murderers. I was a victim, and I try to understand the victim.[2]

Ota Kraus and Erich Kulka devoted their first years of freedom to compiling a massive dossier on the Nazi concentration camps, but when it came to the Nazis themselves they essentially agree with Appelfeld. In spite of 'three years hard training' in various Nazi camps and prisons, their first days at Birkenau had affected them 'so profoundly that we were often scarcely able to find the spiritual and physical strength to bear our utter despair'. They were content to identify the men who had devised that devastating scenario as 'human monsters' – and to leave it at that.

Even Primo Levi, normally so committed to the study of his fellow humans, finds little to say about the men who made Auschwitz. It is true that as a lowly *Häftling* he did his best to avoid the SS, not least because their attention commonly meant death. It is also true that during most of his daily life he saw little of them: routine bullying was left to prisoner subordinates. The closest contact he had with them occurred during the periodic 'selections', occasions of perfect terror and perfect humiliation when naked skeletons puffed out bony chests and lifted barebone knees in parodic displays of 'fitness' before elegantly clad, impassive watchers, whose casual judgment was a matter of life or death.

What is luminously clear is that he hated them. The mature Levi was to refuse to acknowledge that hatred: only fascists and Nazis, he says, hate a man or woman because of their race. He also says, characteristically, 'I'd say that the lasting curiosity I feel about the Germany of then and now excludes hatred.'[3] In his last major work, *The Drowned and the Saved*, he was to include some Germans within the grey zone of moral ambiguity in which he placed Jewish Prominents and the Jews of the death-camp *Sonderkommandos*. On the evidence of his immediate post-Auschwitz writings, however, the Levi who emerged from Auschwitz hated Germans.

This hatred is crystallized in his account of the chemist Dr Pannwitz. In face of their shared specialist knowledge, in face of the superficial civility of their exchanges, Pannwitz offers Levi the immeasurable insult of refusing to acknowledge him as a man. In return Levi presents Pannwitz not as an individual but as a specimen. Even the occasional gestures of kindness by individual Germans rouse little gratitude and less curiosity in this usually responsive, inquisitive man.[4] Only highly eccentric Germans, like the enigmatic, solipsistic Eddy the Juggler, remote from all ordinary sociabilities, are granted life in his prose. To

Levi Germans are reflexes of their culture, and German culture is at once ludicrous and hateful.[5]

Consider a few of the characterisations which freckle his first post-Auschwitz book. Germans 'love order, systems, bureaucracy', but they are cowards when systems break down. 'Rough and irascible block-heads,' they 'cherish an infantile delight in glittering, many-coloured objects.' Their absurdities are endless, some being perverse and de-signed to baffle, most being the consequence of their utter lack of anything but the most brutish humour. They are enclosed in an ar-mour of obstinacy and wilful ignorance: with the Russian army fifty miles away, with the bombs falling, 'they build, they fight, they com-mand, they organise and they kill'. Why? 'What else could they do? They are Germans.'[6]

The SS he sees only at the distance of their authority, but he knows them by their works: by their corruption of language, their 'absurd precision', their vicious deceptions, their taste for degrading the help-less, their delight in the whole mad hierarchy of the camp. They are 'lost in a world of negation'. He therefore dismisses them as 'evil and insane'.[7]

'Evil and insane' – and a decisive stop to inquiry. Through much of his later writings Levi tried to bring the Germans to an admission of their culpable knowledge: to acknowledge their 'willed ignorance' of what was being done to their vanished neighbours, of what their sons and husbands and nephews and brothers were doing to civilians out there in the East. In one of his last writings Levi formally declares his withdrawal from the lists: 'In rereading the chronicles of Nazism, from its murky beginnings to its convulsed end, I cannot avoid the impres-sion of a general atmosphere of uncontrolled madness that seems to me to be unique in history.' He believes that the madness had drawn much of its energy from a 'furious anti-Semitism'. But how had that come about? He had been a Jew in fascist Italy but he had not been made to feel too different – until the Nazis came. He puzzles over the possible 'combinations of factors'. Was it the accident of Hitler's 'ma-lign and twisted personality', and its 'profound interaction with the German people'? Perhaps. The dark remains dark. And Levi, the Ital-ian Perseus who had looked so steadfastly into the face of horror lowers his shield, steps back, turns away. He will not try to understand

the Nazis, because to understand may be to justify, and, more profoundly, because the words and deeds of the Nazis 'are non-human
words and deeds, really counter-human, without historic precedents
. . . comparable to the cruelest events of the biological struggle for
existence'.[8] Classified as non-human, as worse than the cruellest
beasts, the perpetrators of the Final Solution are placed beyond human
scrutiny.

The revulsion of an ex-prisoner from murderous jailers is not, I
suppose, surprising, although I confess I am surprised – I expect Levi's
humane insight to be inexhaustible. What surprises more is to see a
similar position being adopted by some of the major scholars in the
field. The newcomer to Holocaust studies is impressed by a curious
imbalance. The overwhelming mass of scholarly writings bears not on
the few who planned the actions or the thousands who carried them
out, but the millions who suffered them. It is true that one monumental study of the perpetrators appeared as early as the sixties. Raul
Hilberg's *The Destruction of the European Jews* is, as Hilberg robustly
declares, 'not a book about the Jews. It is a book about the people
who destroyed the Jews.'[9] But while it is close to indispensable for
information regarding the development of the institutional structures
and procedures of that destruction, and while perpetrator mentalities
and motivations are firmly outlined, the task of mapping and chroni-
cling is too consuming to leave much space for the kinds of up-close,
detailed case studies we need if we are to grasp why these men thought
as they did, and how they did what they did. This was why I so much
valued Christopher Browning's study of the activities of Hamburg Police Battalion 101 when I happened upon it: here at last were recognizably human men in the process of executing horrifying orders.[10]

There is a further division among historians which is almost as
consequential. Nearly all scholars who focus on the 'why' of events
concern themselves with the decisions of the Nazi high command, not
with the doings of the lower executive ranks. They want to know who
willed what when – to establish the moment when intention coagu-
lated into instructions. They seem notably less concerned with the accounts of those often oblique, often verbal instructions, so these accounts can all too easily appear sanitized, remote from the terror and
anguish of the actualities they purport to explain. Meanwhile, the
many scholars who devote themselves to the analysis of victim experi-

ence give scant attention to perpetrator actions, despite the fact that those actions fall directly within their immediate field of vision.[11] Finally, and to my mind perversely, when scholars turn to more general questions provoked by the Holocaust, questions to do with the nature of humankind, it is the conduct of the victims, not the perpetrators, which is placed in the moral frame and subjected to rigorous scrutiny.

This may be because of an assumption: that men and women best reveal their 'essential natures' when *in extremis*. Bruno Bettelheim defines that condition as 'a situation experienced by the subject as irremediably bound to destroy him'.[12] I have come to think this notion of self-revelation under fatal stress is a romantic fiction, and a dangerous one. What we mostly exhibit *in extremis* is the state of our physical reflexes. In this instance the intensity of focus on prisoners' actions and failures to act has the cruel effect of adding to survivors' already burdensome guilt. If we want to understand the extremes of human capability we must turn not to the victims but to the dark territory of the Nazi leaders' motives and understanding.

What drove the men who made the Holocaust? How did men not previously criminal come to will what they willed, to do what they did? These are the crucial questions to be answered if we are to understand the Holocaust at all. Yet for many committed students these questions remain opaque. Saul Friedländer, a notable scholar, has courageously undertaken to try to explain why that is so.

UNDERSTANDING NAZIS

Friedländer begins by claiming that too many historians evade the problem of perpetrators' motivations 'by concentrating exclusively on specific ideological motives (i.e. racial anti-Semitism, racial thinking in general etc.) or on institutional dynamics'. While such factors may be important, they leave 'an independent psychological residue' which 'seems to defy the historian', and which when recognized is 'usually reduced to a vague reference to 'the banality of evil.'[13] He believes such notions cannot get us far – although, as it turns out, his objection has more to do with the invocation of 'banality' than of 'evil'.

Friedländer launches his own analysis with an excerpt from a famous and often cited Holocaust document: the speech Heinrich Himmler addressed to an assembly of senior SS officers at Posen on 4

October 1943. Hitler had instructed Himmler to breach official secrecy, which to that point had shrouded the fate of Germany and
Europe's Jews. Later that same month Himmler was to deliver a
speech similar in content to the regional bosses of the Nazi Party, and
later again in the new year to an assembly of army chiefs, but in this
first address of 4 October the SS *Reichführer* is speaking to his own,
out of shared experience.

Out of an hour-long speech Friedländer selects this passage:

Most of you know what it means when 100 corpses are lying side by side,
when 500 lie there or 1000. Having borne that and nevertheless – some
exceptional weakness aside – having remained decent has hardened us . . .
All in all, we may say that we have accomplished the most difficult task out
of love for our people. And we have not suffered any damage to our inner
self, our soul and our character.[14]

These are certainly startling lines. Friedländer identifies the emotion
generated by our reading of them as 'horror and uncanniness', occasioned by the dissonance between 'the explicit commitment to breaking the most fundamental of human taboos, that is, the wiping from
the face of the earth each and every member of a specific human group'
(Friedländer is assuming that the corpses are of Jews), and the claim
that such an ambition can be realised without moral danger to the
killers. Friedländer characterises this notion as 'the inversion of all
values'.

Even more important to Friedländer's diagnosis is another sentence
from the same section of the speech: the insistence on secrecy. The
extermination of the Jews, Himmler declares, is 'the most glorious
page in our history, [yet] one not written and which never shall be
written'. Friedländer dismisses the possibility that Himmler's determination to keep SS actions secret related to the social dynamics of 'the
forging and existence of a fanatical elite', pointing to what he calls 'the
fact that for religious movements, as well as for modern day political
religions, the mass killings of enemies of the faith or of the party
generally is part of the well-publicized campaigns of such entities'. He
goes on to provide a mixed bag of rather dubious examples ('the extermination crusades against the Cathars, the witch-hunts and the general practices of the Inquisition, the "Terreur", the Bolshevik killings,
and those perpetrated by the "Khmer Rouge" etc.') to prove his point,

declaring that these killings were all defiantly and deliberately public: 'always linked to the most explicit aims, propagandized with pride . . . and presented as almost self-understood in terms of ideological necessity.'[15]

We could quarrel with the claimed 'fact' regarding the broadcasting of mass killings. While it is true that Stalin's state executioners had a public rhetoric of justification at their disposal, its invocation was frequently well after the fact, and always within the context of the vastly larger silence which blanketed millions of other deaths in slave labour camps and in collectivization campaigns. Meanwhile, dozens of ethnographic studies, those useful close-ups of small examinable societies, have demonstrated the efficacy of even fictive 'secrets' in sustaining the cohesiveness of an exclusive, self-glorifying elite. The secrets of the SS were both real and scandalous, and presumably even more effective in promoting internal loyalty. Hannah Arendt notes an interesting adjustment of Nazi terminology: the men in the Nazi hierarchy who were 'told explicitly of the Führer's order [to solve the Jewish Question by mass murder] were elevated by virtue of that knowledge from mere "bearers of orders" to "bearers of secrets" '.[16]

Properly speaking the murders were not secret at all. The mass shootings of Jewish and Polish civilians by the *Einsatzgruppen* and the German army in 1940, and then of Russians in 1941, were certainly known about by many Germans because they were public affairs in which large numbers of Germans participated, and because while there was a declared official preference for secrecy, there was little attempt to keep them so.[17] Even within Germany the SS had beaten and killed Germans Jews in their homes or publicly on the streets, most especially on *Kristallnacht*, the Night of Breaking Glass.

By contrast the existence of extermination centres and the use of the gas chambers were closely guarded secrets. But even there secrecy was necessarily imperfect, because altogether too many people – the families of the men working 'in the East', the railwaymen who saw people crammed into boxcars or heard the moans coming from closed trucks at stations and sidings, the multitude of bureaucrats involved in the giant enterprise of the dispossession, 'resettlement' and destruction of thousands of people, the factory managers who processed the camps' sinister products – all these people must have been aware that something grave and terrible, something murderous, was going on somewhere out of sight. The official shroud of secrecy added terror to the silence. It could not effect ignorance.

Friedländer, however, sees Himmler's emphasis on secrecy as indicative of something far more sinister and metaphysical than a pragmatic interest in keeping dark things dark. In Friedländer's reading, Himmler's concern for secrecy reveals his recognition of the absolute moral transgression of Nazi intentions and undertakings. The argument runs thus: 'Himmler's vow of secrecy for all times seems to indicate that he saw no higher comprehensible argument which would "justify" such an annihilation in the eyes of posterity.' Therefore 'he and the whole assembly were, in this case, well aware of some total transgression that future generations will not understand'.[18] Thus 'the singularity of the Nazi project seems to lie not only in the act, but, incidentally of course, in the language and the self-perception of the perpetrators'.[19]

Once again we are being invited to put the Final Solution into its singular category of one. And in view of the claimed admission by the perpetrator-in-chief, Friedländer declares that 'the extermination perpetrated by the Nazis is not an ' "inversion of all values" (as would be the case if human beings were worked to death or killed for a very specific political aim) but instead represents an amorality beyond all categories of evil'.[20]

A self-confessed 'amorality beyond all categories of evil'. This is interpretation with a vengeance. Where are we to find the springs of action in this swamp of amorality? Friedländer invites us to dismiss the ideological passions usually assumed to provide the key motivations – for example, 'the centrality of the anti-Jewish obsession in Hitler's world view' – because ideological motivation is not prominent in the Posen address. Instead he suggests that we look for the 'core motivation' for Himmler and the 'higher bureaucracy of death' in non-ideological forces: in psychological and emotional conditions, of which he nominates two: 'If we accept the thesis that Himmler and his generals were not driven by an overriding anti-Jewish ideological obsession . . . we are faced with the *Führer-Bindung* [the 'bond with Hitler'] and with *Rausch*, the 'growing elation stemming from *repetition*, from ever larger numbers of the killed others.' This elation, Friedländer says, 'ties in with the mystical Führer-Bond: the greater the number of Jews exterminated, the better the Führer's will has been fulfilled.'[21]

Here, at last, comes the nub of Friedländer's argument, and the rub for would-be interpreters. Unlike Himmler and his SS, we have not renounced human morality. We are therefore unable to participate in emotions such as Rausch and 'the bond with Hitler':

Precisely at this point – the elation created by the dimensions of the killings – our understanding remains blocked at the level of self-awareness . . . Consequently, the greater the moral sensitivity of the analyst, the stricter the repression will be of a subject deemed too threatening to both the individual and to society. *The historian can analyse the phenomenon from the 'outside', but, in this case his unease stems from the non-congruence between intellectual probing and the blocking of intuitive comprehension of events that happened more or less during his or her lifetime, within his or her society.* [Friedländer's italics][22]

Friedländer is then free to embark on a flurry of speculation on the inner states and processes of the perpetrators, these 'human beings of the most ordinary kind approaching the state of automata by eliminating any feelings of humanness and of moral sense in relation to groups other than their own', who somehow transform from 'bureaucratic automata' into 'beings seized by a compelling lust for killing on an immense scale'.[23] After all, automata might do anything. But we humans are left in a parlous situation. If the perpetrators of the 'Final Solution' could and did place themselves beyond the moral pale ('some total transgression that future generations will not understand'), and therefore beyond the possibility of human understanding ('the blocking of intuitive comprehension of events') by inquirers of any degree of moral sensitivity ('the greater the moral sensitivity, the stricter the repression') – then we mortals can never hope to comprehend the essential dynamics of this vast tragedy. And that is indeed Friedländer's conclusion:

The 'Final Solution', like any other historical phenomenon, has to be interpreted *in its historical unfolding and within the relevant historical framework.* [Friedländer's italics] A priori, therefore, we should be dealing with this epoch and these events as with any other epoch and events, considering them from all possible angles, suggesting all possible hypotheses and linkages. But, as we know, this is not the case, and, implicitly, for most, this cannot be the case. *No one of sound mind would wish to interpret the events from Hitler's viewpoint* [my italics] . . . this past teaches us nothing commensurable with the very enormity of the event; it does not help us to understand the present-day world or the future of the human condition.[24]

This is grim news indeed, given that inhuman policies persist in our world, and given our need to achieve some analytic understanding of them if we are to resist them effectively. Friedländer is covering a great deal of territory here, but the argument appears to be two-fold: the 'Final Solution' has not been satisfactorily (because not globally) interpreted, and it cannot be satisfactorily interpreted because the actions of its agents are not amenable to the analyst's 'intuitive comprehension of events', because 'no one of sound mind would wish to interpret the events from Hitler's viewpoint'.

Friedländer then proceeds directly to what is, in my view, the dangerous conclusion that 'this very perception of limits . . . may indicate that we are possibly facing an exceptional situation that calls for the fusion of moral and cognitive categories in the course of historical analysis as such'.[25]

This conclusion – indeed Friedländer's whole discussion – places us squarely in a conceptual field inhabited by words like 'evil', which are of no use whatsoever when it comes to teasing out why people act as they do, and are likely to lead us to the impasse in which Friedländer finds himself. And not Friedländer alone. As we have seen, Primo Levi also declared his inability to understand the Nazis, I think because Levi, like Friedländer, believes in the central importance of 'intuitive comprehension' in understanding another human creature. Deprived of that sense of intuitive insight he thinks himself lost. Levi writes, 'To understand a proposal or human behaviour means to "contain" it, contain its author, put oneself in his place, identify with him.' But 'no normal human being will ever be able to identify with Hitler, Himmler, Goebbels, Eichmann, and endless others'. Identification, the only route to understanding, is closed. Levi also believes that even to attempt to understand such men is to risk contamination – the 'moral sensitivity' exclusion. Understanding of this kind also threatens to cripple judgment, 'because to understand is almost to justify'.[26]

UNDERSTANDING UNPLEASANT OTHERS

To take the first issue first. In my view understanding does not require anything so heroic as 'identification', which is at best a slapdash procedure and too often a misleading one. Extrapolations from our own experiences and their associated emotions will not take us far in comprehending people of different cultures, or even of different generations and genders within our own culture. We know it can mislead even with intimates drawn from our own immediate circle ('she did *that?*'). It must surely fail with people who appear at first or even second glance to be 'monsters'. So what is to be done?

There is obviously something special about the way human beings 'read' each other's behaviour. This capacity appears to be inbuilt. As Jerry Fodor puts it, 'Children don't have to be taught their native language; they just pick it up. Nor, apparently, do they have to be taught to attribute people's behaviour to the mental states they're in. Children tend, quite naturally, to anthropomorphise whatever moves. What they have to learn is which things don't have minds, not which things do.'[27]

An important distinction. Children also have to work at sociability with the creatures who do have minds if they are to develop a secure sense of self. The two, when all goes happily, proceed in lockstep. When they do not we have varying degrees of autism. Even when we are dumped down in another culture, even when we miss the local cues and mistake the local customs, we can in time more or less 'get along'. To do this we have to begin from a general assumption that the creatures around us are human: that they have minds, and will share at least some of our responses. But it is, in my view, at least as important to operate on the assumption that in any particular they might well be different. A vigorous downward hand gesture which to me says, 'Go away!' in Greece says, 'Follow me now!' In time a reasonable degree of 'understanding' of such local gestures will come, but it will come slowly, out of confusion and by trial and error, which means a long meandering route of observation, inference and experiment, not a shortcut signed 'identification'. And even then our understanding will be as imperfect as is our grasp of all subjectivities, including our own.

As to the second issue, that to understand is to justify or excuse, consider a personal example. I spent a few years of my life attempting to understand Aztec human sacrifice from the Aztecs' point of view, and took some trouble to communicate what I came to think they were up to. I trust that no reader therefore assumed that I favour human sacrifice. I spent another few years thinking about a Spanish missionary friar in sixteenth-century Mexico who had been an effective defender of 'his' Indians against lay exploitation until he discovered what he interpreted as their wholesale relapse into 'idolatry' (they had probably simply continued their traditional observances with a little more discretion). Fray Diego de Landa proceeded to inflict inventive, illegal and hideous tortures on his new converts, thereby managing to extort from them confessions, largely fabricated, to ever more lurid derelictions. These confessions provided him with post-factum justification for his criminal conduct. Supported only by his hand-picked local friars, who were infatuated with their charismatic leader and themselves deeply implicated in the torture campaign, he was denounced by his Franciscan superiors in Spain and Mexico and sent back to Spain in disgrace. Once there, he wrote a great, insightful and tender account of the Indians of Yucatan. Villains are rarely simple men. That he was later rehabilitated and sent back to Yucatan as its bishop was a tribute both to his terrifying self-righteousness and the irremediable quirkiness of Spanish colonial policy.[28]

In such matters it is not enough to weep for the Indians. We must understand their torturers, too. I have no liking for fanatics, no stomach for the punitive infliction of pain on any sentient creature, and no patience with the arrogance of organized religions. Nonetheless, I think I came to understand Diego de Landa, first by retrieving what I could of his dynamic intellectual and social milieu, and then by establishing enough of his actions and statements through time and changing circumstance to recognize characteristic patterns of thought and action – to get to know the kind of man he was. Although he could always surprise me, I came to expect certain things of him, and I was, usually, right. This process is not very different from the way we come to know people in life: learning their typical range of responses, trying out hypotheses, puzzling over the ones we get wrong. I also believe that I have been able to explain something of how Landa came to do what he did, how he persuaded others to join him in exhilaratingly decisive action and how he later contrived to avoid too painful knowledge of what he had done. While I respect him, even have some affection for him, I have not the least impulse to exculpate him. Understanding him better has led me to assess his capacity for harm the more severely, and to decide that I would judge him to be one of those rare beings, a fit subject for assassination. In so far as one can calculate these matters, his premature death would have saved many lives and much misery.

It had taken me some time reading Landa's words to realise that what I had been casually dismissing as ejaculations of conventional piety were at once the stuff of his thought and indicators of emotional intensity. One of my early difficulties in grasping what the Nazis thought they were up to was that I could not take their professed racist ideology seriously. Instead of listening hard to what they were saying, I assumed the violence of the language to be largely rhetorical. That is a natural but completely misleading response. Other people do think differently from us. Himmler declared in the Posen speech that the slaughter of a thousand men is a decent act, while stealing a watch from a corpse is reprehensible: 'We have the moral right vis-à-vis *our* people to annihilate *this* people which wanted to annihilate us,' he said, 'but we have no right to take a single fur, a single watch, a single mark, a single cigarette, or anything whatsoever.' To us the morality is perverse. Was it perverse to the men listening to their much loved leader?

Consider another passage occurring a little later in the same speech:

For the SS man there is one absolute principle; he must be honest, decent, loyal and friendly to persons of our own blood – and to no one else . . . If an anti-tank ditch has to be dug and 10,000 Russian women die of exhaustion digging it, my only interest is whether the ditch is completed for the benefit of Germany . . . If someone comes to me and says, 'I cannot dig this anti-tank ditch with these women and children, it is inhuman, they will die doing it' – my reply will be: 'you are a murderer of people of our own blood; if the anti-tank ditch is not dug, German soldiers will die, sons of German mothers. They are our blood.' This is what I have tried to instil into the SS and I believe I have done so.[29]

These are truly chilling statements, but they are grounded in a coherent if extreme racialist morality – the absolute priority of blood – and in the urgency of war. Should we take Himmler's comments about 'glorious but unwritten pages' as the public revelation of 'an amorality beyond all categories of evil', and a conspiracy to conceal 'some total transgression'? These are surely unusual enterprises for a speechmaker. Or is Himmler making an intensified appeal, at this late and increasingly dangerous stage of the war, to a romantic mysticism alien to us, but which we know to have infused many SS men? Is he also celebrating the exaltation of the top levels of the SS over both 'ordinary' Germans, and their own lesser ranks?[30]

Years ago, in the course of an analysis of the rhetoric of *Mein Kampf*, Kenneth Burke gave warning that 'the drastic honesty of paranoia' may coexist with tough-minded calculations of 'Real-politik of the Machiavellian sort'.[31] In October 1942 the Allies had declared their intention to pursue 'war criminals'. By December of that year they had 'linked this to the German Government's "bestial policy of extermination of the Jews of Europe"'.[32] When Himmler addressed the regional bosses of the Nazi Party later in October 1943, with the intention of formally implicating them in that policy, he was addressing men who possibly did not know just how systematic and bestial that extirpation had been. Two days earlier, speaking to his own SS, he was speaking to men who had been actively engaged in the business of murder since its beginnings.

In none of these speeches did Himmler make any reference to the death camps and their multiple gas chambers. Their existence was not to be broadcast even to the faithful. But Himmler's rhetoric makes dramatically clear how little interest he and his men had in being 'commonly understandable'. At Posen Himmler was addressing comrades who in their own account had arrested Germany's racial, political and economic decline by superhuman efforts, and wrenched it back to its destined path – without losing their decency. Lesser men, meaning everybody else, including all those coming after the Age of Heroes, would never have the moral or the political capacity to grasp the sacrifices made by the elite of the Himmler generation.

HEINRICH HIMMLER

When people who look more or less like us, who seem to 'speak our language', express irrational or immoral beliefs it is inordinately difficult to accept that they might mean what they say. But we dare not decide that ideas cannot be believed in merely because they are preposterous. Analysts have to attune their ears to what is in effect a new language masquerading as a familiar one: a language where a term like anti-Semitism does not mean spite or malice but the active conviction that every Jewish adult, child and infant is a dangerous enemy.

Tone matters as well as text. It is necessary to understand how such extravagant sentences were spoken and such sentiments normalized. Albert Speer, who heard Himmler speak many times, recalled that Himmler 'looked and talked like a schoolmaster . . . When Himmler addressed his young disciples, we can be sure he didn't rant and rave; the enormities he said will have been pronounced firmly but quietly, in middle-class German – very effective'.[33] Effective indeed, especially when the entire subject matter consists of enormities. Himmler was not addressing young, untested disciples at Posen, but men seasoned in murder. What was he seeking to effect, in his schoolmasterly tone, speaking 'firmly but quietly' throughout that long delivery (the speech ran for more than an hour, after a long day of speeches) to his immediate subordinates?

Himmler knew his men better than we do. What he chose to say to them and how he chose to say it are therefore crucial. The speech, which is usually offered to readers in short, shocking snippets, just as I have presented it here, demands to be analysed in its totality if we are to grasp its movement of thought and emotion. It would clearly reward extended analysis.[34] My own reading – in English translation, by one ignorant of German and therefore deaf to every nuance of accent, intonation and local usage – suggests that there was indeed an individual psychological burden attached to the program of killings: a burden that Himmler acknowledged, and was intent on alleviating by recapitulating the moral and political grounds for actions taken and to come. While a close comparison with the other Posen speeches made before rather different audiences is both necessary and beyond me, what this particular speech looks like is not an effusion of nihilistic boasting, but a measured reassurance intended to re-embolden the first tier of his executors, who would in turn reanimate their subordinates right down to the 'ordinary' SS in the camps or in the field. By October 1943 reassurance was required. With the tide of victory turned, and the greater part of the killings done, Himmler saw the need to remind his senior men that they were not ordinary men, but heroes, who had done well and righteously.

As for the 'psychological residue' left after we extract the 'ideological' and the 'political' – we hear of Himmler turning away in distress during inspections of the killing installations he had brought into existence, or trying to find some possible ground for rescuing a blue-eyed, fair-haired boy from a group of Jews about to be shot. Fleetingly we think that his murderousness might arise from some pathological failure of imagination, that had he been present at any of the atrocities he ordered he might have recoiled from them and put a stop to them, that he somehow failed to grasp the enormity of what he was effecting. After all, Hannah Arendt has claimed something rather like this for Eichmann in her emphasis on the sanitizing effect of bureaucratic remoteness from brutal actions in the field.

There can be no such possibility for Himmler. He meant what he said. There is an anecdote I was hesitant to include because it is so extravagant as to test credulity. Martin Bormann, the son of Hitler's trusted secretary, Hitler's godchild, and nicknamed 'Kronzi', or 'Crown Prince', enjoyed the run of the Berghof, Hitler's mountain retreat. Fourteen years old in 1944, he was, as Gitta Sereny tells us, 'a passionate young Nazi, immensely proud of his "strict but just" father and of his Führer'. One holiday afternoon he, his mother and his younger sister were invited to afternoon tea by Himmler's longtime mistress, Hedwig Potthast. Neither she nor Himmler had been fully admitted to Hitler's domestic circle, but they had comfortably installed themselves close by the Berghof, and she was eager to show off her new house. After the chocolate and cake, she told the children she would show them something interesting, a 'special collection' Himmler kept upstairs in the attic, which had become his den. There, the adult Martin remembered, they saw 'tables and chairs made out of parts of human bodies. There was a chair . . . the seat was a human pelvis, the legs human legs – on human feet'. Potthast then displayed one of a stack of copies of *Mein Kampf*. The covers, she told them, had been made by prisoners in Dachau from human skin – special skin, the *Rückenhaut*, the skin of the back.

The children fled down the stairs, closely followed by their mother. In an attempt to calm them Frau Bormann assured her distressed children that when Himmler had sent their father an identical book, he had refused to have it in the house.[35]

A terrible story. Is it true? It is not easy to be a son, especially the son of such a father, and childhood memories can be transformed by later knowledge. But at fourteen Martin was not quite a child; he has made the story public; there were other witnesses. It would be more comfortable not to believe, but I think we must (a sensible scepticism found the rumours of death camps incredible, too). Frau Potthast had made a gaffe: such objects were not for children. Perhaps they were not for anyone beyond Himmler and herself. The prurience her gaffe exposed might seem at odds with the elevated talk we have been listening to – unless we recognize those vile objects were for Himmler icons and trophies of that ideology: artefactual expressions of the final degradation of despised creatures who only facsimilated humanity.

We are a long way from identification here. But it seems that even a Himmler need not be beyond our capacities of clinical comprehension. How did such a man come to power? On Hitler's coat-tails. There are many more difficulties in the way of understanding a Hitler, not least because we know that had there been no Hitler there would have been no Holocaust. This fact is at once obviously true, and so grossly incommensurate with our notions of adequacy regarding historical cause and effect that we recoil from it. It has therefore been a central question for historians.

ADOLPH HITLER

For much of the 1980s the dominant controversy in Holocaust studies was between 'intentionalists' and 'functionalists'. The division lay between those who believed that Hitler and those closest to him had been determined to slaughter Germany's Jews from their first days in politics, expanding that ambition with the war to include all Jews under Nazi domination, and those scholars who argued that the process was more organic: that the 'cumulative radicalization' of the Nazi regime was the crucial dynamic, the decision to kill rather than to expel the Jews being taken late, and opportunistically.

This opposition, too crisp as academic oppositions tend to be, has been all but obliterated by recent publications by Saul Friedländer and Christopher Browning. Browning's collection of essays, *The Path to*

Genocide, seeks to illuminate exactly that: the processes, both personal and political, intentional and bureaucratic, by which Hitler and his henchmen arrived at the decision that the Final Solution to the Jewish Question would be extermination. Saul Friedländer pursues the same question through inquiry into the precise nature and evolution of Hitler's own thinking regarding the Jews, and its slow manifestation in anti-Jewish legislation and action by the Nazi state.[36]

Their findings are reassuringly complementary. Browning does not underestimate Hitler's early, enduring, pathological hatred of Jews. He sees that animus, however, as one part of a larger Nazi vision of a Europe wholly restructured in accordance with racial definitions – a vision that initially did not require the murder of the Jews. Rather, German Jews were to be removed from Germany by emigration, whether 'voluntary' or 'encouraged'. With the conquest of Poland came a grander vision: Jews, both German and Polish, were to be pushed beyond the band of Polish territories marked for resettlement by *Reichsdeutsch* or ethnic Germans, beyond the territories allocated to native and resettled Poles, to be thrust into a remote area east of the Vistula. The final destination was open to revision, at one point it being suggested that all of Europe's Jews could be banished to Madagascar!

There is an immediate implausibility about the notion that any political group, much less any government, could entertain the prospect of such grandiose interventions in Europe's demography, especially in the thick of fighting a war. Surely even the Nazis could not have plotted anything so fantastic? The evidence, however, is compelling. They did. After all, they were to devise and very nearly to carry out an even more implausible scheme for the 'cleansing' from Europe of two historic peoples, the Jews and the Gypsies. We are dealing here with revolutionaries, and revolutionaries of steepling ambition and unfettered power.

Browning argues it was the decision to invade Russia which led Hitler to jettison the resettlement schemes, already proving unworkable, with ghettos crammed and regional bosses protesting, and to fix on the policy of extermination of all Jews who came into Nazi hands: if they could not be got rid of in one way, they would be got rid of in another. Browning sums up: 'Nazi racial policy was radicalised in quantum leaps that coincided with the peaks of German military success, as the euphoria of victory emboldened and tempted an elated Hitler to dare ever more drastic policies.'[37] The speed and the efficiency of the implementation of the Führer's decision were the contributions of a bureaucracy ready and eager to execute its leader's will.

For the perpetrators the step from expulsion to death was not a major one. Commenting on the process of implementation Browning writes:

In retrospect we can see that the inauguration of the Final Solution in 1941 was a monumental event in history, where old notions of human nature and progress were shattered and mankind passed forever into the post-Auschwitz era . . . we should not be surprised that such an appreciation was lost upon many of the murderers themselves . . . For Nazi bureaucrats already deeply involved in and committed to 'solving the Jewish Question', the final step to mass murder was incremental . . . They had already committed themselves to a political movement, to a career, and to a task.

Nazi bureaucrats had already been instructed in cruelty and in indifference to human suffering, from the gassing of the mentally and physically handicapped in Germany, through the agonies of the 'resettlement' projects, to the mass shootings of civilians in Poland and Russia behind the lines: 'By the very nature of their past activities, these men had articulated positions and developed career interests that inseparably and inexorably led to a similar murderous solution to the Jewish question.'[38]

Thus the gulf between 'intentionalists' and 'functionalists' is closed by refined historial research and judicious statement. Browning's essays make a subtle, persuasive case. Friedländer's volume complements them. Peter Pulzer has already written illuminatingly on the changing condition of Jews in Germany culturally, socially and politically.[39] Friedländer adds a close investigation into the origins and nature of Hitler's private anti-Semitism and the process by which that private pathology came to be the engine of public policy: an investigation which confirms Browning's analysis, and extends it back in time. Friedländer's Hitler was early infected with the brand of anti-Semitism hatched inside the 'Bayreuth Circle' formed around the composer Richard Wagner. This version identified two pure races in the world, the Jews and the Aryans, with the struggle between them – the Jews, naturally, were the destroyers and the Aryans the creative force – providing the dynamic for all world history. Hitler had also absorbed the paranoid politics of the 'Protocols of the Elders of Zion'. (The 'Protocols' were an elaborate forgery concocted by anti-Semitic Tsarist secret police, which purported to reveal a Jewish conspiracy to rule the world.) Hitler was convinced of the reality of the conspiracy, and was persuaded that the Bolshevik (Jewish) seizure of power in Russia was its first overt manifestation.

Friedländer dubs this idiosyncratic, very local ideological brew 're-demptive anti-Semitism'. Redemptive anti-Semitism assumes the irreconcilable conflict between Jews and the Aryan state, and the natural opposition of the 'races'. But while it requires separation, it does not logically demand the physical extermination of either one of them. Paul Fussell wisely said, 'Understanding the past requires pretending you don't know the present. It requires feeling its own pressures on your pulse, without any later illumination.' Hitler was a committed 'redemptive' anti-Semite when he came to power, but Hitler himself did not know where his anti-Semitism would lead, or how it would finally come to be expressed in action. Friedländer traces the changing expression of Hitler's vision from the cultural and social segregation of Germany's Jews to his later policy, formulated in 1936, of 'encouraged' Jewish emigration, with the destination preferred by the Nazis being Palestine, conveniently far from Europe.

Friedländer reinforces Browning's conclusion that it was the successful invasion of Poland that sharpened Nazi policy towards the Jews, first to 'resettlement' in eastern Poland, and then, after the invasion of Russia – with mass 'resettlement' proved unworkable, and millions more Russian Jews delivered into German hands – to the most complete political expression of Hitler's 'redemptive anti-Semitism': the capture and murder of all Europe's Jews.

Terminating 'lives unworthy of life' was no novelty in the Nazi state, because Nazism took the politics of race seriously. By the end of 1939 300,000 Germans suffering from mental or hereditary illnesses had been sterilised, and a program of euthanasia for individuals judged 'unworthy of life' was in full swing, with 70,000 to 80,000 German citizens already dead.[40] The deportations of 1939–40 had brought terror and bitter suffering on many people, not all of them Jews, while the euthanasia program had developed personnel and procedures ready for export to Poland. For many of those embarking upon it the Final Solution might not have seemed a major step at all.

Despite these clarifications the pure extravagance of Hitler's beliefs, together with his power to attract and to hold the German popular imagination, continues to astonish. I was shaken to realise that Hitler was not only a vehement anti-Semite, but so systematic a racialist that at the end of 'his' war, with both victory and the future in the hands of 'the strong people of the East', he could declare his total unconcern as to the fate of surviving Germans (he calls them 'garbage') because the fact of their survival in a time of all-out struggle had defined them as 'inadequates' anyway.[41]

I suspect non-Germans have particular difficulty in grasping the appeal both of Hitler's public and private person because he stands in an idiosyncratic relationship to a medium we have come to depend on to catch the distinctive style of a personality. He photographed badly. Stills and documentaries reveal a seedy fellow, flab-cheeked, soft-bodied, awkward in movement, stiff in repose. Among his henchmen on formal occasions he seems by far the least impressive. Our reason tells us we are mistaken – after all, the whole Nazi theatre of politics was built out of this superstar's capacity to dominate huge audiences – but the impression of seediness persists. Churchill, cigar clamped in doggy jaws, is formidable. So, in his fashion, is Stalin. So (but less certainly) is the chronically beaming Roosevelt, whose expansive smile signals self-confidence to Americans, but is disturbing to people used to sterner displays of masculine authority. But not Hitler. Arthur Miller recalls how in 1964, only twenty years after the war's end, the director staging his *Incident at Vichy* showed the young cast a film of Hitler making a speech, so they would know, as it were, what they were up against. 'They watched as Hitler, facing a vast stadium of adoring people, went up on his toes in ecstasy, hands clasped under his chin, a sublimely self-gratified grin on his face, his body swivelling rather cutely, and they giggled at his overacting.'[42]

We whose 'Hitler' was shaped during the anxious days of the war also have to combat the after-effects of brilliant anti-Nazi propaganda. When I hear Hitler's voice I hear a hysterical ranter: when the war leaped into my childhood through the kichen radio it often spoke in Hitler's voice. Remembering my dread of Nazi killers loosed in the family kitchen, I still hate that voice, I still find German hard to listen to. Meanwhile, a wildly funny, wildly popular film like Charlie Chaplin's *The Great Dictator* spread its joke-image over terrifying actuality. Chaplin's little Austrian was comic, pathetic, ludicrous, crazy. He had nothing to do with the actual Hitler – but he imposed himself with the effortlessness of art upon our imaginations. And in Australia, where any pomp and circumstance save that attending major sporting events is regarded with aggressive scepticism, the notion of deifying a leader is comical anyway.

It seems that charisma does not travel well. And despite the grandeur surrounding his public performances, Hitler was in many ways a private man. Looking at his social and economic achievements during the thirties, it is difficult to deny him something close to genius. But much of his politics was secret, because he was mistrustful, and a natural solitary – although a solitary with a charlatan's flair for multiple self-presentations. Despite an abundance of autobiographical writings and recorded table-talk he kept his own counsel, sustaining an air of mystery, a thrilling aloofness, even through his last beleaguered days. This was a man who contrived to remain a hero to his valet.

He was recognised as a hero by the thousands who gathered to hear him speak, and by the dozens who, hearing him, voluntarily relinquished their autonomy to him. If we want to see Hitler's magic, we have to watch not Hitler, but the faces of the people listening to him. We see a people transported. It is no longer possible, if it ever was, to view his rule over Germans from 1933 to 1945 as a seduction turned violent.[43] We cannot feel the magic of the Leader. Germans – most Germans – did.

ALBERT SPEER

To understand the power of the attraction we need accounts from some of those enthralled by that magic. Gitta Sereny's *Albert Speer: His Battle with Truth* appeared in 1995. Sereny's central concern is the peculiar fascination Hitler exercised over a man of sophisticated intelligence, education and apparent sensibility. Speer joined the Nazi Party in March 1931 after hearing Hitler, an obscure would-be politician, speak. (This was a time, Speer is anxious to assure us, when the

Nazis were reticent about their anti-Semitism.) Speer quickly became a member of Hitler's inner circle, and stayed with him to the end, first as his official architect, in charge of the great surge of building, parades and performances which were the visible manifestations of the glory of the Third Reich. Then early in the war he was promoted to Reich Minister for Armaments and Munitions, and later took control of all production inside Germany, civilian as well as military. At one time Hitler considered appointing him his successor. Then the Reich fell apart and Speer faced trial before the War Crimes Tribunal at Nuremberg.

Forty-seven years after his first sight of Hitler, Speer still remembered that powerful attraction:

Above all else . . . I felt he was a human being . . . that he cared about me, about us, the young, individually. I am still convinced now that this was his greatest gift: to convey, not in words but by a kind of mass – and individual – hypnosis, that he cared about each of us, even, if you will forgive the term, that he loved us.[44]

Speer was impressed by Hitler's words, but he thought that the true magic resided in the glance, in the 'piercing blue eyes'. They had the power to compel, or (a favourite term for Speer, with its implication of exonerating helplessness) to 'mesmerize'. Both photography and our propaganda-drenched imaginations will fail to capture that.

Despite his belated recognition that Hitler was a criminal, and a dangerous one, Speer continued fascinated. It is the delicacy of Sereny's analysis of that long fascination which provides us with a kind of understanding otherwise unattainable. Charisma may be invisible to those who do not feel it, but the Speer experience allows us to identify some of its aspects, and to recognize it as dangerously real.

We can retrieve Hitler's appeal, and therefore the true dimensions of his threat, only by conscious intellectual effort. But whether we go back to Hugh Trevor-Roper's account of Hitler's increasingly feeble self-orchestration over his last days in the bunker, or to Raul Hilberg to read the unrepentant testament he wrote on the day he was to kill himself, or to any one among a number of recent studies which expand our knowledge of particular areas of Hitler's life, surely then our understanding is significantly enhanced?[45] We cannot know Hitler's mind fully, but that is an epistemological restriction, not a moral one, and while there are limits to our capacity for understanding others, those limits will be discovered only at the end of inquiry, not before it begins.

ADOLPH EICHMANN

It must be admitted that achieving understanding of unfamiliar others is, like juggling or riding a bicycle, rather more easily done than said, demonstrated than anatomised. Late in 1939 Hitler appointed a young career bureaucrat 'Special Adviser' for evacuation and Jewish affairs. His name was Adolph Eichmann, and his new job was to organize the gathering and deportation of Jews from Germany and later from the occupied countries of Europe, and to deliver them into holding camps, ghettos and slave labour camps or directly to the extermination centres in Poland. Hannah Arendt attended Adolph Eichmann's trial in Jerusalem in 1961, and then spent many pages of a long book attempting to explain the bland ordinariness and intellectual vapidity of this criminal bureaucrat. She finds her essential clue in the idea of 'compartmentalization'. She decides that Eichmann was a petty man, his mind stuffed with clichés which blocked imagination. She further decided that he and thousands like him contrived to preserve themselves from awareness, and so from moral responsibility for the horror they were effecting, by focusing only on their own small part of the vast, complex enterprise. She arrives, finally, at what she claims is 'the lesson this long course in human wickedness has taught us – the lesson of the fearsome, word-and-thought-defying *banality of evil*'.[46]

This seems to be more of a pit-stop than a conclusion, and more exasperation than understanding – what does it mean to call a man 'banal'? Arendt would say, 'a mediocrity, a second-rate bureaucrat obsessed with trivia and incompetent to recognise the vileness of what he was embarked upon'. That was certainly how Eichmann chose to present himself – when he was on trial for his life in Jerusalem. Listening to his testimony we would think him a fussy fellow whose only concern had been to make his trains run on time, and who had been snugly insulated from the consequences of his decisions. Time and again his Israeli interrogator would close in with a blitz of incriminating documents or expose him in a flagrant lie. Eichmann's response was always the same: a self-exculpatory flurry of bureaucratisms –

'*my* signature? Well I can't think how it could have got there, it wasn't my jurisdiction, it must have been sent on by . . . ' And so on and on, in mind-numbing detail, from this very small cog in a very large, complex machine.

The difficulty is that this was not at all how his erstwhile associates remembered him. Those who had worked alongside him in the byzantine structures of the Third Reich knew him as a man of singular ruthlessness and opportunistic ambition, whose careerism – the capacity to 'creatively' interpret, and so exceed his orders – was tempered only by his obsessive determination to hunt down and destroy every last Jew he could lay his hands on, even when, as the tide of war turned, both the time and power to do so were deserting him.[47]

The transcripts of Eichmann's preliminary police interrogation in Jerusalem confirm his colleagues' assessment by exposing the quickness of his intelligence and his calculation, even when he had nothing to gain (his life was certainly forfeit). The transcripts as we read them in *Eichmann Interrogated* have been streamlined for publication. In actuality Eichmann's interrogator fired questions from different periods and projects at him, to trap him into frankness. Despite the fact that he knew he would hang, Eichmann never lost concentration during those interrogations and never yielded an incriminating circumstance.

He also lied, sinuously, and sometimes with breathtaking audacity, as when he claimed never to have felt any particular animus against Jews, that he had at all times simply obeyed orders. It is evident that he despised the crude anti-Semitism of the more blatant propagandists, but I think more for their vulgarity than their sentiments. And since his trial historians have been steadily exposing how chaotic the German bureaucracy was in its daily workings, for all its superficially precise vertical divisions and elaborate protocols. No one could have risen to Eichmann's authority by merely 'obeying orders'.

Eichmann was an earnest and efficient organizer who took pride in the smooth delivery of human cargo to the extermination camps. Throughout his trial – in Israel, surrounded by the kin of the Jews he had helped to murder – he continued to insist that he did not have a bad conscience about any of his actions; that, faithful servant that he was proud to be, he would have had a bad conscience had he *not* done as he had done.[48] If we did not know the nature of his offence he would appear to be a conscientious, equable fellow, eager to please superiors and inspire inferiors, and distinguished, if distinguished in anything, only by a tendency to exaggerate his own importance.

Arendt is altogether too impatient of woolliness in sentiment or thought to decipher an Eichmann much further. Most people live in a comfortable jostle of not quite formulated, even potentially contradictory ideas, while Arendt's are burnished, honed and set out for use like a craftsman's. While his ideas were sadly muddled, at least by Arendt's standards, Eichmann persistently represented himself as an 'idealist'. He was thrilled by what he saw as the glamour of his leaders and their imperial vision. It is disturbing to be faced with the contrast between the vapidity of the man and the horror of his deeds, but we will not understand an Eichmann unless we grasp not only the individual character, but the exhilaration infused into that drab character by his context of revolutionary excitement and urgent high purpose, so that bullying brutal action was transformed into heroism. It is unsurprising that Eichmann was sickened by any direct contact with the actualities of his killing trade, because actuality poisoned the exaltation.

Was Eichmann 'evil'? For me that word carries no resonance. What I find most disquieting is his moral opacity, and his strangely constricted imagination: he seems genuinely incapable of visualizing anything he does not actually see. These twin deficiencies are not restricted to Eichmann: we see them time and again at Nuremberg and in the later trials, where the prosecution can sometimes seem to be boxing with uncomprehending shadows. Recently I was enveloped in that same haze when I attempted to read the autobiography of Rudolph Hoess, Commandant of Auschwitz, written in a Polish prison over a couple of months in 1947 as he was waiting trial for his wartime activities.[49]

RUDOLPH HOESS

Hoess had time to think about his story. Captured in 1946, he was first interrogated by British Security, then questioned at Nuremberg that same year. In April 1946 he talked with an American prison psychologist, and later, in Poland, with a Polish criminologist who had prompted him to write his autobiography.

He was under no obligation to please his captors: like Eichmann he knew he would hang. He had the literary facility to communicate what he wanted to communicate: his prose is fluent and flexible, and he constructs the best short narrative on the development of the processes of mass extermination I have seen. When he says he enjoyed writing the autobiography, I believe him.

It is that freedom from literary and political constriction which makes the autobiography frightening reading. Hoess declares – insists – that he never wantonly harmed a prisoner, that he had merely followed the directives set down by Theodor Eicke, his admired superior at Dachau, the first of the Nazi concentration camps. Hoess grants that Eicke may have been overly zealous in teaching his SS guards to hate the 'enemies behind the wire'; that their training possibly made them too harsh. As for himself, he had done his duty and followed Eicke's principles and precepts. His autobiography rehearses all the platitudes we were to hear so often at the Nazi trials. Hoess presents himself as a simple family man, a patriot deceived by the golden tongue and the golden vision of the Führer, a disciplined, loyal officer simply doing his job.

It is also clear that these platitudes are sincerely meant. We are given access to a Nazi officer so complacent that – even in defeat, even awaiting trial before his enemies, even when being occasionally cuffed about by a prison guard who 'says he is a Polish Jew' – he simply cannot accommodate the possibility of a hostile view being taken of his actions.

Hoess was no more a minor functionary than was Eichmann. Not long after his Dachau experience he was given charge of the small camp at Auschwitz, which he was to make a huge work camp, and the largest and most efficient of all the death camps. Like other camp directors, Hoess made his entire career within the concentration camp system.[50] He gives an aggrieved account of his endless problems with unsympathetic superiors and ill-disciplined staff in effecting those results. While capable of astounding understatement ('The Jews in Dachau did not have an easy time') he is unfailingly tender towards his own discomforts, as in this passage:

I had to watch coldly, while mothers with laughing or crying children went into the gas chambers . . . I had to see everything. I had to watch hour after hour, by day and by night, the removal and extraction of bodies, the extraction of the teeth, the cutting of the hair, the whole interminable business. I had to stand for hours on end in the ghastly stench, while the mass graves were being opened and the bodies dragged out and burned.

And through all this, he tells us, 'my pity was so great I longed to vanish from the scene'.[51]

We don't believe him. His pity is all for himself. But what chills more than the self-pity is the conventional gesture towards conventional sentiment. The man we see is energetic, vain, and much too frank in damaging self-revelation to be classed as a hypocrite. His anti-Semitism is at once so casual and so profound that, even in a document he knows will be read by his opponents, he spends several luxurious paragraphs meditating on the multiple ways in which Jews continued to exhibit their noxious racial characteristics in the work camp, in the changing rooms, even into the gas chamber. The Gypsies, 3000 of whom Hoess and his men had murdered one hot night, were by contrast 'although . . . a great source of trouble to me at Auschwitz . . . nevertheless my best loved prisoners – if I may put it that way'.[52]

That sentence catches the man: the querulous note, the self-tenderness – and the grotesqueness of a sentimentality equally divorced from actuality and morality. It is the world of an autist, with insignificant details highlighted and the significant lost in shadow. His notion of what constitutes comparability is bizarre. One is his choosing to use the case of the assaults by that Polish-Jewish guard, in 1946 a man with many reasons to hate Germans and this German in particular, as an instance of the general difficulty of controlling guards everywhere, and therefore an exculpation of his own SS guards' murderous, authorised conduct: 'so it can be seen that even in a small prison the governor is unable to prevent such behaviour; how much more difficult was it in a concentration camp the size of Auschwitz!'[53] While there may be some lawyerly point-making here, the gross incommensurability of the two situations seems, quite simply, to escape him.

Hoess was tried in Warsaw in March 1947 and executed (in Auschwitz) in April. He presumably died as content with himself as he had been three months earlier when he settled at his writing table 'to tell the story of my innermost being'.[54] It is possible that the document does tell that story – he was, as I say, not a conscious hypocrite, and his occasional efforts to deceive are transparent.

For all that, Hoess and his text remain opaque, at least to me, and therefore profoundly troubling. I am bewildered by that persistent, eerie displacement and misplacement of emphasis and emotion. I do not understand what mix of inheritance and experience could have shaped a creature so efficient in managing the material world, yet so impervious to the moral import of his actions. I do not understand how a man of at least average intelligence could fail to see the non sequiturs, the contradictions, the lacunae in his tranquilly expressed ideas, or the gross misrepresentations which blot his narrative. His text is here in front of me – and I can do nothing with it.

Is my bafflement an instance of that 'opaqueness . . . at the very core of the historical understanding' which Friedländer complains of? Ought I conclude that such men are 'monsters' and as such beyond human understanding? Or is Hoess an example of the 'banality of evil' Arendt saw manifested in Adolf Eichmann, another man infatuated with clichés, incapable of self-scrutiny, who did evil without recognising it as evil? Eichmann was, for most of the time, physically remote from the killings he was facilitating. Hoess built Auschwitz, designed and controlled its workings, lived in the thick of it.

What seems most remarkable in both Eichmann and Hoess is the blandness of the surfaces presented for our inspection. What I need at this point of paralysis is neither grand theory nor a dismissive classification, but a good biographer: someone sufficiently sensitive, informed and intelligent to help me see how a particular man could come to be what he was. What I need, as I have come to realise, is a Gitta Sereny.

Sereny's representations of the subtle, riddling Albert Speer, first Hitler's architect and then his Minister for Armaments and Munitions, and of the most unsubtle Franz Stangl, commandant first of the death camp of Sobibor, then of Treblinka, have made these two very different men accessible to my understanding in a way their self-representations alone could not. Here I will concentrate on Stangl because he was directly implicated in the business of killing in a way that Speer was not, and because he was in character, role and complacency much closer to the opaque Hoess.

FRANZ STANGL

Stangl was a high-ranking Austrian policeman, and probably a secret Nazi, at the time of Austria's brusque 'reunion' with Germany. He began to learn his killer's trade when appointed Police Superintendent at Schloss Hartheim, one of the centres of the German euthanasia program, which had begun as early as December 1939 and continued into 1941 and (illicitly) beyond, and which saw the death, by gassing or injection, of more than 80,000 physically or mentally disabled Germans.[55] The process of those killings – secret lists, the secret transport of victims in blacked-out buses, their reception and 'assessment' by doctors whose 'hospitals' had neither wards nor beds, the gassing, the obliteration of the remains in specially constructed crematoria, even the conveyor-belt technology to convey the corpses into the fire – was in style and structure a sinisterly precise model for the mass killings to come.[56] (The process was, in fact, continuous: after the program's official ending, thousands of concentration-camp prisoners – politicals, 'habitual' criminals, Jews – were briskly certified as incurably insane, and gassed.)

Stangl was then sent to serve as commandant of the death camp at Sobibor from March to September 1942, and then to Treblinka, where current organisation was slipshod but which had the potential to process 5000 to 6000 people into ashes in a day.[57] At Treblinka he stayed, a most diligent administrator, until August 1943, when the last transport of Jews rolled in and (after a desperate uprising of worker-prisoners) the demolition of buildings and the camouflaging of the wounded earth began. In October of that year Treblinka's surviving work-Jews were shipped to Sobibor, and to the gas. Stangl was captured by the Americans in 1945 and handed over to the Austrians in 1947. Put in an open prison, he 'escaped' to Rome, where he was hidden by Bishop Aloïs Hudal, confessor to the German Catholic community and protector to many SS officers on the run, who was protected in his turn by Pope Pius XII himself. Stangl's wife joined him there, and they travelled to Brazil (under their own names) in 1951, and registered (still under their own names) with the Austrian consulate in São Paulo in 1954. There they lived until Stangl's dramatic arrest in February 1967. He was extradited to Germany, and sentenced to life imprisonment by a Dusseldorf court in December 1970.[58]

Sereny's study of Stangl was one of a spate of publications following Arendt's 1963 analysis of the Eichmann trial. Sereny had attended Stangl's trial. Early in his imprisonment when he was waiting for his appeal against a life sentence to be heard, she visited him and proposed a series of interviews. Stangl agreed. It was in the course of those private interviews – seventy hours of them – that she came to know Stangl and to develop a relationship with him.[59] We are made privy to the manner and the development of those interviews. We 'get to know' Stangl (and, less directly but quite as effectively, Sereny) progressively, as we get to know people in life: through what they say and how they act, and then (as Sereny turns to research), what other people who knew them have to say about them.[60]

Sereny's concern throughout was to elicit her subject's own account of what he had done, assaying his account against those of others to measure its reliability. She was also intent on reconstructing the context of his actions through detailed research. Her task was to decipher what her subject had meant by what he did, what meanings his actions held for others and what meanings those actions and understandings might hold for us. She brought a rich array of qualities to the task. An intrepid researcher, she tracked down surprised and sometimes reluctant witnesses around the world. She brought guilty, long-concealed secrets into the light, most particularly the shameful conduct of the upper levels of the Roman Catholic hierarchy in shielding leading Nazi criminals running for safety at the war's end.

Sereny is also a fine psychologist with a knack for highlighting a revelatory movement of a mind, as in the following textbook example of the self-protective strategy psychologists call 'compartmentalization'. Stangl, intent on establishing the innocence of his role at Treblinka, is recalling the definition of a crime as he had learnt it at police training school. Four elements had to be present: a subject, an object, an action, and an intent. He tells Sereny, 'if the "subject" was the government, the "object" the Jews, and the "action" the gassings, then I could tell myself that for me the fourth element, "intent," was missing'. He had committed no crime because his role had been merely administrative. He had not personally released the gas. That, he informs Sereny, had been the duty of two Russian prisoners, from which it follows that given that the Russians were prisoners and under coercion, 900,000 or more deaths had been effected with no one being guilty at all.[61] As for himself – he had done no more, he said, than administer and redistribute the fruits of these non-crimes by disposing of valuables removed from the victims.[62]

Sereny's capacity to pursue and to retain detailed information, to recall the small fact needed to thwart an evasion, is remarkable. But her most useful characteristic is her terrier curiosity. She is curious about everything, and she is never satisfied. She knows that humans, however easily classifiable they may seem, are complicated creatures, with much of their inner workings concealed not only from observers but also from themselves. Out of that insatiable curiosity comes her fathomless capacity for alert listening and the concentration to note the smallest hesitations, even changes in skin colour and tone, over interviews that sometimes lasted for more than seven hours. She has the forensic skill to analyse elaborate, calculated statements as she hears them, and to pose a precise and destabilising question in response. And she has what I take to be the key skill of the great interviewer: the ability to engage with her subject so deep inside their own territory that the urge to justify, to explain or simply to gossip with someone 'in the know' becomes irresistible. Again and again she seduces the wary Stangl into frankness, as he realises that here at last there is someone who might understand.

But not excuse. While she has the discipline to restrain expressions of outrage or scepticism, Sereny never conceals her detestation of what her subjects had done. What is most remarkable to me about her interviews with both Speer and Stangl is the steady acuity of her moral intelligence. In a morass of self-and-other deceptions and delusions, she keeps her footing. She is neither shocked nor shamed by Stangl's lies: she merely notes them – and bides her time. She has perfect moral pitch.

She is consistently honourable in her relationship with Stangl, as with all her interview subjects, because she is by nature honourable, and because her concern is ultimately moral. Towards the end of the Stangl interviews, when they were both weary (when they had both come to trust each other) she remains careful not to take advantage of either the weariness or the trust: 'my professional interest notwithstanding, it [was] important to me not to persuade or fatigue this man into disclosing more about himself than he wished to. If the sum total of what he could tell, and possibly teach us, was to be valid and of real value, I felt he had to offer it freely, and in full possession of his faculties.'[63] Thus for Sereny morality, reason and the quest for truth commingle.

Sereny has an ulterior and ultimate motive. Because her subjects are indeed subjects to her and not specimens, she is concerned for their reformation. She subtitled her Stangl book 'An Examination into Conscience'. Conscience? In a Stangl? Over the years he had obstinately sought to evade any admission, even to himself, of the least legal or moral responsibility for his actions.[64] At their first meeting she rejected his attempt to move into a routine set of justifications: what she wanted, she told him, was his own story, the story of himself 'as a child, a boy, a youth, a man: to tell me about his father, his mother, his friends, his wife and his children'. Stangl, invoked as a person, not a criminal, responded: he wept, agreed, and began.[65] In their last interview Sereny believed she saw the first indications that he had begun to reflect on his past actions, to recognize what degree of choice had been in them – and how selective, self-serving and dishonest his practised narrative had been.

Stangl died of heart failure nineteen hours after that last interview. Sereny believed his death had been hastened because of the 'monumental effort' he had made in the course of the interview, when he had finally, briefly, faced himself and 'told the truth'. Truth wears no shudder marks in Sereny's vision. At Nuremberg Albert Speer had grandly declared himself culpable by association for Nazi atrocities – atrocities of which he insisted he had been personally ignorant. Sereny's persistent question to Speer was, 'What did you know?' For Stangl her question was, 'What did you feel?' In each case the initial answer was 'Nothing' and the core drama of each narrative the increasing unease of that response, until, at last, the protective denial is abandoned, and a different, more painful truth begins to emerge.

We are a long way from monsters here. We are almost equally far from the invocation of large-brush psychological states to explain consistent, coherent, long-term actions across large numbers of individuals, like the influential notion of 'the Auschwitz Self' put forward by Robert Jay Lifton in his remarkable analysis of Nazi doctors.[66] Sereny did not attempt to 'identify' with either Franz Stangl or Albert Speer beyond that first, essential assumption of a shared humanity, yet through her scrupulous work we are brought to understand those two men immeasurably better. I do not pretend that 'understanding' men like Hitler, or Himmler, or Stangl is an easy matter. I would only insist that the problem is not qualitatively different from the problems inherent in understanding any other human beings – and that our understanding of our fellow human beings will not be and cannot be complete.

My final and largest anxiety arises from what might seem Friedländer's least consequential statement: that the Final Solution confronts the would-be investigator with so exceptional a situation that it 'calls for the fusion of moral and cognitive categories in the course of historical analysis as such': that is, that in the course of analysis objectivity cannot and ought not be the aim. That, to my mind, is a disastrous step. While the moral burden placed on humanity by the fact of the Holocaust is exigent, history will be able to educate morality only for as long as the categories are kept as separate as human imperfection allows. The capability to judge is not at issue. These men were murderers and inciters to murder. They should have been tried and punished in sufficient numbers and with sufficient publicity to restore the honour of their victims, to discourage potential imitators, and to repair battered human confidence that justice will sometimes prevail. But it is only after the scrupulous retrievals and analyses of 'good' history that we can hope to understand enough to engage in the essential task of diagnosing the circumstances of their rise to dominance, and of their successful recruitment of others to act as their agents.

How are we to understand the conduct of those agents, the actual killers? Are they little more than 'inhuman automata', as Friedländer suggests? Are they infected, like Hitler's closer associates, by *Rausch* or *Führer-Bindung*, the 'bond with Hitler'?[67] Hypotheses of this level of generality are difficult to assess. Sereny's investigation into Albert Speer certainly reveals Hitler's capacity to inspire devoted love in a superficially unpromising candidate, while the weird little world of the last days in the bunker illuminated by Trevor-Roper shows us other loves enduring until death.[68] Eichmann is also reported to have told his men during the last days of the war, with the Thousand Year Reich crumbling, 'I will jump into my grave laughing, because the fact that I have the death of five million Jews on my conscience gives me extraordinary satisfaction.' He went on repeating the damning sentence 'to everyone who would listen' in Argentina and elsewhere. Arendt sourly dismisses the claim as another example of Eichmann's vapidity, describing his pretension to primary responsibility for the deaths as 'absurd', and the whole statement as a bragging inflation of his role when he first said it, and an exhilarating lie when he repeated it.[69] What we must recognise is that Eichmann's exhilaration was real and transforming, and that when Hitler decided to enact the most extreme fantasy of his private ideology, the Nazi state moved with astonishing speed and efficiency to fulfil his dream, despite being engaged in warfare on two fronts. Christopher Browning supplies the essential figures:

In mid-March of 1942, some 75 to 80 percent of all victims of the Holocaust were still alive, while some 20 to 25 percent had already perished. A mere eleven months later, in mid-February 1943, the situation was exactly the reverse. Some 75 to 80 percent of all Holocaust victims were already dead, and a mere 25 to 30 percent still clung to a precarious existence. At the core of the Holocaust was an intense eleven-month wave of mass murder . . . The German attack on the Polish ghettoes was not a gradual or incremental program stretched over a long period of time, but a veritable blitzkrieg, a massive offensive requiring the mobilization of large numbers of shock troops at the very period when the German war effort in Russia hung in the balance.[70]

If those in high office could do their planning and their triumphing in private, the men who executed their orders – the SS of the concentration camps and the mobile killing squads, the soldiers and police who shot civilians in Poland and Russia or forced them into swollen, disease-ridden ghettos or directly into the death camps – had to do their work in public. What will we see when we look at them in action?

Primo Levi, who excluded the leaders of the Nazi action as beyond his comprehension, never doubted the necessity of understanding how they recruited their agents: 'those faithful followers, among them the diligent executors of inhuman orders, who were not born torturers, who were not (with a few exceptions) monsters: who were ordinary men.'[71] It is time to meet these ordinary men who became killers.

7

THE MEN IN THE
GREEN TUNICS
The Order Police in Poland

... in many cases it is considerably easier to lead a company into battle than ... to hold down a hostile population ... to carry out executions, to deport people, to remove shrieking, weeping women, to move our fellow Germans across the frontier and then look after them.

I will tell you something – throughout the Waffen-SS we must begin to recognize the other great services rendered by the SS as a whole and by the Police. You must regard the business of the man in the green tunic as something just as valuable as the service you yourselves render.

– SS *Reichsführer* Himmler to officers of the Waffen-SS, 7 September 1940

In the course of his researches into Nazi activities in Eastern Europe Daniel Goldhagen retrieved a number of photographs. One, taken in the course of the slaughter of the Jews of Ivangorod, Ukraine, in 1942, is iconic in its distillation of German atrocity.[1] In what appears to be a rough field a German soldier in battledress levels his rifle at a young woman, about two metres distant, who is in the process of turning away. It is possible she is trying to run – her left foot is slightly lifted. She clasps a child, bare legs dangling, close to her shielding body.

In the case of Nazi 'desk murderers' it may be possible to estimate how far ideology and how far ambition (not to mention lack of imagination) worked to sustain their enthusiasm for murder through examination of their verbal and written statements without too much reference to their daily round, although I would not envy the task. With the 'hands-on' killers the problem is at once more visceral, and more opaque. We know they killed, and killed on a massive scale. The question is: how could they do it? How were young armed men brought at a pitch to kill not other armed young men but old women moaning in their beds, or frightened toddlers, or this young woman desperate to protect her child? How could they come to do these things routinely, without evident hesitation, and sometimes with evident relish?[2] Until Hitler came to power the German army had been distinguished by its exemplary discipline and its strict adherence to the conventions of war. Less than a decade later, and we have the incident caught in the photograph.

Faced with that image, it is easy to flinch and declare that such men must be monsters, creatures too unlike us to be amenable to understanding. This response is reinforced by the knowledge that some army men, and some SS men too, had been sufficiently affected by the killing of civilians to persuade their superiors to hand over the bulk of the work of mass shootings and disposal of corpses, whether in Polish villages or Ukrainian fields, to less valuable aides. The directors of the killings also developed new techniques for the killing centres established in Poland, where thousands could be gassed 'hygienically', with minimal contact with their murderers.[3] While the Germans made widespread use of 'willing helpers, the *Hilfswilliger*, or 'Hiwis' recruited from among Ukrainian, Latvian and Lithuanian prisoners of war and trained for their duties by the SS, the crucial work of the organisation and direction of the mass killings, and often the killings themselves, remained in German hands.

Daniel Goldhagen has chosen to focus on the German engagement in civilian killings and, among those killings, on the swift, ferocious and fatal assault on Europe's Jews. It is this which provides the evidence for his central thesis, that 'the vast majority of the German people . . . were aware of what their government and their countrymen were doing to the Jews, assented to the measures, and, when the opportunity presented itself, lent their active support to them', to become Hitler's 'willing executioners'. Why? Because Germans had nurtured a deep-rooted hatred of the Jews, an 'eliminationist anti-Semitism', long before the Nazis came to power. Hitler's own rabid anti-Semitism provided no more than the opportunity for action.

To demonstrate his thesis Goldhagen analyses the conduct of SS guards during the strangely purposeless, often murderous 'death marches' which followed on the closure of the camps in the last days of the Reich, paying special attention to a brutal march involving women prisoners. He also uncovers the obscure links that convinced anti-Semites saw between Jews and physical labour, and exposes the hidden dynamic of those otherwise bizarre ritual humiliation – the scrubbings of pavements with toothbrushes, the 'physical jerks' – that Nazi thugs inflicted on Jews from the first days of Nazi rule: humiliations which were to flower into the mindlessly punitive labour and 'sports' inside the concentration camps.[4]

These actions, however, were carried out by men – SS guards, Nazi hoodlums – we may assume to have been already ideologized. Goldhagen's best chance of persuading us that Jew-hatred was a general German obsession and not a specifically Nazi one lies in the involvement of the army and of civilian police in the mass shootings of civilian Jews in Poland and Russia in the first years of the war.

Goldhagen's book, informed by a passionate determination that the gruesome actualities of German cruelties and killings not be sanitised by academic abstractions, made a great public clamour and attracted a wide readership, especially within Germany. Historians remain unimpressed. They have acknowledged Goldhagen's work on the death marches and on the mad Nazi conviction of Jews' antipathy to physical work, but his central thesis has been roundly rejected.* As one respected commentater puts it: 'the majority of Germans, although undoubtedly influenced by various forms of traditional antisemitism and easily accepting the segregation of Jews, shied away from widespread violence against them, urging neither their expulsion from the Reich nor their physical annihilation.'[5]

My concern here is not with those larger criticisms, although I agree with them, but with the methodology of Goldhagen's reconstruction of the actions and attitudes of the Hamburg Reserve Police Battalion 101 in Poland and Russia in the first years of the war. Here his area of research overlaps with Christopher Browning's study of the activities of the same battalion, published four years earlier. Until that date almost nothing had been published on the police formations, the reg-

---

* Hear Gordon Craig, *New York Review of Books*, 23 May 1996, p. 52: 'The specificity and variety of history finds no place in Goldhagen's book . . . Goldhagen's relentless argument by implication that the population of Germany consisted exclusively of two groups, the Jews and the Germans who hated them, bears little resemblance to the facts of life.' See also Raul Hilberg, 'The Goldhagen Phenomenon', in *Critical Inquiry*, Vol. 23, Summer 1997, pp. 721–28.

ular, uniformed municipal and county police (militia-like regional units, although one writer calls them 'the equivalent of the English "Bobby" ') who were abruptly sent into Russia and Poland to clear pockets of partisan resistance, and to shoot civilians – whether Polish or Russian hostages, or Jews. The police battalions' main work quickly came to be 'cleansing' Poland first of its own Jews, and then of Jews imported from other areas as they came under German control. In what follows I want to compare the approaches of Browning and Goldhagen to the problem of understanding and explaining the actions of these men – men who appear to have been, at least until the time of those actions, ordinary Germans, ordinary men.

In his opening chapter Goldhagen tells us that 'explaining the per-petrators' actions demands . . . that the perpetrators' reality is taken seriously'. Accordingly he promises to bring an anthropological per-spective to bear, a perspective he claims hitherto absent from Holo-caust studies. He promises a 'thick' description of perpetrator actions, in order 'to bring to life their *Lebenswelt*'.[6]

From the phrase 'thick description' we know which anthropological perspective he means: the semiotic approach associated with the Amer-ican anthropolgist, Clifford Geertz. A methodological approach, espe-cially a complex and subtle one, cannot be reduced to a paragraph, but I will do my best.

Geertz writes: 'Believing, with Max Weber, that man is an animal suspended in webs of significance he himself has spun, I take culture to be those webs, and the analysis of it to be therefore not an experi-mental science in search of law but an interpretive one in search of meaning.'

The job is to reach a sufficiently detailed understanding of how the particular group under study think to be able to differentiate, in a famous example, a twitch, an involuntary and therefore meaningless physical spasm, from a wink, which comes freighted with particular social significances and exquisitely depends on circumstance. The aim is to arrive at 'thick description', the 'setting down [of] the meanings particular social actions have for the actors whose actions they are': as we might say, what they think they are up to. 'Thick description' once achieved, it is possible to proceed to diagnosis.

This is not a simple matter:

The distinction, relative in any case, that appears in the experiential or ob-
servational sciences between 'description' and 'explanation' appears here as
one, even more relative, between 'inscription' ('thick description') and 'spec-
ification' ('diagnosis') – between setting down the meaning particular social
actions have for the actors whose actions they are, and stating, as explicitly
as we can manage, what the knowledge thus attained demonstrates about
the society in which it is found, and beyond that, about social life as such.[7]

Thus speaks Geertz. The advantages to a historian of this approach
are obvious. It reduces the role of untestable 'intuition' by making the
business of interpreting actions a public affair, it inhibits the casual
offloading of our own expectations onto unlike others, and by locating
the individual firmly within his or her particular milieu it gives hope
that we may be able to identify what is distinctive to the individual as
well as to the society. Geertz has had a deep and continuing influence
on social historians over the last twenty years, but it is fair to say that
historians of politics have been relatively unresponsive. This, then, is
the 'new anthropological approach' to which Goldhagen commits
himself.

As it turns out 460 pages later, he does not quite achieve his intention. This is in part because, despite the most diligent research, the
material remains too thin to allow a sufficiently detailed retrieval of
actions to achieve 'thick description', save in one singular instance: the
Hamburg Reserve Police Battalion's first day of mass murder at the
little Polish town of Józefów. More damagingly, Goldhagen tends to
confuse detailed external descriptions of actions ('They did this, they
did that') with the 'thick description' which Geertz would have us
aspire to, where the actors' meanings are the quarry ('She'd gone too
far, so I hit her').

That confusion points to what is Goldhagen's greatest disability. He
is not curious about these men and what they did, because he believes
he already knows why they – indeed, why all Germans – did as they
did. He details their actions, but as an outraged prosecutor: 'Look
what they are doing!' The 'Why?' is already determined: these men
were Germans, and therefore heirs to a deep-rooted, pathological anti-
Semitism which had nothing to do with experience, needed no habituation, but simply awaited the ascendancy of Hitler and the opportunity of war for its lethal expression.

Goldhagen rejects discriminations like 'Nazi', or 'SS man', which might imply a hierarchy of ideological commitment and of moral responsibility. In his view such distinctions are no more than 'convenient, yet often inappropriate and obfuscating labels'.[8] What matters is that these men are Germans.

Christopher Browning titled his earlier and more modest study of a single police battalion 'Ordinary Men: Reserve Police Battalion 101 and the Final Solution in Poland'. Goldhagen and Browning are agreed that the 450 or so men of Hamburg Police Battalion were sufficiently ordinary to constitute a fair cross-section of German society. While Himmler had contrived to bring the civilian Order Police under his control in 1936, there were still only a few SS men to be found in its ranks.[9] Except for their regional loyalty the Hamburg men seem to have been a motley crew, most of them blue-collar workers, and most settled family men, too old for any youthful infatuation with the dogmas of national socialism. In politicised Germany few were overtly 'political'. Ordinary men indeed.

And untested men. Other police battalions had already been killing Jews and fighting partisans in the Soviet Union and elsewhere in occupied Poland. Some had even fought, briefly, on the front line.[10] While Battalion 101 had two earlier tours of duty in Poland on its record, and while some of its men assisted in the forced deportation of Hamburg's own Jews in the autumn of 1941, the battalion trucked out from Hamburg in June 1942 was essentially a new organisation with nearly all of its men unblooded.

Not many days after their arrival in Poland, with no preparation beyond uncertain rumour, these men were set down in early dawn before the sleeping village of Józefów. Their commanding officer told them their duty: they were to round up and kill all the Jews of the village, exempting only the able-bodied men, who were to be temporarily reserved for labour. Nearly all the men from Hamburg did as they were ordered. By the end of a long day at least 1500 Jews of all ages and conditions were dead, their bodies lying unburied in the woods. In a matter of weeks most of the men of Police Battalion 101 were reliable Jew-killers, and some, it would seem, dedicated ones.

Although Browning's study draws on only some of the material explored by Goldhagen, it is to my mind more penetrating, more subtle, and more interesting both methodologically and morally. Although it does not invoke the term, it comes as close as such material will allow to 'thick description', which given the nature of the material is a formidable achievement. Out of the elisions and evasions of more than 200 trial testimonies taken twenty years after the event, in the face of the immense difficulties arising from systematic concealment, obfuscation and denial compounded by the oddities of the postwar German legal system, Browning contrives to reconstruct in detail the actions of that chaotic day.[11] He needs that detailed narrative to reconstruct and reflect on the distinctive emotional 'narrative' of each identifiable participant.

We learn from several witnesses that the battalion's commander Major Trapp wept as he explained to his men what they had to do. He represented their duty as a terrible one, 'entirely not in his spirit', but as an order to be obeyed because received from 'a higher authority'. He was to weep again in the course of the day during the execution of his duty. Before the killing began he offered to excuse any older men who felt unable to undertake the task. About a dozen men stepped forward, some eliciting the anger of their immediate superiors. Others sickened during the day and were released from duty, or contrived to evade it. Most did not, and continued to the end. Alcohol had been distributed during the course of the day's work. When it was over, some remembered, there had been heavy drinking and little talk.

Through Browning's scrupulous labour we now know much of what happened on that day in Józefów. We know how the men were deployed; who said what, who did what; who refused to act; who complied, for how long, and how willingly. We know how those who demurred expressed their demurral. We know that some men began sturdily enough – and then wept, or vomited, or fled the action to hide in the forest or among comrades assigned less horrible duties. We know of one lieutenant who vehemently declared his opposition to the killing of Jews, and who refused to participate further in that action or in any other like it. Later, when the illness of a colleague left him in charge of a similar action, he quit the scene and wrote to his superiors demanding a transfer – which he was granted. We also know that another lieutenant, unremarkable during that initial July action, quickly distinguished himself both as a great drinker and a great Jew-hater. Within a month a drunken Lieutenant Gnade was amusing himself by making his men strip elderly Jews and beat them as they

crawled naked beside the execution pits.[12] By November he had insti-
tutionalised the humiliation of nakedness: now all Jews of whatever
sex and age were strip-searched at Lieutenant Gnade's 'undressing station' before being packed, naked or in their underwear, into the cattle
trucks which would carry them the hundred kilometres to Treblinka.
And we know that by February 1943 Trapp was recommending the
dismissal of a company commander who despite a great deal of fire-
breathing talk always contrived to suffer disabling stomach distur-
bances before major actions. The persistent coincidence spelt coward-
ice to Trapp. We might interpret it differently.

Browning's marvellously detailed narrative provides descriptions
sufficiently 'thick' to give us some access to the actors' states of mind.
With his account of Józefów he provides us with a coherent account
of an episode previously unknown, and of historical and moral importance to us all. We come to know something of the particular circumstances of the deaths of these thousands of people who would otherwise drown in statistics. We are also forced to be attentive to clear
indications of uncertainty or revulsion in the behaviour of men it
would be both simpler and more comfortable to dismiss as brutes.

The evidence thins radically for all of the battalion's later actions.
Józefów stayed in the men's minds because it was their first major
killing and because their lack of experience had made the task more
distressing. In this, their first exercise, the executioners paired with
their victims for the walk into the woods, and some of the victims
were children, or mothers with infants in their arms. Being novices,
the men had also tended to give the 'neck shot' too high, so that skulls
exploded and faces and uniforms were splattered with bone and tissue.

With time they were to acquire techniques which better preserved
their equanimity and their uniforms. If most remembered their initiation vividly, later killings were often blurred in memory. After Józefów
Browning had to work with patchy material. As a historian he lacked
the anthropologist's privilege of checking inferences by further interrogation and observation. Instead he had to deal with the veils of time
and the vagaries of memory, and by the 1960s his informants had
good political reasons for selective amnesia. Unsurprisingly, individuals were apt to remember the slightest indicators of non-compliance,
while dismissing gross compliance as prudent submission to 'orders'.

Browning also noted a great silence – the lack of reference to anti-Semitic feelings. Whatever the realities of 1942, such attitudes were no longer acceptable in the Germany of the sixties.

By contrast, Daniel Goldhagen is persuaded that murderous anti-Semitism was a German obsession which the Hamburg policemen brought with them into Poland. He interprets individual hesitations and avoidances at Józefów as signifying no more than a transitory physical fastidiousness, a visceral revulsion soon overcome and forgotten. Looking for evidence of a principled rejection of the murder of Jews, he finds none: after all, even the recalcitrant Lieutenant Buchmann had only declared he would not participate in any action where 'defenceless women and children were shot'.[13] During his tearful speech to his men apologising for the horrible nature of their duty, Major Trapp made reference to the fact that German women and children were at that very time dying under aerial bombardment. Goldhagen is convinced that this statement was spoken and heard as a coded ideological statement which betrayed Trapp's Nazified conception of the Jews as the key agents for the war. How else, he asks, 'could such a statement make sense to him and to those who heard and understood it?'[14]

The interpretation appears far-fetched. These men, not long away from the domestic hearth, had just been ordered to drag women and children from their beds and to kill them. Trapp reminds them that German women and children are also dying. There is nothing in his conduct, in that first episode or later, to indicate that Trapp thought all the people his men were to kill that day were enemies – although one policeman remembered him saying that Jews had instigated the American boycott, while two others recalled he had claimed that some Jews in Józefów were involved with partisans. It is true that he killed Jews with less distress than he killed Poles, as when he selected his quota of hostages to be shot in retaliation for a Polish partisan action largely from Jewish prisoners – prisoners who he knew would be killed sooner or later. But there is no indication, on that first day or later, that he found the murdering of Jewish civilians a congenial task.

Goldhagen sacrifices the opportunity to discern difference and change in the men's attitudes by discussing the Józefów killing together with an *Aktion* at Lomazy some weeks later. Here the men from Hamburg were forced to take over a gruesome mass execution from drunken Hiwis, and the company was in the charge not of 'Papa' Trapp, but the overtly anti-Semitic Lieutenant Gnade. Those intervening weeks may have had major effects on attitude and behaviour. Under the impact of remarkable new experiences and under close military discipline, attitudes can transform swiftly. Armies function on that assumption. We cannot assume that the men who killed at Lomazy were still the same men who had clambered out of the trucks at Józefów.

Sequence matters. Goldhagen argues that because many ordinary Germans came in time to commit mass murder readily, they had always been ready to do so. He concludes that therefore any and all Germans must have been ready to become killers. He dismisses the possible influence of intervening experience – the fear of partisan attack, absence from home, the vulnerabilities of the individual in a garrison situation and subjected to extreme internal and external pressures – as trivial.

By contrast, Browning is concerned with process and alert for influences shaping the group sensibility. Through close attention to temporal sequence he traces what looks like a process of 'education' during that first brutal day, when a revulsion against killing civilians was overcome by a generalised notion of 'duty' to one's country and one's comrades rather than by the invocation of a particular ideology.*[15] Given the lack of adequate documentation for any later action, he cannot hope to trace the crucial process of 'habituation' by which some men developed from nervous or nauseated beginners into practised killers. All he can do is suggest what may have influenced the men of the police battalion as they 'adjusted to their duties' from small clues in their conduct, and by comparison with other, better-documented and reasonably analogous situations.

To suggest how briskly the coercion of immediate circumstance and authority can overrule individual resistance, even where the victims

---

* Armies know the difficulty of making men kill. Military historians tell us that only a small percentage of men are ready to shoot to kill in their first engagement, at least when they can see the enemy. The solution for effective collective action is drill, drill and more drill, to drown individual impulse in mechanical response. For small-group action, as in jungle warfare, one of the rare fellows ready to kill without compunction is placed among five or six of 'ordinary men', most often but not necessarily as leader. Once the action starts his example will be followed through self-pride and group loyalty.

are helpless civilians and the killers not motivated by formally ideologised racism, Browning makes the obvious comparison – United States
military actions in Vietnam. He borrows Ervin Staub's chilling account
of a U.S. veteran recalling his initiation as a skyborne killer flying high
over the Geneva conventions of war:

> Flying over a group of civilians in a helicopter, he was ordered to fire at
> them, an order he did not obey. The helicopter circled over the area and
> again he was ordered to fire, which again he did not do. The officer in charge
> then threatened him with court-martial, which led him to fire the next time
> round. He vomited, felt profoundly distressed. The veteran reported that in
> a fairly short time firing at civilians became like an experience at a target
> shooting gallery, and he began to enjoy it.[16]

A number of things are going on here, among them fear of authority,
fear of punishment, fear of shaming oneself before one's fellows. Compliance also brought rewards: re-incorporation into the group, the experience of power, the practice of a skill, a god-like immunity. What
happened to 'our boys' in Vietnam has forced us to be attentive to
what can happen when informal racism, frustration and a near-
monopoly of advanced weaponry meet. The men of Charlie Company
did not begin by hating 'gooks', but they slaughtered between 500 and
600 unarmed Vietnamese villagers in a space of days, among them the
people of My Lai. To understand why they did that, and why some
members of the company did not, would require a great deal of careful
work, but we would consider it relevant that the company's combat
briefing the night before My Lai had incorporated a funeral service for
members of the company, among them a well-loved sergeant, who had
been killed by mines, the archetypal weapon of treachery.[17]

Their situation was, like all situations, distinctive. In Vietnam all
parties knew they were caught, however unwillingly, in a civil war, in
which any civilian, however apparently innocent, could be a combat-
ant. Nonetheless, since Vietnam – for Australians, since the Pacific war
– we can no longer pretend that atrocity is an aberration belonging
to the enemy, or that soldiers licensed to kill and maltreat non-
combatants will not commit 'gratuitous' atrocities as well.[18]

There are, of course, a multitude of other possible factors to consider. Combat soldiers have long acknowledged the high value of physical toughness and, in circumstances which 'require' it, of inventiveness

in cruelty. Listen to old soldiers in relaxed mood, and you will hear what soldiers will boast of. The adrenalin rush of uninhibited physical power over others is notoriously addictive even at second hand, which may explain the present taste for dead-pan gangster movies in the Tarantino mode.[19] How far civilians remote from military coercions will go in inflicting pain or humiliation on protesting, even screaming victims has been demonstrated by the famous experiment devised by the psychologist Stanley Milgram more than twenty years ago, and the even more apposite investigations by Philip Zimbardo into what make-believe 'guards' will do to make-believe 'prisoners' when they have them in their power.

Milgram inveigled naive subjects (which means you and me) into his investigator's web by leading them to believe they had enlisted as paid volunteers in an experiment on the effectiveness of punishment in learning. He then set them to giving graduated electric shocks to their error-prone 'partners', whom he had placed in an adjoining room, out of sight but within earshot. The partners were in fact Milgram's accomplices and, we have to assume, accomplished actors, although to save costs and to maintain conformity their responses were often taped and replayed after the initial genial introductions.

More than two-thirds of the 'teachers' proceeded through complaints, shrieks and sinister silence to inflict what they thought to be extreme pain, unconsciousness, and possibly death, while they themselves exhibited signs of acute distress.

In the early eighties Philip Zimbardo selected Stanford undergraduates for 'normality' and divided them into two groups, one being assigned the role of guards and the other of prisoners in a simulated prison situation. Direct physical violence was specifically prohibited, but after six days the experiment had to be terminated because of the escalating and increasingly inventive cruelties of nearly all the guards.

These outlines are no more than cartoon versions of subtle, continuously refined experiments whose findings and meanings take some teasing out, but their relevance to the police battalions' actions in Poland is obvious. While Browning discusses these experiments at some length, Goldhagen dismisses Milgram as someone who claims that 'humans in general are blindly obedient to authority', although he is a little more expansive and slightly more just in a backnote. Zimbardo he ignores altogether.[20]

To go a little further afield into theory: Ervin Staub, a psychologist who translates psychological theories into admirably concrete examples, presents the discomforts attending what is called 'cognitive imbalance' thus: 'If a person likes Hitler, given Hitler's hatred of Jews, there is imbalance if that person likes Jews. To create balance, either the attitude towards Hitler or the attitude towards Jews has to change. In Nazi Germany, all the pressures acting on this person would favour Hitler over the Jews.'[21] We must also remember that in his study of firing rates and of the ratio of kills to ammunition in military situations the American historian David Grossman finds that while 2 per cent of recruits kill easily, the rest must be brought to do so by careful military training. Increased kill-rates in Vietnam were accompanied by a high incidence of post-traumatic stress disorders. This kind of correlation leads Grossman to argue that the history of warfare is the history of conditioning men to overcome 'their innate resistance to killing their fellow human beings'.[22]

Anthropologists have demonstrated how a taste for carnage can be cultivated in young men even within the home territory. Michelle Rosaldo's enthralling account of the instruction of young Ilongot men in the Philippines in the 'proper' complex of emotions which should attend the 'tossing' of the heads of ambushed enemies, heads which could be those of men, women, children or infants, all being generically 'the enemy', might seem a long way from Józefów, but awareness of such studies and the social plasticity of emotion they exhibit helps keep imagination supple, and alerts us to possibilities too easily masked from us by our casual assumptions as to what constitutes the normal.[23]

The handful of low-range theories touched on here may well seem too piecemeal to frame and explain the murderous behaviour of Police Battalion 101, but given the lack of material which would permit 'thick description' there is not much more the historian can do. The utility of particular interpretations can be assessed by the relevance of the theories invoked, and their power to illuminate, however obliquely, the situation under analysis.

We are fortunate to have a few recorded facts on behaviour from the months when the Hamburg battalion was routinely engaged in killing. The wife of Lieutenant Brand, visiting from home (outsiders are usually good for revelatory observations) was surprised, shocked and embarrassed to discover that all Germans, not only those in uniform, were at all times to be treated as members of a master race by the local population. Poles were required to step into the gutter when Germans approached, and to quit a shop should Germans of any rank and either gender enter. 'Ideology' is too cerebral a word for the consequences of daily experiences like these on the once 'ordinary' men' of the Hamburg police, now lording it in conquered Poland.

The men were also offered continuous ideological instruction. Police battalions received minimal physical and ideological training on intake, but there was a surprising amount of indoctrination in the field, with the men scheduled to receive daily, weekly and monthly instruction. Goldhagen dismisses this ideological training as 'laughably perfunctory and ineffective', on the grounds that no special preparation was required, and that 'all educational meetings [were] conducted by the pedagogically innocent officers of the police battalions themselves'.[24] The dismissal is too cavalier. Given the destabilisations and the extraordinary experiences which had begun with that summer day at Józefów, in-house discussions must have been charged affairs. In their own company, secure from the interventions and impositions of outsiders, the men were free to find a way of thinking, talking and feeling about what they were doing. The consequences for the clarification, the confirmation and the radicalisation of 'ideology' by its daily actualisation, and the radicalisation of daily action by its developing ideological justification, can be no more underestimated than it can be precisely measured.

Goldhagen also informs us that 'once a month, the men were instructed in a designated theme supplied by Himmler's office, the purpose of which was to treat thoroughly a topic of contemporary ideological significance'.[25] These discussions may have been less than sophisticated, but the monthly reminder that even when culling desolate villages of Poland the men of the battalion were not forgotten by the centre of power and were informed and valued agents of that power, is likely to have added purpose to their 'work' – especially when other police battalions were winning glory fighting deep inside Russia.

We are powerfully reminded of the gruesome nature of the police battalion's work by the photographs offered by both Goldhagen and Browning, and which constitute Goldhagen's trump card. The killer in the iconic instance discussed at the beginning of the essay was a soldier, but the Hamburg Reserve Police engaged in similar actions.[26] While the dirtiest work was left to the Hiwis, all members of the battalion, including the few individuals who contrived to avoid direct killings, participated in the exercises of clearing ghettos and herding Jews to train stations, or to the meadows where they would be shot.

They were also ready to be photographed while they did it. The images the group's unofficial photographer chose to record are crisp visual statements of the master race at its work of destroying a lesser people. A ghetto is being liquidated. Pale, thin-featured men, bearded, wearing striped prayer shawls, kneel before other much bigger, clean-shaven well-nourished men, in solid boots and snugly-belted overcoats. One man, phylacteries wound around his arms, is being forced to say Kaddish over the bodies of murdered companions. The overcoats are carrying switches or guns; they grin at the camera. In one photograph a haggard Jewish man is having his beard hacked. In another, a hunchbacked woman, tiny, barefoot, already stripped to her shift, turns a face ugly with fear and incipient tears towards the camera. Large smiling men, boots dark against the dust, stand close around her. One, on the right, seems to be holding a small whip. Another has a rifle negligently tucked under an arm.[27] This is Lieutenant Gnade's undressing station at Miedzyrec, where Jews were stripped of clothing and valuables before being crammed into the train for Treblinka or herded to a local killing field. In other photographs the big men loom over cowering figures, or stride beside shambling processions. They are at once businesslike, and very much at ease.

Such photographs shock, and shock profoundly. They are also a reminder of the exoticism of both the appearance and conduct of Polish Jews to provincial German eyes.[28] Under interrogation, in the different world of Hamburg twenty years later, the men recollected little of their many slaughters of Polish Jews, but several recalled the names and fragments of the histories of German Jews, some from Hamburg, and acknowledged some uneasiness at killing them. Was this because, as Browning suggests, those identifiable individuals could not be made to conform with the developing stereotype of 'the Jew' as the unutterably foreign and less-than-human enemy?

A squad from the Third Platoon spent a couple of uneventful weeks quartered in the Jewish schoolhouse at Lomazy while the life of the little community swirled around them, but there is no evidence of hesitation when they and their comrades were called to take over that botched execution from drunken Hiwis. Even after months of 'habituation', however, some men found it hard to kill Polish Jews they had come to know as individuals. When two kitchen workers, already 'allowed' to escape a round-up, were caught with other Jews hiding in a bunker, one of the men who found them, and who knew them, refused to shoot. (They were, of course, shot anyway.)[29]

For Goldhagen the photographs constitute direct and unequivocal evidence of the battalion's early and ongoing pride in its Jew-killing work.[30] He tells us that such snapshots, while officially illegal, were laid out so that the men could inspect them and order copies for wives and families back home – postcards from Poland. Some must have taken up the offer, or we would have no photographs. But persuasive as this evidence is, we still cannot know how many disapproved, whether overtly or silently. Furthermore, the photographs obscure evidence of process. At this distance and with the evidence we have it is impossible to distinguish confidently between dour acceptance of unpalatable duty, placid obedience, and eager participation, or the switches and changes which may have occurred between those attitudes.

It is true that some police seemed to require no 'hardening' at all. Both Browning and Goldhagen tell of a touring entertainment unit of Berlin police ('Welfare at the Front') who, hearing of a Jew-shooting scheduled for the next day, begged permission to be allowed to participate. Permission was granted, the troupe forming the majority of a squad of fifteen to twenty-five men who took their victims, including women and children, into a field, made them lie face down, and then shot them in the back of the neck.[31] Willing executioners indeed. Were these singers and musicians committed Jew-haters? Or were they driven by bravado, the desire to show their comrades in the field that even 'soft' Berliner entertainers could be tough too? Lacking any detail as to their behaviour before, during and after the killings, we cannot know. We do know that the few individuals in the battalion who refused to participate in the killing of Jews, or who begged off particular duties, did so without significant penalty beyond the contempt of their fellows – but in the garrison situation of a foreign posting that can be penalty indeed.

In his determination to expose the Germans as anti-Semites *sans pareil*, Goldhagen attempts to blame the Hiwis' extreme and gratuitous savagery on the example of their German masters. This is unpersuasive, especially in the light of Goldhagen's own account of the spontaneous massacres of Jews by Lithuanian mobs after the arrival of the Germans, when, 'in a frenzied orgy of bludgeoning, slashing, and shooting, [they] slaughtered 3,800 Jews in the city's streets'.[32] These men – young, far from home, drawn from countries with long histories of active contempt and hostility to their Jewish communities, and accustomed to levels of everyday violence which would terrify us – were granted arms, power and impunity, together with large amounts of alcohol. It is perhaps not surprising that their aptness for brutality could shock SS superiors. To my knowledge they have not yet found their historian.

Within Police Battalion 101 it is clear that the unsteady compliance and morose silences which marked that day in Józefów in time gave way to a different mood. Here Goldhagen and Browning are in broad agreement. Despite the peripatetic nature of their duties, police battalions worked out of settled environments, with some slender apparatus of normality – darts nights, concerts, and a milieu which, for officers at least, could pretend to the domestic. It is therefore reasonable to speak of a 'battalion culture', and what we can see of that culture is ugly.[33] One officer, admittedly a member of the SS, arranged to give his pregnant wife a special treat by taking her with him to watch a major massacre at Miedzyrec. We know about his gesture because it was disapproved of by other members of the battalion, on the grounds that a pregnant woman ought not be exposed to such sights.[34] Frau Brand tells us that on her holiday from Hamburg she was breakfasting one morning in the garden with her husband when they were interrupted by one of her husband's subordinates. He came into the garden, 'stood stiffly at attention', and said: 'Herr Lieutenant, I have not yet had breakfast . . . I have not yet killed any Jews.'[35]

The interrupted breakfast occurred at the time of the 'Jew-hunt' to eradicate the last Jews hidden in the forest. We glimpse in this fragment a small theatrical performance, a 'presentation of self' undertaken in order to impress.[36] The swaggering intruder clearly thought himself admirably tough. Frau Brand, a civilian visitor from a different world, thought it an outrageous intrusion and its agent a disgusting fellow, and reacted accordingly. Lieutenant Brand's response was to dismiss the man – and then to rebuke his wife, warning her that her fastidiousness could bring trouble down on both of them. While the underling's studied flamboyance was clearly an individual performance, both the action and the reaction suggest that the dominant culture of the barracks had come to be the kind of bully-boy geniality exhibited in the photographs, with dissenting voices few or silenced altogether.

In that remote, barely glimpsed police culture we see scant indication of Saul Friedländer's notion of 'the bond with the Führer', or of *Rausch*, the surge of exhilaration and exaltation attending outrageous action.[37] What we do see is, in its way, more disturbing. It would seem that, while these ordinary men had felt initial reluctance, even aversion to the killing of civilians, reluctance and aversion were largely and quickly overcome. Habituation, a complex and largely invisible process, assisted by the active dissemination of an ideology vested with power to impose its vision on the world, had done its work. These ordinary men had become efficient, untroubled killers of helpless civilians.

Given the restricted evidence, the precise 'how' of the transformation remains veiled from us, as it may have remained veiled from the men who experienced it. But if some individuals felt and continued to feel scruples, others, probably most others, came to beat and bully and kill with apparently easy consciences. Whether they killed with more enthusiasm when their victims were Jews cannot be demonstrated from the evidence we have, although both researchers identify some individuals eager to inflict specific, ideologically-sourced humiliations on Jews.

What is encouraging is that neither Browning nor Goldhagen feels the need to look beyond the realm of the human to explain these killings, or the massacres of Jews carried out by local populations in Latvia and Lithuania on the arrival of the German force, or the enthusiasm of the SS-trained Hiwis for the foul work they did for their German masters. They do not invoke notions of Evil. There are no implied extra-human capitalisations at all. Accepting the killers as human, both historians are intent on understanding them as fellow humans. Goldhagen titles his book, very deliberately, 'Hitler's Willing Executioners', but his subtitle firmly designates them 'Ordinary Germans' – that is, ordinary men whom he believed to have been culturally imbued with a homicidal anti-Semitism. Christopher Browning is determined to bring his readers to a wider acknowledgment that 'the men who carried out these massacres were not monsters, but human beings'. He therefore titles his book, with only the faintest breath of irony, 'Ordinary Men'. Browning has persuaded me that that is exactly what the men of Police Battalion 101 were.

That recognition has large consequences. If they were indeed ordinary men made murderers by the state, how are we to judge them? In my view there is no difficulty: both their intentions and actions were murderous, and they should be declared so. It is unwise to let men think they can make murder not murder first by slander, and then by fiat – although deciding what degrees of punishment would be appropriate is a different and more difficult matter. But Browning reminds us of something historians can sometimes forget, and points to troubling consequences:

> Explaining is not excusing; understanding is not forgiving. The notion that one must simply reject the actions of the perpetrators and not try to understand them would make impossible not only my history but any perpetrator history that tried to go beyond one-dimensional caricature . . . I must recognise that in such a situation I could have been either a killer or an evader – both were human – if I want to understand and explain the behaviour of both the best I can.[38]

He asks us to ask ourselves: could I, in the circumstances described, in a country where I owed no affection, in time of war and subject to persistent propaganda, have been moved by loyalty and solidarity with comrades to carry out similar actions? Could I have been brought to a conviction or at least a temporary acceptance of their legitimacy? These are questions we cannot answer, but their posing forces us into the serious, imaginative reconstruction of particular circumstance, temperament and personal history, and of the uncertainties haunting the whole enterprise of retrieval, which together constitute historical understanding. If these men were ordinary after all, that recognition does nothing to diminish the horror of their actions. It increases it.

Of necessity, Browning and Goldhagen focus on the perpetrators. In their pages and photographs we see the victims, but we learn nothing of them. Another researcher has rescued an entire community from the silent side of the equation. Theo Richmond, growing up in England as an English boy, chose to spend several years trying to recover something of the texture of the life Jews once lived in the small Polish town of Konin before the Nazis came. His parents and most of their friends had been born in Konin, but while he had heard the name and vague talk about it from earliest childhood, in maturity he realised he knew almost nothing about the place which had been his forefathers' homeland, and which had been obliterated in a matter of weeks.

The search was arduous and necessarily incomplete. Nonetheless, Konin lives again, if only in Richmond's pages. Among a gallery of characters we come to recognize and respect the town's rabbi. Rabbi Lipschitz was an impressive, tolerant man, whose rulings sometimes offended the more fiercely orthodox of the local Chasidim. In 1939 he was one of the first hostages taken by the Nazis in an early attempt to intimidate the Poles and terrify the Jews. The rabbi appears not to have been terrified: after his release he continued to negotiate robustly in defence of his people.

Richmond reports that Rabbi Lipschitz was among the second batch of Konin deportees sent first to the local countryside, and then, in March 1941, to Józefów. It was at Józefów that the rabbi met his death, almost certainly on that July day, at the hands of Hamburg Reserve Battalion 101.

8

THE AUSCHWITZ SS

I tell you it is not a sanatorium you have come to but a German concentration camp from which the only exit is up the chimney.

If anyone doesn't like it, he can go and throw himself against the high tension wires straight away.

If there are any Jews in the convoy they are not entitled to live more than two weeks; priests have one month of life and the remainder three months.

> – Speech of welcome to newcomers selected for work by SS Fritsch, Commandant of Auschwitz I[1]

You stand as matchless soldiers even in peacetime, day and night, against the enemy, against the enemy behind the wire.

> – SS-*Oberführer* Theodor Eicke, Commandant of Dachau, to his SS guards, June 1933[2]

Torturers notoriously come disguised. The affectation of smoked glasses, impassivity and anonymous uniforms increases the impenetrability of affectless power, as it distances the perpetrator from the human flesh he torments. Nor do torturers readily offer their confidences. Intent for their whole period of rule on keeping most of their actions at least formally secret, the Death's Head SS who survived the war had little interest in remembering, and less in telling what they remembered. Some died before a tardy justice sought them out. Others contrived to vanish. More were re-absorbed into a wounded, incurious community. Most of those interrogated before a legal tribunal discovered memory to be a diminishing resource. Others, ready to remember, were also ready to abrogate their moral being by presenting themselves as mindless executives of a higher, implacable will. Or it may be that this was how they remembered themselves: that they experienced the same sense of radical disjunction between the selves of the 'then' and the 'now' which afflicted survivor-witnesses. Fractured identity is not confined to the innocent.

Despite the difficulties genuine or manufactured, a great deal of information about the SS who ran the camps has been retrieved, some of it from superficially innocuous administrative documentation, some from surviving SS members, some from victims who had daily endured their attentions and survived them. There have been fine analyses of the SS as an institution – its organisation, its modes of recruitment and training – and others, although fewer, on the SS in action. Well before the outbreak of war the SS had a history of public violence, from the lethal ambush of their rival Brownshirts on the Night of the Long Knives to the torching of synagogues and the public assaults on German and Austrian Jews on the Night of Breaking Glass, and the secret executions inside the SS concentration camps. With the coming of war, opportunities for mayhem multiplied. While some SS military units were distinguishing themselves fighting alongside the *Wehrmacht*, others were enrolled in the *Einsatzgruppen* or mobile killing squads and operated well behind the lines, implementing Hitler's order to kill Polish political leaders, commissars and Jews, and spearheading the general Nazi assault on the civilian populations of Poland and of Soviet Russia.

It was the Death's Head formations of the SS who devised and administered what was to become the defining institution of the Nazi regime – the 'camp': concentration camps, designed to protect the public peace whether from dangerous 'politicals', which meant anyone thought to oppose the Nazi regime, social deviants (homosexuals, Gypsies), or social recalcitrants (Jehovah's Witnesses); slave labour camps inhabited by those groups and by 'prisoners of war', a definition loosely interpreted; and the six camps established in occupied Poland specifically to destroy the thousands of Jewish traders, artisans and professionals, mothers, children and babies the SS defined as enemies too dangerous to be allowed to live.[3] The Auschwitz SS had multiple duties, as controllers of the socially dangerous, managers of the work camps, and as organisers and directors in the extermination sector at Auschwitz-Birkenau.

Inside Auschwitz, as in every SS-run camp, distinctions between 'guard' and 'prisoner' were highly visible and deliberately dramatised. On the German side authority was elevated by remoteness from routine elements of discipline, the kickings, clubbings and whippings being inflicted by underlings. Their elegant, emblematic uniforms and cultivated ease of bearing was in constant contrast with the physical squalour, ludicrous clothing, cropped heads, and histrionically abject demeanours imposed on their prisoners.

The discipline imposed on those designated as 'enemies behind the wire' was public, detailed, and violently enforced. The historical origins of the disciplinary practices are mirrored in the biography of the Commandant of Auschwitz, Rudolph Hoess.

Hoess made his SS career in concentration camps. Chosen by Himmler in 1933 to serve as a block leader in the first Nazi concentration camp at Dachau – a camp largely comprised of political enemies to the new regime – he served a term at Sachsenhausen before taking over command of Auschwitz-Birkenau in May 1940, when the work camp was expanded to include the work of exterminating Nazism's civilian enemies.

Hoess was also experienced in German military discipline. In 1916, when he was no more than fifteen, he had responded to 'the soldier's blood that ran in [his] veins' by joining his father's regiment of Dragoons. By the end of the war he had accumulated the Iron Cross, First and Second Class, the Iron Crescent, the Baden Service Medal and two wounds. In the twenties he expanded his experience by serving five years in a Prussian prison for his part in a political murder. As he says, 'Serving a sentence in a Prussian prison in those days was no rest-cure'. Discipline was ferocious, with every detail of life regulated, although as a 'political' initially kept in solitary confinement he escaped the 'hideous bullying' by other inmates he accepted as a natural accompaniment to prison life.

Hoess's account of the internal workings of the penal system – the corruption, the ferocious cruelties manifested 'where no form of moral restraint applies', the crazy power of rumour ('the really naive prisoners were ready to believe absolutely anything they were told') – is in prophetic conformity with later conditions inside Auschwitz. What he learned in his own flesh and person was the effectiveness of a discipline which sought to regulate every action, and which rewarded energetic compliance with minutely differentiated increments in title and privi-

leges. The young Hoess rose like froth through the complicated 'reward for virtue' prisoner hierarchy: he was, he proudly tells us, 'the
first of approximately 800 prisoners to reach the third [highest] degree'.[4]

The men like Hoess who went on to shape the routines and regulations for the concentration camps clearly drew on the widely admired
traditions of German military culture – traditions which permeated
not only German penal institutions, but German civilian culture. The
primary assumption was that strict discipline and submission to rule
will build character and train individuals both to command and to
obey. It ought not surprise that we find precisely same values extolled
and exemplified in the regulations governing SS training schools.[5]

These suave cultural explanations for strenuous camp discipline do
not, however, fully satisfy. One difficulty is that the great majority of
the people who were its objects, the Jewish and Gypsy inmates of the
camps, had been ideologically designated as incapable of reformation.
Perhaps that does not matter: ideologies are rarely fully coherent or
ideologues consistent. But the explanation also fails to comprehend
the apparently gratuitous 'disciplines' inflicted inside camp boundaries
but outside official hours of work, and inflicted with sinister enthusiasm. Nor does it acknowledge that those subjected to camp discipline,
the prisoners themselves, obstinately read it as ridiculous: a ludicrous
manifestation of an SS obsession with meaningless outward show.

Consider 'the business of the caps', best described by Elie Cohen
but remembered with the clarity of loathing by many survivors: the
parody of military elan which kept scarecrows drilling and drilling
until at 'Caps off!' these ramshackle recruits could snatch caps from
heads and slap them against hollow sides with an audible crack. Punishment for 'slackness' was immediate, violent, and sometimes fatal.
Cohen and his fellow scarecrows nonetheless thought the drill an utterly ridiculous activity, even as they strained and trembled. There was
a plethora of other equally bizarre exercises conducted with equally
ferocious intensity. Cohen remembers:

the behaviour of the SS often struck us as unreal, we could not understand
it. We repeatedly asked, 'How is it possible for a human being to be like
that?' In addition to this, we often found the behaviour of the SS ridiculous.
Their excitement at some petty offence struck us as exaggerated, unreal . . .

Sometimes we thought all their activity, however disastrous to ourselves, a mere waste of time . . . There are some feelings held by all the prisoners: the contempt in which they hold the SS, and the hope of leaving the concentration camp alive.[6]

'Ridiculous', 'exaggerated', 'unreal' behaviour, regarded by its victims with 'contempt'. Scarcely an effective disciplinary exercise. So why the insistence? Outside the camps Nazi ideological aims were often in tension with what we would see as sound sense, not least in their overriding determination to destroy functioning communities of useful workers in time of war. Inside the camps we see persistent indulgence in other apparently non-instrumental exercises – exercises which consumed radically limited energies and resources not only of the prisoners, but of the SS themselves.

Consider the rollcalls, a feature of the first concentration camp at Dachau, and at every camp afterwards. It was obviously necessary to keep a count, even a daily count, of prisoners, for general reasons of control and to discourage escapes. Rollcalls were also sometimes used as selections for death, as when inmates of hospital barracks were exposed for hours in rigorous weather conditions. They could also be directly punitive. But do those reasons fully explain the rollcalls? Reading descriptions of those interminable counts we can be so mesmerised by the ordeal endured by the victims that we forget to wonder at the energy of their overseers. For the sweating *Kapos* much of that energy must have come from the awareness that laxity could mean demotion, that they might be cuffed off their precarious perches to flounder again in the general misery. But what benefits did the exercises bring their SS supervisors? It is difficult to find much purpose in those marathon parade-ground performances. To force already exhausted men and women to stand for two, three, five hours after a gruelling day's work will deplete physical endurance. It will also 'select' some for death, but the Nazis had much more efficient ways of doing that. What else does it achieve? The further humiliation of the prisoners? Surely a redundant exercise, and if that was indeed a major part of the intention, a failure. Those who survived to give accounts of the agony of enduring it have made clear that even at the time it was judged to be an absurd and mindless routine, if a dreaded one.

Primo Levi's account of camp discipline is all the bleaker because he finds these men and their motives impenetrable. Faced with the SS –

indeed, with all Germans, save those so eccentric as to escape categories altogether – his capacity to follow the movement of other minds
deserts him. He describes their actions carefully enough. He records
their obsession with the racial discriminations they inscribed upon the
bodies of their slaves, and gives a full account of the pictorial vocabu-
lary of the racial hierarchy figured forth in tattooed numbers, colours,
strips and stars and triangles. He notes with scorn how these scraps of
coloured cloth governed conduct and treatment. But he is content to
read such expressions as yet more reflexes of 'absurd German precision', or German 'love [of] order, systems, bureaucracy'. He cannot
begin to grasp what these signs might signify to those who read them
with a racist's inflamed eye: that here, at last, however pathetic, however derelict, was a seemly, ordered, properly labelled world. He sees
debilitated shadows drilled again and again to snatch caps from heads,
and explains these actions instrumentally, as yet another exercise in
deliberate humiliation: he does not wonder what gratifications salutes
from the skeletons could carry for the well-nourished men who received them. He watches the masters watching the march of the puppets which framed the working day, but he does not inquire into what
complicated satisfaction the sentimental music and the jerky march of
grey-faced stick-figures might bring. He is content to infer a troglo-
dyte's pleasure, that the SS enjoy 'this choreography of their creation,
the dance of dead men' as a sign of their triumph.

Levi records with particular bitterness how the SS chose to surface
the paths of their 'village':

The human ashes coming from the crematoria, tons daily, were easily recognised as such, because they often contained teeth or vertebrae. Nevertheless,
they were employed for several purposes . . . especially notable, they were
used instead of gravel to cover the paths of the SS village near the camp. I
couldn't say whether out of pure callousness or because, due to its origins, it
was regarded as material to be trampled on.[7]

For Levi all these performances, from the obsessive camp parades and
the strippings and beatings to the slopping buckets of human waste in
the railway transports, were manifestations of 'being German', or, in
the case of the SS, being 'insane'. But what did these uses and misuses
mean to the SS who devised them with such devotion? The little societies of SS men quartered inside the concentration camps had some

need of solace. Concern for the psychological health of the killers had been a major motive for the establishment of the death camps, with their apparatus of 'changing rooms' and 'shower rooms', because it was felt that mass death by gassing was less personal and therefore less psychologically taxing for the killers than the slow, messy business of shooting great numbers of individuals.

The Death's Head formations working inside the concentration camps may have enjoyed the physical security of being far from the front, but they had their own threats to morale: the isolation, the monotony, and the all-too-evident weakness and pathos of the prisoners, their 'enemies behind the wire'. Men claiming membership of an intellectual, moral, physical and genetic elite were marooned at a time of national crisis in a bleak corner of Poland, remote equally from home and from the centres of significant political and military action. The fiction that their shuffling charges were steely opponents, that they themselves were 'matchless soldiers' on a permanent state of alert, must have been difficult to sustain in the squalid reality of life as it was lived 'behind the wire'.

Under these conditions it is reasonable to pursue the hypothesis suggested by the words of their prisoner-observers: that some of the daily activities constructed by the SS inside the camps can be considered as rituals enacted for the psychological gratification of their directors and impresarios, rather than as instrumental exercises in discipline. It would be unreasonable to expect Cohen, Levi or any camp inmates to spend time puzzling over the motives and obscure gratifications of their masters when all their concern was to endure and survive them. But these involuntary witnesses record what they see and can tell us more than they know. Much of what they categorise as 'insane' or bizarre behaviour looks at this distance rather like what anthropologists would identify as 'ritual conduct': that is, conduct apparently excessive or unproductive but nonetheless persisted in, which suggests that the actions, however futile they may seem to outsiders, carry significant meaning and rewards for those who perform them.

Anthropologists would also tell us that the rewards and meanings embodied in such actions are unlikely to be, and probably could not be, articulated, which means that in interpretations of ritual conduct we have to forgo the historian's usual reassurance of confirmation from written sources. We do not even have rules to help define what is and what is not ritual conduct. My own work on the Aztecs forced me to recognise how poorly what their post-conquest spokesmen declared to be ritual actions fitted my suburban western notions of what rituals might be.* If some Aztec rituals were formalised into grave, theatrical formality, they also offered moments when control vanished, so that to the naive observer they looked like riots. Others were so muted as to melt invisibly into the mundane.[8] They were rituals because the explosions and diminutions were contained within an established script, with the stages marked, the high and low points scheduled and the denouement fixed.

These repeatable, choreographed experiences were powerfully effective in confirming very specific notions about the nature of the Aztec self and the Aztec world: that is, they worked. For the historian such participatory rituals are most usefully thought about as texts-in-performance; and these acted texts, whether preserved in continued performance or an observer's description or by being filmed are invaluable, because they are at once public and viewable: the heart-made creation of whatever group it is we are trying to understand.[9]

What can be deciphered of the meanings the activities of the Auschwitz SS held for the men who performed them? Their working lives appear as a glum, unvarying round of rollcalls and selections, of bullying pathetically ineffectual 'workers', of herding largely unresisting civilians to their deaths and preparing for the next train-load. Few had access to the excitements enjoyed by a Mengele, with his unlimited supply of 'research' subjects.[10] If early recruits to the SS were moved by the perverse but austere understandings of honour, obedience and abnegation of self encoded in the SS oath, as the years wore on recruitment became much less selective, and we must assume such loyalties to have been attenuated by the toll of war, age, and increasingly promiscuous enlistment. How then was morale inside the camps to be sustained?

Various suggestions, a few of them narrowly ideological, most of them broadly psychological, have been made to answer that question.[11] Some analysts have emphasised the importance of 'escapes' into

---

* Aztec elders discovered the words along with the need to tell of these matters after their defeat, when the world they had cherished was being destroyed by Spanish conquerers, colonists and imported disease. In this as in too many other cases, historians know the life of societies before European contact only from the funeral bells of their passing.

alcohol or the profits of corrupt trading, and there was certainly plenty of heavy drinking and urgent trading. Others point to the physical comfort and security of a concentration-camp post in contrast to the rigours and dangers of the front.

I want to add the suggestion that the rounds of disciplinary procedures so ardently enforced by the Auschwitz SS not only met cultural criteria of discipline and punishment, but were also consciously theatrical, and that these pieces of SS theatre, constructed and enacted daily, reanimated the SS sense of high purpose and invincibility, authenticated the realism of their absurd ideology, and sustained both morale and self-image in what was, indubitably but inadmissibly, psychologically a hardship post. I would further claim that the excitements of those enactments and entertainments worked to maintain the glamour still attaching to their gruesome calling, and that the manic theatricality imposed on camp inmates was primarily addressed not to its cowering audience, but to its SS impresarios.

Historians typically set aside their often meagre and shop-worn handful of anthropological insights when they examine the social dynamics of the concentration camps or, indeed, any aspect of the Nazi regime, perhaps because such approaches seem at once too trivial and too mundane to comprehend enormities. It is also true that, now that the blunt instrument of class has been hung on the wall, intellectual fashion has drifted through literary theory towards a focus on individual psychological motivations. In my view it is precisely for apparently aberrant phenomena like the camps that anthropological approaches are likely to be fruitful. I therefore want to consider Auschwitz as an anthropologist might consider a newly encountered 'exotic' society, looking beyond apparently instrumental actions to seek out the theatre of emotions and status those actions sustained.

Let us begin as incoming prisoners' experience of Auschwitz began, with the reception. Primo Levi has described the phantasmagorical aura surrounding arrival, with the sudden cessation of all movement and the impenetrable darkness in the railway car. Then 'the door opened with a crash, and the dark echoed with outlandish orders in that curt barbaric barkings of Germans in command which seems to give vent to a millennial anger. A vast platform appeared before us, lit up by reflectors'. The exhausted passengers stumbled out into a pool of light – which also became a pool of silence; a 'silence as of an aquarium, or as in certain dream sequences'. SS men, aloof, indifferent, low-voiced, 'with faces of stone', moved among the people, separating them into two groups by the movement of a finger.[12] Anxieties were soothed, a few requests granted with others calmly denied. Refusal to obey was swiftly punished, but few failed to obey. Why would they not obey?

In that space of subaqueous silence ('We had been expecting something more apocalyptic') momentous things were effected: 'In an instant, our women, our parents, our children disappeared. We saw them for a short while as an obscure mass at the other end of the platform; then we saw nothing more'.[13] Ninety-six men and twenty-nine women had been selected for the labour camp. More than 500 others had been sent to the gas. There had been no ripple of protest, because the miasma of silence drowned panic and stifled complaint.

We know from other accounts how often that same choreographed sequence – the silence, the eruption of noise and action, then unnatural stillness again – was applied for the reception of victims into Auschwitz. One reason such scenes have been so easily theatricalised in representations in films or words is that they are already theatrical: the silent waiting, the calculated urgency to empty the trains (will they baulk?), the entry of the victims into the light – and then the quiet, mesmerically calm processing that lends panic no purchase. The sequence did not always work, and then the resort to violence was swift. But consider the range of gratifications for the key players when the scenario unrolled smoothly to its desired conclusion. The 'factory' metaphor, apt as it is to catch the surreal 'rationality' of the overall planning of the camps, misses the emotional involvement of those engaged in the work of management. Eliciting the desired performance from trusting, deceived players is at once the perfect experience and the perfect expression of one kind of power.

Initiation into camp life was also theatrical. Levi recognised that the nakedness, the hair-shearing, the hours of waiting, the sudden blows, the orders screamed in real or simulated rage, even the seemingly gratuitous insults and assaults from fellow prisoners were all scripted, designed to effect first bewilderment, and then moral and physical collapse. 'It was all staged and this was quite obvious', he says, contemptuously.[14]

As always, Levi's eyes are on the cowed victims. He has no interest in how the charade might affect the stagers, who were also the leading players. Instead, he constructs a victim-oriented category for these and a multitude of similar episodes. They are all 'useless violence', their only instrumental dimension the humiliation of the hated Jew.

I doubt the violence was 'useless', or the time wasted. Consider, for example, those paths. Although there was an SS 'village' complete with houses and gardens, children, rabbits and pet dogs, most of the Auschwitz SS lived in barracks. Even for those officers with households, the place and the life must have been dreary. Levi does not think to wonder whether one of the virtues of gravelling those SS paths, and only those paths, with human bones was to provide the recurrent experience of their crunch under the boot, a crunch which could make a small walk from camp to barrack at once an exercise in superiority, and an aural and tactile celebration of the toughness of the true SS man. Elie Cohen describing 'the business of the caps', did not consider the effect on the recipient when every striped figure within an eight-foot radius would stiffen, uncover and walk rigidly 'at attention' until released from one's invisible field of force.[15] Ota Kraus and Erich Kulka tell us that while 'all the SS guards and wardresses had but one aim: to get rich as quickly as possible, to acquire luxury goods which could not be bought elsewhere', that 'paradoxically, it was often the strictest SS who were the greatest traders in goods of all kinds'.[16] The pursuit of luxuries and high living serves to pass the time and to feather future nests, but living flamboyantly high also carries a special frisson in a setting of mass abject deprivation, and is a gratifyingly insistent outward sign of inner superiority. Himmler made clear in his October 1943 Posen speech to his top SS officers that he dreaded the risk of corruption in SS ranks, but Himmler's kind of puritanism was hard to maintain among those constantly made to see and experience themselves as superior, not in some abstract and cerebral way, but viscerally, in every physical detail, and for every waking moment.

Robert Lifton recognised that Auschwitz was 'a staged melodrama'. But, in an echo of Elie Cohen's response, he judges the reiterated performances to be largely unwitting expressions: an inadvertent self-exposure in which 'the authors had so indulged their wildest fantasy as to render it completely absurd'.[17] We must remember that the SS at Auschwitz, like the SS in all the camps, knew that their SS comrades were fighting at the front, against 'real' enemies, enemies with guns, enemies who fought back. I doubt that Lifton appreciates the importance of the SS camp theatre for men and women who could cast themselves as star players in what would otherwise have been a dumbly squalid everyday. Even the most brutish of the SS had played their parts in the mass theatre of party rallies and national celebrations. They had been sensitised to the transformative power of theatre long before their arrival at the camps, and they brought that predilection with them. In Auschwitz they set it to work, to transform unpromising circumstance into a theatre of ideology realised.

Theatre was everywhere in Auschwitz. Apart from their careful construction of the milieu (those gravelled paths, those gaunt barracks) what I will call street theatre flourished. The Auschwitz authorities, who permitted so little, encouraged 'holiday' spectacles within the camp, as when the giant Jacob, rumoured to have been the sparring partner of the legendary German boxer Max Schmeling, would bend iron rods in his bare hands on Sunday afternoons, or when the dwarf Elias screamed and cavorted for his masters' diversion.[18]

The authorities also provided their own Sunday theatricals, in the form of 'sports'. The essential scenario was always the same. Already debilitated prisoners were badgered into committing some trivial 'offence' and then forced to perform meaningless physical exercises – running, doing push-ups – until they collapsed. The *Kapos* then subjected them to savage beatings, punishments which often ended in death.

It is important to be clear that these punishments were in no sense disciplinary. The 'culprits' were at all times desperate to obey; they were merely physically incapable of doing so. All prisoners dreaded failure at any routine the SS demanded of them. We may therefore assume that these performances served some other interest or interests. One strand of the aggressive anti-Semitism uncovered by Daniel Goldhagen seems to be being enacted here: the pleasure to be had in forcing Jews to perform physical work or 'sport', which was taken to be inimical to them.[19]

There were, however, other less fully ideologised elements in play. Filip Müller chose to open his 'Eyewitness Auschwitz' account with a description of one such 'sports day'.[20] The passage repays examination, for the apparently gratuitous form of the exercise, the form of the drama, and for the opportunity it provides for closer diagnosis of the preferred SS style.

It began with 'the business of the caps'. Men who had performed the manoeuvre with inadequate crispness were plucked out of the ranks, arranged in lines of five, and ordered to carry out a routine of tough physical exercise. As each man collapsed, he was bludgeoned to death. There could have been a reminiscent masculine competitiveness here: SS man Carl Jacob Burkhardt later acknowledged that extreme public humiliation through enforced exercise was a feature of SS train-ing – although naturally without the lethal outcome.[21]

In Müller's telling the routine beatings were inflicted by a sweating, bellowing block clerk (a 'green triangle', that is, a German and a crim-inal) and his subordinates. Müller counted thirty bodies laid out on the ground beside their living comrades before the 'sports' were judged to be completed.

All this was effected under the occasional, casual eye of an SS offi-cer, who watched, strolled away, strolled back, watched again. The drill completed, he received the count of the living and of the newly dead from the block clerk, and proceeded to check the number by a slow, steady walk along the quivering lines.

Despite his insouciant style he was indubitably the star of the show being staged for him. He sustained his impassivity until there was an unscheduled interruption (a protest from a naive prisoner, Müller says) when he erupted in brief anger – and then returned to his histrionic composure. A very conscious performance by a man who knew he was the cynosure of a thousand eyes, and surely a fine and gratifying way to pass an otherwise tedious Sunday morning.

The preferred demeanour for the Auschwitz SS when supervising or inflicting cruelties was typically one of theatrical detachment and un-shakeable 'cool'. Adolescents of all ages have been sensitive to the eloquence of lethal violence encased in elegant correctitude. The most notorious camp killers were notoriously dapper. Lieutenant Muhsfeld, a famously efficient killer, always donned rubber gloves before dis-patching batches of victims by shooting them in the back of the neck. He was jealous of his reputation for imperturbability. When Dr Ny-iszli, in the course of a routine check-up, suggested that his elevated pulse-rate might have something to do with 'the little job' he had just carried out in the furnace room (he had just shot eighty men), Muhs-feld was indignant: ' "Your diagnosis is incorrect," he said. "It doesn't bother me any more to kill 100 men than it does to kill 5. If I am upset, it is merely because I drink too much" '.[22]

The theatre of the Birkenau extermination complex developed its own scenarios and its own gratifications. The SS were always on show, and always dressed to kill. Their immaculate presentation contrasted, and was meant to contrast, with the dilapidated squalor of the lesser creatures who stumbled out of the boxcars, or the grotesques in striped pyjamas who marched into the light to take charge of baggage. The same attentiveness to the appearance of things was demonstrated in the SS orchestration of the mass killings. Primo Levi did not see the performance staged for the 500 men, women and children from his convoy selected for the gas, but he would have recognised the 'chang-ing rooms', the anterooms to the gas chambers, as overt stage sets, with their numbered pegs for clothing ('Remember your number!') and the signs in various languages advertising the benefits of hygiene. When the episode was over and the rooms emptied, there would be a frantic rush to remove all traces of the last audience and to reset the scene for the next intake and the next performance.

There was a range of possible scripts in the anterooms to death. We see different scenarios played out and then assessed in accordance with their capacity to control and direct 'audience response', and achieve an orderly, brisk processing. Müller, our best informant inside the crematoria, describes one model performance in which the SS, playing affable and courteous guides, ushered their victims through the neces-sary sequence with 'no shouting, no goading, guns . . . carefully tucked away . . . not a word of abuse passed their lips'. After a couple of reassuring speeches, the crowd of people was successfully cozened and sealed into the gas chambers with no time-consuming fuss. The SS officer in charge turned to his underlings: 'Well, you two, have you got it now? That's the way to do it!'[23] Again we have an example of that chilling Nazi perversity which combines a readiness to manipulate their victims as humans while effecting their extermination as vermin.

Good staging made the work go more briskly, but we must also grant that there was a separate pleasure to be had from successful performance. Levi, taking Nazi hatred of the Jews as the motive for the humiliations heaped upon them, seizes on the response made by

Franz Stangl, Commandant of Treblinka, to Gitta Sereny's question: what was the point of the humiliations? 'To condition those who were to be the material executors of the operations. To make it possible to do what they were doing.'[24] There can be no doubt that much SS behaviour inside the camps was predicated on an active hatred for Jews and an active desire to degrade them. Contrast the very different treatment, accorded the Gypsies, the other 'race' declared unfit to live, who were nonetheless permitted to retain their clothing, hair, family and personal dignity inside Auschwitz, and whose passage to the gas shook the nonchalance of the SS who presided over it. Filip Müller recalls their embarrassment: 'One could see that most of the SS men had a bad conscience. They hadn't shown any scruples about annihilating Jews, the killing of whom was now a daily routine for all of them, yet they clearly found it unpleasant and distressing to exterminate people with whom they had been on quite good terms up to now'.[25] But hatred of Jews cannot adequately explain the smiling affability displayed by the SS up to the moment of entry into the gas chambers. Only the gratifications attending successful play-acting will do that.

Alcohol was a major indulgence among the *Sonderkommando* SS, as among the Auschwitz SS more generally, but few drank on duty.[26] Duty offered its own rewards. Time and again we note fine ensemble playing from the permanent members of the troupe. We should not underestimate the cohesive effect of the main players' immediate exhilaration and consequent gratification when the scenarios worked, nor the steady accrual of contempt for their manipulated audiences. Even when the script faltered, the team recovered quickly: time and again we see a swift, concerted move to panic-inducing violence when cozening fails and the victims begin to resist.[27] If we were watching a theatre rather than a charnel house, we would applaud the sleekness of the performance.

When *Hauptscharführer* Moll arrived at the Auschwitz-Birkenau extermination plant to speed up production and streamline procedures he brought vast and terrifying energy to the task. That energy seems to have been fuelled not only by a vivid loathing of Jews and rawly sexual sadism, but by an active devotion to his leader – the *Führer-Bindung*, the 'bond with Hitler' emphasised by Friedländer. At all times, including his frenetic exertions during excavations of huge new cremation pits, Moll wore the medal with which his Führer had personally invested him. Müller notes that among all the Auschwitz SS associated with the *Sonderkommando* only Moll firmly held to the rule that prohibited 'helping themselves to valuables belonging to *Rassenfeinden*, members of the enemy race'.[28] He also took a technician's pride in his ability to reduce hundreds of thousands of living people into ashes in a span of a few months. But will concepts like *Führer-Bindung* explain the almost equally sustained and strenuous activity of Moll's men? What we mainly hear from them are complaints as the mountains of corpses pile up faster than their capacity to destroy them. What we see is increasing drunkenness. Moll's preference from first to last is brute force. What has gone from SS lives are the recurrent gratifications of theatrical stagings and the psychological manipulation of victims.

Stage-setting at Treblinka appears to have been even more extravagant. In the 'slack' period of spring 1943 Stangl took the opportunity to have the railway station freshly embellished with paint and decorated with false direction signs, ticket windows and a fake clock. The whole lower camp – separated from the gas chambers and the corpse-burning racks of the upper camp only by the changing rooms and a pine-wreathed barbed-wire fence – was beautified with the construction of a street, '800 metres, all bordered with flowers', garden beds and walks, quaintly carved signs (a bent Jew pointing to 'The Ghetto'), with the whole topped by a guardhouse 'in Tyrolean style'. Stangl happily remembered: 'I tell you, I had the best carpenters in the world – everyone envied me. It was all done in wood – stylistically perfect.'

Stangl also acknowledged that 'the whole place stank to high heaven from kilometres away'. At Treblinka incoming train-loads received different receptions, depending on their place of origin and their consequent level of suspicion. Those from the west, and therefore relatively unsuspicious, alighted at the charming railway-station and encountered gentle courtesies and soft-voiced requests for cooperation – until they were running naked under the whips. Trains from the east, carrying people who knew to expect terror, were met by some of Treblinka's eighty Ukrainian 'helpers' wielding their whips and bludgeons.[29]

Richard Glazar, the tough Prague Jew who survived ten months as a clothes-sorter in Treblinka Camp I until his escape in the great

breakout of August 1943, was constantly impressed by the theatrical-
ism of the SS, both in the shepherding of naive victims into the undressing rooms, and in the 'disciplining' of workers. Two men had
been discovered trying to escape. 'The other SS officers are just standing around, as if waiting for a show to begin, a show featuring humans
who have come to look much like naked scarecrows'. Then Master
Sergeant Franz makes his entrance:

> He doesn't walk; he strides. He is aware of every one of his steps. He knows
> that everything about him is flawless, perfectly pressed, polished bright: the
> black boots, the grey leather jodhpurs with the large yellow patches stretch-
> ing across his rear and down to his knees, the green uniform jacket, the grey
> deerskin gloves, the skull and crossbones cap worn at an angle. SS Master
> Sergeant Kurt Franz knows only too well that here he is the most highly
> cultivated, the most handsome of all. What he doesn't know is that among
> the damned here in Treblinka his appearance, his red cheeks, his sparkling
> brown eyes, have earnt him the Polish nick-name Lalka – the Doll.

The would-be escapees are stripped, and dragged naked (beaten all the
while) to a beam between two trees outside the mess, where they are
suspended by the feet:

> An image turned on its head, as in a funhouse mirror, intrudes into the steam
> rising from the bowls in the raw cold and the stale odours of the kitchen:
> bluish bodies, heads forced back, protruding Adam's apples, eyes seeming to
> spill out over their foreheads, thick ribbons of blood between the nose and
> the lips, thin ribbons of blood from the corners of the mouth to the tem-
> ples.[30]

The two men take some time to die.

Inside the work camps, dealing with long-term prisoners, SS man-
ners were different. The Auschwitz camp style of command has been
well documented. While the top officers spoke once and softly, the rest
of the German ranks, along with their imitators among the *Kapos*,
'screamed', 'bellowed' or 'barked' their orders.[31] Intelligibility was not
the issue. Many of their listeners could not understand even the bas-
tardised German of the camps, much less these animal bellowings. We
know the intended (and achieved) effect on those who heard and who
did not understand: terror. But we ought also remember the effect on
the bellower: the strong intake of breath, the tensed muscles of the

throat and belly, the violent exhalation. Soccer hoodlums know the exhilaration of the bellow as a preparation for physical violence – they even set it to music. The uninhibited bellow is at once the expression and the experience of unmitigated physical domination.

The pleasures of unrestrained violence were always available, along with more refined versions. Consider the SS use of dogs. Dogs were useful as cheap, eager and effectively tireless instruments of terror. But they were more than that, both for those who dreaded them and for those who trained and controlled them. The dogs were habituated to attack any human in prison garb. In their training programs they had been confronted by man-sized puppets in striped jacket and pants, which were flopped and shaken before them until they attacked, and rags and stuffing flew. They therefore had to be held on a short leash in the vicinity of prisoners. It is possible to become used to the sight of a truncheon, but not a bristling, snarling dog. Panting, straining, they were in a quite unmetaphoric way leashed violence, barely controlled animality – until the voluptuous release into action, when the script blurred excitingly, when no one could know the precise nature or the extent of the damage. Outcomes, however, remained certain: prisoners torn and bleeding, or prisoners dead. Or almost always: when the Auschwitz SS tried to set their dogs on the rebels of the *Sonderkommando* during the October uprising the dogs whined and skulked. They knew only their predestined prey. They dared not attack these men who did not wear the striped garments of the less-than-men.[32]

We know the public play *Hauptscharführer* Moll made with his alsatian as he rode around the camp in his white uniform, Hitler award on his breast, the brute alert in the motorcycle sidecar, because Filip Müller has told us about it. We know how he used the dog as his physical extension in his sexual play with the naked women he tormented on the rim of the pit of fire, with both dog and man unendurably excited.[33] Guards' opportunities were less flamboyant, but there was always excitement to be had with the dogs, especially when they were used against the women, who were terrified of them.[34] Animal accomplices in the theatre of power, they were well worth the feeding.

In such scenes it is profitless to separate 'emotion' from 'ideology': experience, reward and reinforcement are manifestly simultaneous. The psychological significances of collective performances are more difficult to unravel, particularly for historians, whose vision is narrowed because it is restricted to the happenstance of available documentation, and further clouded by the distance between experience and the record, which is almost always the record of an outsider, not a participant.[35]

Nonetheless we can sometimes glimpse the raw edge of what look like contrived occasions for ecstatic violence. Take the performance orchestrated by Joseph Kramer, commandant of a large part of the Auschwitz complex, on the occasion of the clearing of the so-called 'women's hospital'.

Kramer normally kept aloof from the daily workings of the camp, preferring to keep out of sight within the administrative area. When he did appear he cultivated a 'heavy and ponderous' walk and a mannered imperturbability: 'Everything about his bearing gave him a Buddha-like air'. However, on selected occasions that sublime calm could fracture.

Auschwitz Camp I had been largely evacuated as the Russians approached, but a thousand ailing women, together with their prisoner attendants, remained in the hospital barrack. The barrack was to be emptied and the patients transported direct to the crematoria.

In the early dawn of the appointed day the first ambulance-truck drew up at the barrack entrance (in Auschwitz ambulances were routinely used for such work), and Kramer's underlings – Mengele and twenty SS guards – took their places in the ward.

The star kept them waiting, but at last in he strode. 'Without replying to the greeting of his subordinates, [he] halted in the middle of the room, his legs apart, his hands behind his back. He barked orders at his subordinates'. The clearance began. At first it was orderly enough, but the women were slow and some of them unable to stand, so the SS began to hit them with truncheons and whips. Some of the women dragged from the upper bunks sustained further injuries.

At this point the chaos cannnot have been too great, because the prisoner attendants were ordered to take the womens' blouses (their last garments) from them, and did so, despite their protests. But then, as more screaming women were dragged from their bunks and beaten into the waiting ambulances, wild violence erupted. 'Kramer himself had lost his calm. A strange gleam lurked in his small eyes, and he worked like a madman. I saw him throw himself at one unfortunate woman and with a single blow of his truncheon shatter her skull'.

Blood and tissue were everywhere: 'on the floor, the walls, the SS uniforms, their boots'.[36]

A scene from a bad movie. But the blood is real. The performance offends the protocols of conduct of the Auschwitz SS, who did not typically do their own dirty work except on display occasions, as when would-be escapees were subjected to extreme, inventive (and theatrical) violence. While the attack was made possible by the inhumanity of the controlling script, which demanded the transportation of the sick and dying to a place of instant death, the smashings and crushings did not speed that work. They slowed it. The SS valued their reputation for coolness. Here they sacrificed it. So why did Kramer do what he did? Why did his men follow suit? It is true that anxiety must have been high, with the Russians closing in and the future bleak. Was it panic? Kramer and his SS were certainly working fast: Olga Lengyel tells us that Camp I was evacuated within twenty-four hours, with 20,000 people deported to Germany. The most likely date for the hospital evacuation, however, is late October, so the Russians were not yet perilously close. Had some particularly unwelcome news come from Germany? At least in its beginnings the action was, I think, another staged event, its shape implicit in Kramer's mind from his unhurried entry. Was the explosion into violence therefore an aberration, an accidental chain-reaction of individual responses? Or was the violence implicit from the beginning, with those tension-building moments of confrontation between poised men and terrified women? Consider Kramer's entry, his immobility, his eruption into action – and then the frenzy, which must have lasted some time: there were, after all, a thousand women in the barrack. Rituals – real rituals, exciting rituals – often tremble on the edge of uncontrol.

The theatrical perspective helps expose understandings otherwise left implicit, and flush into light some of the sadistic impulses which lurk along the boundaries of consciousness. It can expose the determined 'othering' by the SS of their 'enemies behind the wire'. It can take us a certain distance into even this action sequence – into what Olga Lengyel, who saw it, diagnosed as one of the 'fits of destructive insanity' she thought occasionally possessed the SS. But I do not believe it can take us to the heart of the scene described, or into the hearts of similar scenes scattered through the record.

Neither, however, can anything else. There was no issue of 'discipline' here, no question of anything but token resistance, no audience beyond the SS themselves, the doomed women and a handful of medical aides. Did these well-armed, well-fed men see their victims as detested Jews? They knew there were non-Jews among them. Did they see these tottering creatures as women and therefore apt for abuse? For a time I thought this kind of violence restricted to males, but Nazi women in authority were capable of behaving in much the same way. Was the violence a reflex of disgust, for the abjectness of their victims, for the vileness of their own role? Or was it a piece of self-indulgence, a Dionysian reward for isolation, an ecstatic antidote to boredom?

It is episodes like these – planned, yet deliriously extravagant – which can be categorised easily enough, but which continue to escape final diagnosis. When the work of the imagination is done, we ourselves remain the measure of plausibility. Tracing the experiences of a member of the Order Police set down outside that Polish village in that July dawn, in his exact circumstances, I can imagine – barely – how in the knowledge that my country was deep in war, in the strangeness of an unfamiliar place inhabited by people I cared nothing for, linked to familiar comrades by shared isolation and loyalty and a need for their respect, I might have tried to follow the orders given me by a trusted commander. I might have walked with a man, a woman, a child into the wood, and asked or forced them to lie down, so I could deliver the 'neck shot'. I also believe that in the event I could not, finally, have carried out that order.

Mystery shrouds the Kramer episode. That violence was planned, chosen, but quite gratuitous. The gratification must have resided in the action itself. Yet even within the compelling frame of theatrical expectation (and there is compulsion in theatre) how is it possible to smash a truncheon into a human face? How is it possible to take living flesh into one's hand, to feel its warmth – and then to injure it, for pleasure or to exact a graduated measure of pain? The gratuitous yet stylised cruelties of men like Kramer continue to confound me.

Men like Kramer decline interrogation: they die serenely mute. Fiction offers some close-to-persuasive sorties into such minds, but I think the real world does not.[37] We have no access to them beyond their actions. Must we therefore retreat to pathological psychology, to the notion that actions like these are indeed the 'fits of destructive insanity' that Olga Lengyel called them, here framed and sanctioned by a complaisant state? Are there always sadists and psychopaths enough distributed through any society apt for such work, ready for action whenever opportunity and political circumstances allow?[38]

If the motivations of Kramer and his men unleashed in the hospital remain obscure, the social and political implications are clear. If such creatures live among us, we must be careful to deny them the conditions and opportunities for their self-realisation. Civilised values are a chosen state, not a natural condition.

The path to Auschwitz-Birkenau.

Jews waiting in the birch wood, Auschwitz-Birkenau.

German soldier firing at a woman and child.

Jews being loaded into railway trucks, Siedlce Station, 22 August 1942.

Clearing the ghetto, Luków, Fall 1942

Clearing the ghetto, Luków, fall 1942. A Jew (companions prostrate beside him) forced to pray by order of police.

Lieutenant Gnade's Undressing Station, Miedzyrec

9

REPRESENTING THE HOLOCAUST

What shall I take to witness for thee? What shall I liken to thee, O daughter of Jerusalem? What shall I equal to thee, that I may comfort thee?

— *Lamentations*, Chapter 2, Verse 13.

In his *Contingency, Irony, and Solidarity* the distinguished American philosopher Richard Rorty pointed the way to a utopia: a utopia at once utopian, post-metaphysical, and liberal. The trick was to learn to recognize that people physically and culturally remote from us were moral realities too, as worthy of our compassion and regard as our own kin and kind. Once educated in 'the imaginative ability to see strange people as fellow sufferers', we would be readier to count the costs of our own gratifications, and to temper our quests for autonomy and abundance.

Rorty entrusted the central task of the extension of the reach of the moral imagination to 'genres such as ethnography, the journalist's report, the comic book, the docudrama, and, especially, the novel'. A couple of sentences on he added film, recognizing that 'the novel, the movie, and the TV program have, gradually but steadily, replaced the sermon and the treatise as the principal vehicles of moral challenge and progress'.[1] History was, rather pointedly, excluded.

The exclusion rankles, at least with this historian.[2] Rorty's identification of fiction and film as the prime educators of the popular imagination is obviously justified, especially if we allow that the effects may be ephemeral or unpredictable, and will largely elude measurement and analysis. My interest here is with one great process of public suffering which has been notoriously difficult to represent, whether in film or in the various forms of literature whose end is art. I mean, of course, the Holocaust.[3]

The poetry which came during the decade after the ending of World War I distilled and certified a transformation in a generation's understanding of what war, peace and politics mean. No comparable distillation of meanings has come out of the Holocaust, now more than fifty years past. It continues to defy assimilation. Even piecemeal appropriations typically fail. In her last and finest poems, Sylvia Plath tried to tap the power of Nazi and concentration camp imagery to convey her personal sense of dread, isolation and betrayal, as in these lines from 'Daddy':

> An engine, an engine
> Chuffing me off like a Jew.
> A Jew to Dachau, Auschwitz, Belsen.
> I begin to talk like a Jew.
> I think I may well be a Jew.[4]

The response to the poem was general consternation, followed by general rebuke. (There was no equivalent critical reaction to lines like that from 'Fever 103': 'Like Hiroshima ash and eating in'.) Artists often play with fire, but this incandescence seemed to carry with it the whiff of actual burning flesh. Even admirers acknowledged that Plath's attempt to marry her personal psychological afflictions to such grossly incommensurate sufferings imploded the delicately building structures of her art.[5] When D. M. Thomas chose the mass shootings at Babi Yar as pivot and the dramatic denouement of his long, fraught and intricately worked novel *The White Hotel*, and despite his attempt to invoke authenticity and acceptance by the reproduction of the words of one of the few survivors of that most barbarous massacre, the effect was immediate: the queasy trivialization not of the events, but of the writing which sought to exploit them. The extraordinary coda, which involved the revivification and reunion of people we had seen murdered in a heavenly 'Israel', only compounded catastrophe.[6]

I am not concerned to criticise Plath and Thomas here. What interests me is the inversion effect. Normally we expect the magic of art to intensify, transfigure and elevate actuality. Touch the Holocaust and the flow is reversed. That matter is so potent in itself that when art seeks to command it, it is art which is rendered vacuous and drained of authority.

The most effective imagined evocations of the Holocaust seem to proceed either by invocation, the glancing reference to an existing bank of ideas, images and sentiments ('Auschwitz'), or, perhaps more effectively, by indirection. Martin Amis in *Time's Arrow* conjures Auschwitz skimmingly through the swift manipulation of familiar clusters of icons. The pathos of Anne Frank's diary derives not from the words before us, which are in fact rather chirpy, as we might expect from so irrepressible a young woman, but from our knowledge of what is to come. The horrors in Aharon Appelfeld's laconic novels are always extratextual, or at the least offstage.[7] What makes Toni, the central figure in Appelfeld's *To the Land of the Reeds*, so moving, and our anxiety for her so painful, is that she is innocent: so endearingly trivial in her vanities, so incapable of imagining the unimaginable fate which is being prepared for her. The standard iconography is all there – the winter coat, the hastily gathered possessions, the docile, even eager travelling towards an increasingly problematic destination – but she has no notion of what is to come.

We do not see her lose her innocence: when the trap springs she is already gone from our sight. We do not see her climbing into the boxcar, or stumbling on the ramp. Instead we flick to the identikit image of 'the Holocaust' we carry in our heads – and are relieved at that point of the terrible burden of specific, systematic imaginings. Appelfeld's technique is superbly effective in rousing our imaginative sympathies, but essentially it still draws on existing capital. However much it may enlighten us as to the condition of the victims in the process of becoming victims, it does not challenge and expand imagination with a representation of the Holocaust in process.

Dan Pagis, as great a poet as Appelfeld is a novelist, employs a technique not of indirection, but of misdirection: the bodily assumption of the actual into the mythic. This is most perfectly effected in the small poem he titles 'Written in Pencil in the Sealed Railway-Car':

here in this carload
i am eve
with abel my son
if you see my other son

cain son of man
tell him that i[8]

In this carload, Eve. There is no strain in the coupling of the biblical reference and the commonplace railway-car, because the title has already catapulted us into the archetypal world of 'The Holocaust'. Pagis does not seek to tame the tiger. He rides it. We do not need the vaulting pole of imagination to leap the gap between the actual and the figurative because there is no gap to leap: we are already in the icy uplands and infernal gullies of myth. The intricacies of particular human suffering are left far behind.

That same mythic potency has come to suffuse normally banal words – 'oven', 'chimney', 'smoke', 'hair' – when those words are invoked anywhere within the broad range of the Holocaust context. Within that context they are instantly charged with explosive, undifferentiated emotional force: the genie effect. It seems that Holocaust material is by its nature already so freighted with significance that the figurings of the individual aesthetic imagination to render actuality visible can easily reduce to puny scratchings.

This may have been part of what Theodor Adorno meant by his famously gnomic reflection that to write poetry after Auschwitz would be a barbarism. His dictum takes our paralysis before the great fact of the Holocaust and elevates it to a moral act, a reflex of humane sensibility. Or does he mean that the companionable shared silence which is so large a part of poetry, the silence charged with trust in an opened humane sensibility, is not possible after Auschwitz, because now our confidence in one another is gone? Yet great poetry has been written not only after Auschwitz, but out of it. Paul Antschel (or 'Ancel', as it was sometimes written) was another remarkable artist to be born, like Pagis and Appelfeld, in Bukovina, at Czernowitz, that extraordinary enclave of High German culture. After the war he renamed himself 'Paul Celan' in repudiation of what Germany and Germans had done to him and his. He had survived his years in a work camp in Romania, but both his parents had died in a Ukrainian concentration camp, his father of typhus, his gentle, adored mother of a German bullet in the back of the neck.

After the war Celan at first chose to live in Vienna and to write his poetry in German: his mother's preferred tongue, the tongue of the

poets they had read together, the tongue of her murderers.[9] It was in
that tongue that he wrote a poem soon after the war which delivered
the language from its Nazi barbarizations, and reclaimed it as a language fit for poetry. It begins:

> Black milk of daybreak we drink it at evening
> we drink it at midday and morning we drink it at night
> we drink and we drink
> we shovel a grave in the air there you won't lie too cramped
> A man lives in the house he plays with his vipers he writes
> he writes when it grows dark to Deutschland your golden hair
> Marguerite
> he writes it and steps out of doors and the stars are all sparkling he
>   whistles his hounds to come close
> he whistles his Jews into rows has them shovel a grave in the ground
> he orders us strike up and play for the dance.[10]

'Todesfuge' comprehends the cruelty, the terror and the pity of the
murder of Jews by Germans in a steadfastly human voice, with no
mythic evasions, indeed with no transcendental referents at all. In image and attitude it is rooted deep in camp actuality. Celan initially
titled the poem not 'Death Fugue' but 'Death Tango', the name given
a tango composed by a concentration camp orchestra on the orders of
an SS lieutenant. Hitler, who rejected jazz as 'decadent', approved of
the tango. The camp orchestra was recorded; the record still exists
somewhere; it could be played, and we could hear it. The poem itself
is rightly named a fugue for the complex reiterations and reworkings
of its themes and their final, inexorable resolution, while it retains all
the concreteness and immediacy of its first title. It is at once a lament
and an indictment.

But Celan's poem does not seek to extend our knowledge. It assumes it. Poetry may be written after Auschwitz, but despite Rorty's
confidence I am persuaded there are innate difficulties in the successful
literary representation of the process of the Holocaust. Readers of
fiction typically expect to be seduced into concern for particular characters, who are then pursued through time and different contexts to
some plausible and emotionally satisfying outcome. In the Holocaust
case the context is at once stable and unendurable, time is at once
suspended and arbitrarily abbreviated, and the closure is at once pre-

dictable, and utterly bereft of meaning and comfort. In such circumstances *any* good outcome, *any* act of dignity or defiance, appears as a falsification or sentimentalisation of the general condition. Production-line killing allows small space for drama, while the huge contextual fact of the death of the multitude must trivialise the fate of the fortunate few. The Jews huddled on Schindler's ark live, Styron's Sophie survives to relive her impossible choice – but can such stories help us grasp how it was in that place, where everyone lived in the realistic expectation of death, and where nearly everyone died? Ordinary rules of dramatic narrative must at least suspend if they do not implicitly deny that great fact.

The representations discussed so far all draw on what I have called existing capital. I must exempt at least one writer (the reader will already have half a dozen in mind). Tadeusz Borowski's stories, written soon after his release from Auschwitz, were collected for publication in a volume entitled *This Way for the Gas, Ladies and Gentlemen*.[11] Every one of them augments our understanding and exercises our imaginations in new and extraordinary ways. We watch a new recruit to the squad which relieves incoming victims of their possessions accommodate both to his duties, and to their rewards. In a dreamily pastoral setting (milk, eggs, a bountiful woman) we follow the events of an ordinary day in the work camp at Harmenz, a subsidiary camp to Auschwitz. A young man expert in the dubious arts of survival practises his necessary skills, at the cost, as it turns out, of the life of a competitor. Meanwhile an unusually benign *Kapo* decides to teach two raw recruits (Greek, terrified, knowing no German) how to march. If they do not learn quickly, they will surely be 'selected' and die. They cannot be instructed or reassured. So, ingeniously, their teacher ties sticks to their legs to keep them rigid, and drives the men in small circles in the hope that they will somehow catch on, and so survive. The bizarre little exercise draws the irritated attention of an SS officer, who orders the *Kapo* to kill his pupils. So he does: he knocks them down, places a stick across a throat, steps on it, rocks . . .

What is happening here? What kind of story is this? In another story, a deputy *Kapo*, already stuffed with food, allows a Jew selected for the gas to eat his fill from his surplus and take the leftovers with him into the Cremo. An act of compassion, or of irony? Or of contempt? How can we tell?

Such actions, narrated in Borowski's studiously offhand style, take place within a vividly realized physical space, but in a moral void. Men speak, men act, and there is no moral echo. As we read, any wistful hopes of heroism, or even of secure moral location, leak away. And we have no notion of what will happen next, how 'the story' will develop, because while the space illuminated by the prose is sharp and clear, we know it to be rimmed by other utterly unpredictable forces, forces which may at any point explode the patterns we think we see. In these fictions it is the reader, struggling for a foothold, finding none, who is the protagonist, and feeling – at a remove, but feeling – the moral vertigo investing that cursed place.

Borowski's technique is masterly, his images cinematic-vivid. He engulfs us in the strange world of the camp. Does that achievement give the palm to fiction? Like Isaac Babel before him, Borowski raises in acute form the question of the relationship between I-was-there history and the fiction which comes out of that experience. I do not deny that much of Borowski's effect is the result of art: the writing is so economical, so finely poised, the surface so densely textured, that it is only as we try to pull away that we discover that this is glue paper; that we are caught, bound, and implicated by more than the magical weavings of an individual sensibility. We realise that Borowski has taken us by the shoulders and shown us how it might have been in that place, back then.

Might have been? Or must have been? I am persuaded that the authority of a Tadeusz Borowski or an Isaac Babel or those other writers who present us with 'fiction' made out of experience owes a great deal both to the fact and to our knowledge that they have 'been there'; that they are reporting (and selecting, shaping, and inventing) out of direct observation and participation. I cannot effectively separate their texts from the greatest texts of that other genre, 'survivor testimony', where subjective experience can be represented, with high art, by such consummate artist-witnesses as Primo Levi or Charlotte Delbo, or from the sustained poignancy of Anne Frank's diary, a poignancy which arises in part from our knowledge of its context, but also because of the literary talent of this adolescent, preternaturally gifted writer.

Our knowledge that Borowski has indeed 'been there' supplies an undertext of intimate moral implication never present in 'pure' fiction.

This is a difficult issue, especially in these post-postmodernist days, but it is central, and worth taking time over. In my view the largest single difference between History and Fiction (at moments like these they require capitalization) is that each establishes quite different relationships between writer and subject, and writer and reader. Had I discovered the nature of Humbert Humbert's secret joys in real life, I would have had him locked up. I may have tried to 'understand' him, but only after I had destroyed his happiness. Snug between the covers of the fiction called *Lolita* I can revel in his eely escapades, his delirious deceptions; weep with him when his child slave escapes; yearn with him for her recapture. Through giving me access to the inner thoughts and secret actions of closed others, fiction has taught me most of what I know, or think I know, about life.

This fictional world, however, contains a curious absence. The reason for its exhilarating freedom is that it is a kind of game, a circumscribed place of play. Once inside I have no responsibility beyond my responsibility to respond to the text. I may tremble for its people, I may weep for them – but I want to relish their anguish, not heal it. I do not want Anna reconciled with Karenin and living to plump and comfortable grandmotherhood. I want her dead under that train. I want Emma Bovary to dream her dreams, to act them out, increasingly shabbily, and then to drink prussic acid and die in agony. I have no human responsibility towards these people. Although they may be more intimately known than my most intimate actual others, although they may often seem very much more 'real', in the end my compassion is a fiction too, because I know they are fictions.

Contrast this with what happens when I read a story which claims to be true. I will know very much less about the protagonists. There is no creator to strip away their veils, so they will be somewhat opaque to me. Nonetheless, I engage with them differently because I stand in a moral relationship with these people, because they are my fellow-humans, whose blood is real and whose deaths are final and cannot be cancelled by turning back a page.

As a reader I will also assume a different contract with the writer depending on whether that writer is offering me fiction, or claiming to report on this mundane world. Listen to Flaubert, writing to a friend and gleefully pointing to the joke he tucks into the last lines of his *Légende de San Julian l'Hospitalier*. They run: 'and that is the story of

Saint Julian the Hospitalier, more or less as it can be seen on a stained-glass window in a church in my part of the country'. A most elegant finale, bringing us back from wonderland, depositing us gently adjacent to the real. Flaubert imagines the befuddled consternation which would have occurred had he been so foolish as to append an illustration of the cathedral window to his literary text: 'Comparing the image to the text, one would have said: "I don't understand anything. How did he get from this to that"?'[12]

How did he get from this to that? For Flaubert, by the pole-vault of imagination, which carried him from the muddled ambiguities of the mundane to the glorious symmetries of art. In that leap anything goes – provided you get there, which Flaubert, being Flaubert, does. However devotedly he researched his novels, whenever actuality impeded aesthetic effect he tossed actuality out the window.

I think that is the way of it with the best of the so-called 'realist' novelists. Flaubert can freely offer us rich accounts of physical circumstance and interior states. Those freedoms and riches are the privileges of fiction. However much historians may covet them, they must not be either facsimilated or simulated in historical writing, because to do so is to violate the historians' unstated but binding contract both with their readers – to stay in close contact with the ascertainable evidence – and with their 'characters', the once-real people they have chosen to represent.

There are some costs attaching to fiction's freedoms. Nabokov is a master in the representation of cruelties – he is one of Rorty's major nominees for the 'activation of imaginations' job. To return to the Holocaust: Nabokov chooses not to represent the horrors of Nazi actions against their chosen victims directly. His nearest reference to the Holocaust comes, with typical obliqueness, in a short story which refers briefly to an anxious Aunt Rosa who lived in tremulous anticipation of catastrophe 'until the Germans put her to death, together with all the people she had worried about'.[13] Instead he offers his *Bend Sinister*, published in 1947, a kind of parable of contemporary totalitarian regimes. In it Nabokov describes the physical destruction of David Krug, aged eight. We come to know of the child's death and the manner of it by watching a film, which is also being watched by his father, Adam, who is under interrogation by officials of an unidentified but generically totalitarian state. Krug has already agreed to confess to everything and anything to save his son, but there has been a small bureaucratic bungle. The hideous death we are watching has probably been ordered by 'mistake'. The idiocy only adds to the horror.

The horror is very well done. Yet for me the master fails, because he is writing 'only' fiction, and I am therefore not compelled to heed him. Nabokov the fabricator cuffs us lightly: 'Attend now'. In *Lolita* I attended, for the pleasure of it. But I am under no obligation to attend; I could, should I choose, simply close the book. I made that choice with *Bend Sinister*. The pages dealing with the death of David Krug are stapled together in my copy. I do not wish to see them even inadvertently. Nor have I forgiven Nabokov for installing those images in my mind, because they are gratuitous, things of his own invention.

My response may well be idiosyncratic, but I am persuaded that we listen differently to stories which are 'real', however naively or awkwardly reported, from stories, however beguiling, which we know to be invented. With a work of fiction we marvel at the fictioneer's imagination. With real thought and actions presented for our scrutiny we are brought to wonder at ourselves.

Other media also claim to expand our imaginative understanding of the human condition. Photographs stand at their own distinctive angle to the actuality they pretend to preserve. All photographs do something magical, fixing transient actuality into durable, perusable form, into iotas of transfixed time. Personal photographs do something more, converting the bright, frail moments of memory into an array of masterful images, unchallengeable kings of the cannibal empire they effortlessly establish in our heads. Theo Richmond has called photography 'an inherently morbid medium', and he is right.[14] All photographs are melancholy; the vanished moment caught at the moment of its vanishing. All photographs are ominous: who are these special people, framed in space? All photographs are poignant: we feel the chill of an irretrievable past, the threat of an invisible future, the mortal vulnerability of the innocent, ignorant creatures caught on the silvered paper. The photographs relating to the Holocaust are melancholy, poignant and ominous to an exquisite degree, as they catch men, women and children huddled at railway stations, harassed into cattle trucks, or trudging down roads towards vaguely glimpsed clusters of buildings, trees, and tall chimneys.

In those moments of passage we see that the people are still alive.

They are still capable of hope. But not of rescue. Again, context is all. As with the fictional or poetic representations discussed earlier, to 'make sense' of photographs of people climbing into trains or walking along roads we have to know they are what they are: 'Holocaust photographs'. We already know that context. But now we 'know' these people were once as alive as we are, living in this same green world.

That capacity to persuade us of the actuality of the past belongs exclusively to the camera. Roland Barthes rightly celebrates the photograph as a 'new, somehow experiential order of proof'. 'Photography's inimitable feature', he says, 'is that someone has seen the referent (even if it is a matter of objects) *in flesh and blood*, or *again in person*'. He recalls his fascinated horror when as a child he saw a photograph of a slave market – not a drawing, not an engraving, but a photograph:

the slave-master, in a hat, standing; the slaves, in loincloths, sitting . . . there was a *certainty* that such a thing had existed: not a question of exactitude, but reality: the historian was no longer the mediator, slavery was given without mediation . . . We look at the paper inscribed by the alchemy of photography by the light rays which once emanated from some actual object, and the connection is unequivocally made: *That-has-been*.[15]

The photographs of the Holocaust do more than persuade us of its reality. They are also suffused by bitter affect: like the after-the-event photographs of the dead and the ambulant corpses of Buchenwald and Belsen, they are direct records of our failure, and of our guilt. We were alive at the time of their agony; we did nothing to alleviate it. In time (because of that powerful affect?) we come to refer to them with the unconscious fluency we reserve for personal memories. As a result we may also grant them the immunity from scrutiny we grant our own memories. They are, nonetheless, historical texts, and must be analysed, evaluated and interpreted, like any other text.

That we have these indispensable photographs at all underlies the contingency of the historical enterprise. Unsurprisingly, photography within Auschwitz, as in all the other camps, was officially forbidden. We have the photograph of the small girl walking alone to her death with which I began this study only because an SS man had been given special permission to photograph the arrival, separation and selection of victims in the interests, we are told, of 'scientific racial research'. The man had maintained a home in Czechoslovakia. After the war a

Jewish woman moved into his house, found the photographs, and sold them to the Jewish museum in Prague, where years later they were recognised for what they were by a former Auschwitz prisoner.[16] By some miracle the frail pasteboard had not curled or cracked. Only this long trail of happenstance preserved them for us, so we can look into the wary faces of the children, the haggard adults, and know them as living beings, as real as the people we might jostle on a railway platform today. We have photographs of people being loaded into cattle cars for Treblinka, with three barefoot boys, one carrying his little brother pickaback, nervously hanging back behind the crush, because an Austrian soldier called Hubert Pfoch was travelling through Siedlce Station on his way to the front on 22 August 1942 and saw the loading in process – saw the people being forced into the cars, saw them beaten – and dared to photograph what he saw. The photographs were presented as part of the evidence against ten former Treblinka guards on trial at Dusseldorf in 1964. When Gitta Sereny spoke with Hubert Pfoch in 1972 in Vienna, he recalled that seconds after he had taken the photograph the tall Ukrainian guard in the background 'had hit out so hard at the children who were "slow to move" that he split the butt of his rifle in two'.[17]

Photographs tell the moment. Documentary film makes the claim to record moments-in-sequence; to capture Barthes's '*that-has-been*', too. A genre which can range from Leni Riefenstahl's heroic mythologising of Germanic fantasies to the apparent innocence of the amateur hand-held camera is too protean to be discussed here – although even brief reflection suggests that, given film's expansiveness, truth is a greased pig, to be caught, if caught at all, in flight. 'Fictional' film, with its visual vividness, its magical simulation of reality, is only marginally less complex. Most commercial films about the Holocaust have vulgarised events even more grossly than popular novels. Consider the American series 'Holocaust', where terrible actuality is subordinated to, and suborned by, a standard girl-boy romantic narrative, or the German series 'Heimat', where exculpatory sentimentality takes unchallenged precedence. Hear Elie Wiesel on what the populace gets from the 'cheap and simplistic melodramas' that pretend to represent the Holocaust: 'a little history, a heavy dose of sentimentality and suspense, a dash of theological ruminations about the silence of God, and there it is: let kitsch rule in the land of kitsch'.[18]

These are the deformations typical of popular fiction, and ought not be blamed on the medium. Nonetheless, I confess to a mistrust of film as a vehicle for conveying authentic, which must mean tentative and unstable, historical understanding. Film is a treacherously expansive, not to say uncontrollable medium, both in the exuberance of its communication of information – settings, styles, physiques, behaviour, *everything* must appear – and in its swift, various and incalculable effect upon the individual imagination. Steven Spielberg's ghetto-clearing sequences in *Schindler's List* are testimony of film's incomparable capacity in the hands of a great director to represent the scope and the staccato pace of such mass 'actions', without obliterating the individual – although it is as well to remember that while the representation brilliantly presents the ruthlessness of the action's execution and design, it does not represent any individual's experience of it. It is a director's view. Even Schindler on his horse on his hill could not have seen a fraction of what the roaming, swooping camera allows us to see. And even Spielberg sweetens the horror of his concocted scenes in providing the consolatory figure of the little girl in red, herded with the victims, then making her perilous way back to precarious safety. We follow her uncertain passage the more easily because of the darkness around her. Cinematically her image works to distract us from the contexting horror, to supply a spurious comfort.

By its nature, film cannot be made properly respectful of the mysteries and the ambiguities of actual experience. Even less can it be made respectful of the kind of fragmentary and ambiguous documentation on which history depends. It must at once say too much, in its expert mimicry of the richness and density of actuality, and too little, in its concealed selectivity, its beguiling, invisible anglings and strokings. And even at its most mannered, it insists on its own existential veracity. For all its apparent realism, its glory is its remoteness from the actuality it mimes so eloquently. Its home territory is not the actual, but the mythical.

An example from my home territory. Despite borrowing its title from the historical record, Werner Herzog's *Aguirre, the Wrath of God* represents no conquistador that even was. As an account of any actual Amazonian exploration it is irretrievably melodramatic. But it is also a superb distillation of the fantasies and potentialities simmering within the heads of many expedition leaders, and their followers too. It is a demonstration of how easily reckless visions of conquest can degenerate into nightmares of murder and self-delusion. Film is the incomparable medium for dreams which have been choreographed to be shared by the waking. We watch Reisenstahl's extravaganzas unfurl like banners to display the Nazi vision for Germany, the sophistication of Nazi theatrical skills, and the ecstasy those skills unleashed in the throbbing thousands gathered for the ritual of affirmation, and we are enlightened as we could not be by any other medium. But film remains a drunken giant, inept for the delicate imaginative and critical work of transmitting our uncertain understandings of the worlds which have closed behind us.

There is, however, one remarkable film, part documentary, part most conscious work of art, which forces the most committed champion of the literary text to admit the importance of the human contexts concealed behind the words we puzzle over on the page: Claude Lanzmann's *Shoah*. That film demonstrates the process of 'increasing understanding' in, as it were, slow motion – or, as I think about it, in real, human time. Who can forget the opening shot of gentle meadows, of two men strolling, quietly talking? Who can forget how, as they talk, the innocent pastoral before us changes? We stare at silent fields, at rusting railway tracks with soft grass tufting between them, and are forced to locate and reconstruct buildings, sidings, walkways, chimneys. Then, the structures having been inexorably established in the imagination, we are made to people them: to people them out of information slowly being fed to us, in interaction with banks of memories we did not know we held. We are being educated in horrors. The very length of the film – more than nine hours of it, in recollection – mimics the 'abnormal' elongation of misery, the monotony of exhaustion and anguish, endured by those immured in the camps.

Throughout, Lanzmann is omnipresent, forcing his witness-sources to ever more precise recollection, establishing places, times and actions with chilling exactitude. His concern is solely with the killings of the Jews, and with their killing in the gas chambers. He begins his film at Chelmno in December 1941. Throughout, this cinematic auteur sustains the relentless critique of sources I would urge as the central organising narrative for all serious historians. Who can forget the barber, recalled from retirement to a Tel Aviv shop, clipping the hair of a customer as he struggles to respond to Lanzmann's questioning; laying down his scissors, shaking his head, slowly, painfully weeping – and Lanzmann's voice insisting that he go on? And go on he does, taking up his scissors, 'collecting himself' by the routine exercise of routine skills, going on, slowly, painfully, as if wading through waist-deep mud.

In the course of an analysis of filmed testimonies James Young, an American cultural analyst, explains some of the processes we have been watching:

> . . . these memories are still part of the survivor's inner life, still an inner wound; if, in watching these memories pass from the private to the public sphere, we also feel some of the pain in this transition, we may understand something about the consequences of both the experiences and the telling of such experiences. In the testimonial image, we also perceive the traces of the story the survivor is not telling; these traces are in his eyes, his movements, his expressions – all of which become part of the overall text of video testimony, suggesting much more than we are hearing and seeing. We grasp here that memory is being transmitted not merely through narrative but by body movements and behaviour as well . . . we thus find transmitted a universe of non-verbal memory – signs no less than language to be interpreted and decoded.[19]

Lanzmann privileges we who are new to the analysis of video testimony to watch that moment when memory transforms into language. (He also introduces historians to what must become a major source for future work: as I write, the Shoah Foundation's enterprise of interviewing men and women directly affected by the Holocaust is in full swing in my home city of Melbourne.) Writers must destroy silence in order to represent it. In filmed testimony silence is as present, and often more eloquent, than speech. 'Silence that cannot exist in print except in blank pages is now accompanied by the image of one who is silent, who cannot find words'.[20] We watch as 'memory' is selected and verbalized; a most crucial transition for the historian, who typically must be content with the inscriptions left after that painful birthing. Lanzmann insists that we watch, and watch again, because by that repetition we are forced to awareness of a truth that the daily work of living (like the daily work of 'doing history') tempts us to forget: that heard words are the products of obscure interactions of fluctuating circumstance and unstable memory; that words inscribed on the page, made though they are out of human experience and human emotions, have an apparent solidity which denies and conceals the exigency of their origins. There can be no unmediated access to the experience of others – that is a dullard's fantasy – but just how great the distance is between experience and texts, and how masked from us the circumstances of their making, is here made manifest as we watch these men and women hesitating, rejecting, searching for the words which will best seize and hold any one out of the shoal of possible and potential 'memories' flickering behind their eyes. We are being shown memory in process, not memory encrypted as sacred relic.

The *Shoah* interrogations also mimic the confusion of tongues which existed in the camps, with its attendant demoralisation of perception. Lanzmann speaks French and German, but he does not speak Polish, Hebrew or Yiddish, so questions and answers ripple through transforming veils of language; witnesses and interrogators strain to understand, to respond to what they think they understand; we strain to absorb the import of fleeting English subtitles, and fume at their inadequacy. As witnesses speak, we see they are visibly abashed by the grotesqueness of what they must say. And Lanzmann is a brutal interrogator. Under his insistence, witnesses writhe away from the cameras, resist, refuse. We watch something like torture when the man who years before had been forced to cut the hair from the heads of naked women and children before they were sent into the gas is asked how he felt 'when he saw those naked women'. We experience a kind of visceral recognition of the impossibility of response to such a question. We see that indeed there is no 'why' here: only the abasement and anguish of utter physical and cognitive helplessness. We also glimpse, unwillingly, and, I think, as no part of Lanzmann's intention, how other coerced agents of the perpetrators – *Kapos*, the men of the death-camp *Sonderkommandos*, even the perpetrators themselves – could have arrived, in time, at a sort of doomed detachment, once the obscene system had been kicked into action.

Having been made to watch the barber's anguish at his helplessness, we can better understand why the legends cherished by camp inmates usually had to do with heroically purposeful, confrontational actions. In prisoner testimonies prisoners rebuke guards, look them in the eye, offer defiance – and against all reason and all experience get away with it. The young woman dancer recognised by an SS officer and ordered to dance is magically released by the kinetic energy of her art from the oppression of accumulating circumstance. She dances up to her persecutor, seizes his revolver, and shoots him. Sometimes she dies in the next instant, sometimes she scores a couple of further hits before disappearing into the crowd. What matters is the defiance, the denial of abjection, the glorious, definitive action.

The whole of *Shoah* is a controlled product: an object of Lanzmann's contriving. We hear Lanzmann's voice, cajoling, prompting, bullying; then he appears, filling half the screen. Concealed from our sight, he cuts kilometres of film into the metres he decides we should see, and choreographs the positioning of these fragments to concoct tiny narratives set within a frame of his choosing.[21]

Nonetheless, and despite his total power, Lanzmann has been criticized on the grounds that his film offered 'no over-all interpretation'. The comment is true, but grounds for congratulation, not censure. He names his film *Shoah* not to locate it in some transcendental upland of myth, but to describe its contents: these partial, contested memories, this past and present pain, is what the Shoah was, and what the Shoah is. Then, watching this thing of his making, we further clothe what each of us sees out of our individual understandings and imaginings. It is precisely the film's stoical review of the range and flux of human experiences, the inadequacy of 'simple' interpretations, the impossibility of closure that makes it what it remarkably is: an accurate representation of the piling horrors as they, bewilderingly, occurred; as they continue to bewilder and to horrify us today.[22] It is at once a record, an argument in the process of its making, and a series of problematic interpretations constructed out of a conspiracy between director and viewer. Because of all of these things it is also superb history.

The theorist Hayden White, lamenting the inadequacy of 'literary modernism' confronted by the task of representing 'events such as the Holocaust, which are modernist in nature', has urged the development of a 'middle voice', in which the writing is not a distanced setting-down but is itself 'the means of vision or comprehension', with the reader no passive recipient, but called upon to be closely engaged in the writing process.[23] While White is notably coy when it comes to indicating what such a mode of writing might be like, I would argue that with *Shoah* we have a filmed example of this 'middle voice' in action, with the controlled incitement and deployment of the viewers' critical imagination working upon written, visual, aural and material texts.

This is the process which lies at the heart of the historical enterprise. I would also argue that we already hear something very like this 'middle voice' in good historical writing today: writing whereby the reader is brought into a constructed, controlled, directed engagement with the texts, and is invited to join the writer's search for their meanings. With these historians – Peter Brown, E. P. Thompson, Robert Darnton, William Taylor, we each have our favourites – the writing is already 'the means of vision or comprehension', and the reader 'no passive recipient', but called upon to be 'imaginatively involved in the writing process' – or, rather, in the intellectual movements mirrored in the prose.

All these works in their different media seek to represent the Shoah of the victims. Lanzmann presents both victims and perpetrators, but his style changes radically when he confronts the perpetrators and their accomplices. With them he is not concerned to probe memories and emotions. What he intends is to expose them. Thrusting the camera in close, he pins them, holds them, frames their confusion, their shiftiness, or, in the case of those unforgettable Polish peasants and railway men, their sinister, tainted geniality. He wants to shame and humiliate them. When he has SS *Unterscharführer* Franz Suchomel in the frame, filming him without his knowledge and against his expressed wish, he wants, he says, to 'kill him with the camera'.[24] He wants us to share his rage.

Those are appropriate and understandable emotions, and for the duration of the film he has the art to make us share them. But when that same Franz Suchomel was persuaded to speak with the historian-biographer Gitta Sereny we begin to see something of the man he was. If we want to achieve some measure of understanding of the men whose thoughts and actions created such places and effected such despair, men who typically concealed their subjectivities from others and often from themselves, whose intentions and emotions must be inferred from cautious self-protective statements and glimpses of routinized action – then only the patient burrowings, the slow-motion assessments and retrievals, and the fastidious, rule-bound interpretations of the historian will serve.

THE NECESSITY OF HISTORY

Sixteen years after the end of the war and the disclosure of the depth and extent of Nazi atrocities, David Ben-Gurion arranged to have Adolf Eichmann kidnapped and put on trial in Jerusalem, because, he said, 'it is necessary that our youth remember what happened to the Jewish people'.[25] Ben-Gurion mistrusted memory. Half a century after the opening of the camps the same fear is abroad, exacerbated by another: now, with the external facts of the Holocaust established and with other atrocities reported daily, might not the Holocaust be forgotten, and simply set aside?[26]

However, as Ben-Gurion recognised, 'remembering' is not a steady state, but rather, as Roland Barthes puts it, a 'frequent waking out of forgetfulness'. The past stands still, but the present moves, and every generation must discover the history of its parents' generation for itself. I doubt that the Holocaust will ever be cancelled from the human account. For all its apparent temporal shapelessness, it has not ended: not for the survivors, not for the perpetrators, not for us who seek to understand it. And do we ever achieve closure, in history or in any significant human affair? Does the nature of human curiosity allow it? The sense of an ending is a privilege reserved to art. The elements of the Holocaust which most threaten us are precisely those which will draw us back, again and again. Whenever we are granted the time and the courage for reflection, it will be there, grim, implacable – but not, finally, indecipherable.

Pace Celan's essential distillations, *pace* Lanzmann's marvellous panorama, I would argue that the great enterprise of representing both the span and the depth of the Holocaust is best done in writing, and in historical writing at that. Writing is a highly controlled medium, capable of nuance, but not, or not easily, of successful elision or evasion, because it grants the reader the opportunity to read and to re-read, to reflect, to reject, to modify, and so opens itself to critical evaluation in ways which other modes of communication, like visual representations, or music, do not.* Historians have much to learn

---

* More correctly, writing *did* allow all these things, when it came in the cheap and portable form called The Book. These advantages may be lost if we are returned by irresistibly advancing technology to that most archaic vehicle for the conveying of written information, the scroll.

from the word-artists created inside and by the camps; from the preternaturally clear-sighted Tadeusz Borowski or Primo Levi, or from Charlotte Delbo dauntlessly piercing the thickened membrane of deep memory to retrieve those images of degradation which she has now engraved upon ours. But those writings essentially belong to the category of art. Secular 'professional' historical writing, the writing which declares itself not or not primarily art, is open to interaction, selection and revision, all processes which art, in its necessary absolutism, rejects.

Historians take the large liberty of speaking for the dead, but we take this liberty under the rule of the discipline, and the rule is strict. There are many who would use the images of the Holocaust for their own purposes, some sinister, some trivial, all deforming. If the people of the past are to be given a life beyond their own, beyond the vagaries of fashion and of political exploitation – if these particular dead are not to be surrendered to those terrifying children the neo-Nazis, strutting in their stylish black, living in a fantastical history of their own invention – historians must retrieve and represent the actualities of past experience in accordance with our rule, with patience, scepticism and curiosity, and with whatever art we can muster – provided always that the art remains subject to our rule.

The enterprise is not impossible, merely quixotic. Even if it were impossible, the attempt would have to be made. Historians are the foot soldiers in the slow business of understanding our species better, and thereby extending the role of reason and humanity in human affairs. Humankind saw the face of the Gorgon in the concentration camps, petrifying the human by its denial of the human both in itself and in its prey. The shadow of the Holocaust has lengthened with the years. In that shadow, none of us is at home in the world, because now we know the fragility of our content. If we are to see the Gorgon sufficiently steadily to destroy it, we cannot afford to be blinded by reverence or abashed into silence or deflected into a search for reassuring myths. We must do more than register guilt, or grief, or anger, or disgust, because neither reverence for those who suffer nor revulsion from those who inflict the suffering will help us overcome its power to paralyse, and to see it clearly.

The Final Solution appals most by its inhuman dimensions: it counts in millions. Levi and Delbo and others like them have defied that cruel reduction, first by opening their own experience to us, then by retrieving a gallery of people who remained irreducibly individual in the lowest circle of hell. Perhaps that is what their art most teaches us. Some months ago I tried to write an essay on death, and learnt by failure what any survivor could have told me: there is no category. Every death is its own discrete catastrophe. Within the mass of the only apparently anonymous we must seek and hold the individual action, the individual situation. There are a thousand snapshots of such actions and situations recorded in documents generated by the Holocaust, as in the handful of photographs which survive it. The energy for the historical enterprise is inherent in the material. The woman surrounded by thugs at Lieutenant Gnade's 'undressing station' has done her persecutors no injury – she could not if she tried. She is terrified, as those millions of others who were humiliated and brutalized were terrified. We know what has been done to her, as we know what will be done. We look, and our muscles tighten. We are as roused as ever Rorty wished us to be. We burn to intervene.

The desire is futile. While some of her tormentors might still live, the woman is dead. But the moral and the intellectual energy generated out of that photograph provides the essential fuel for action. An awakened, outraged sensibility demands systematic inquiry. And, as that photograph makes clear, it is not enough to loathe the perpetrator and to pity the victim, because in that scene they are bound together. We must try to understand them both.

Milan Kundera has observed that the 'struggle of men against power is the struggle of memory against forgetting'.[27] That is true. But human rememberings, whether individual or collective, are not inert archives. They are factories of dreams, and hopes, and illusions. They are also our surest individual homeland, essential evidence of our essential being, and our impulse is to defend them against all comers. The men and women who lived through the Holocaust will manage their memories as they must, to render present circumstance endurable, to authenticate the present self. Collective memory, created out of shared experience, will go on functioning in much the same way – if it is allowed to do so. Since Kundera produced his aphorism we have learnt again what self-indulgent collective memory can do when yoked to political interest and murderous impulse. Only disciplined, critical remembering will resist the erasure of fact and circumstance effected

by time, by ideology, and by the natural human impulse to forget. It is
not the duty of my apple-rich friend in her orchard to live in her past.
It is mine.

Whatever the virtues of novelists and historians, it is still the poets
who say most, and most succinctly. I conclude with the words of a
Polish poet who only recently became known to me, but who has, as I
discover, even more recently won the Nobel Prize for Literature, who
says much of what I have been trying to say over these many pages in
as many words.

It could have happened.
It had to happen.
It happened earlier. Later.
Nearer. Farther off.
It happened, but not to you.

You were saved because you were the first.
You were saved because you were the last.
Alone. With others.
On the right. The left.
Because it was raining. Because of the shade.
Because the day was sunny.

You were in luck – there was a forest.
You were in luck – there were no trees.
You were in luck – a rake, a hook, a beam, a brake,
A jamb, a turn, a quarter-inch, an instant . . .

So you're here? Still dizzy from
another dodge, close shave, reprieve?
One hole in the net and you slipped through?
I couldn't be more shocked or
speechless.
Listen,
how your heart pounds inside me.

Wislawa Szymborska[28]

NOTES

BEGINNINGS

1 John Keegan, *The Face of Battle*, Jonathan Cape, London, 1976, and Paul Fussell, *The Great War and Modern Memory*, Oxford University Press, New York and London, 1975.
2 Inga Clendinnen, *Aztecs: An Interpretation*, Cambridge University Press, New York, 1991.
3 *Probing the Limits of Representation: Nazism and the 'Final Solution'*, ed. Saul Friedländer, Harvard University Press, Cambridge, Mass., 1992; *Lessons and Legacies: The Meaning of the Holocaust in a Changing World*, ed. Peter Hayes, Northwestern University Press, Evanston, Ill., 1991.

IMPEDIMENTS

1 Christopher R. Browning, *Fateful Months: Essays on the Emergence of the Final Solution*, Holmes and Meier, New York and London, 1985, p. 6.
2 Hans-Adolf Jacobsen, 'The *Kommissarbefehl* and Mass Executions of Soviet Russian Prisoners of War', in Helmut Krausnick, Hans Buchheim, Martin Broszat and Hans-Adolf Jacobsen, *Anatomy of the SS State* (1965), Walker and Company, New York, 1968, pp. 505–35, p. 531.
3 Isabel Fonseca, *Bury Me Standing: The Gypsies and Their Journey*, Chatto and Windus, London, 1995, esp. pp. 252–75. For pre-Nazi legislation by German states against the Gypsies, see Fonseca, *Bury Me Standing*, p. 257.
4 'Among Roma . . . "forgetting" does not imply complacency: its tenor is one of – sometimes buoyant – defiance'. Fonseca, *Bury Me Standing*, pp. 273–6.
5 See esp. Yael S. Feldman, 'Whose Story Is It, Anyway? Ideology and

Psychology in the Representation of the Shoah in Israeli Literature', in Friedländer, *Probing the Limits of Representation*, pp. 223–39.

6 See e.g. the collection of essays, Alvin H. Rosenfield and Irving Greenberg (eds.) *Confronting the Holocaust: The Impact of Elie Wiesel*, Indiana University Press, Bloomington and London, 1978. For the Jewish quest for a term which would restore coherence to their collective narrative, see Saul Friedländer, 'Trauma, Memory, and Transference', in *Holocaust Remembrance: The Shapes of Memory*, ed. Geoffrey H. Hartman, Basil Blackwell, Oxford and Cambridge, 1994, pp. 252–63, esp. pp. 254–5. For the realisation of the importance of community and the meaning of tradition in a time of persecution, see Saul Friedländer's moving memoir of his own disrupted childhood: Saul Friedländer, *When Memory Comes*, trans. Helen R. Lane, Farrar, Straus & Giroux, New York, 1979. For Hannah Arendt's energetic efforts to render these issues as problems in international law, see Hannah Arendt, *Eichmann in Jerusalem: A Report on the Banality of Evil* (1963), Viking Press, New York, 1965.

7 Elie A. Cohen, *Human Behaviour in the Concentration Camp*, trans. by the author, Free Association Books, London, 1988, xviii.

8 For an incisive intervention and clarification of some of these matters by a distinguished 'insider', see Christopher R. Browning, 'German Memory, Judicial Interrogation, and Historical Reconstruction: Writing Perpetrator History from Postwar Testimony', in Friedländer, *Probing the Limits of Representation*, pp. 22–36. See also, in the same volume, Dominick LaCapra's exploration framed by the psychoanalytic concept of 'transference'. LaCapra, 'Representing the Holocaust: Reflections on the Historians' Debate', pp. 108–27, esp. p. 110.

9 Elie Wiesel, 'Pilgrimage to the Kingdom of the Night', in his *From the Kingdom of Memory: Reminiscences*, Simon and Schuster, New York, 1990, p. 110.

10 Eberhard Jäckel, quoted LaCapra, 'Representing the Holocaust', p. 112.

11 Arendt, *Eichmann in Jerusalem*, pp. 267–9.

12 Saul Friedländer, introduction, *Probing the Limits*, p. 3. Habermas went on to represent Auschwitz as shredding 'a bond of naiveté . . . a naiveté from which unquestioned traditions drew their authority, a naiveté that as such had nourished historical continuities' – until the catastrophe of the extermination camps'. Jürgen Habermas, 'Historical Consciousness and Post-Traditional Identity: The Federal Republic's Orientation to the West', in his *The New Conservatism: Cultural Criticism and the Historians' Debate*, ed. and trans. Shierry Weber, Nicholsen, Polity Press, New York, 1989, pp. 251–2.

13 Or so I argue. See Clendinnen, *Aztecs*.

14 Cf. Vincent P. Pecora, 'Habermas, Enlightenment, and anti-Semitism', in Friedländer, *Probing the Limits*, pp. 155-71. 'In the same decades when the United States was putting into practice a constitution which many consider the first true political product of the Enlightenment, it was also systematically eradicating a supposedly inferior native population in its search for *Lebensraum* and calmly pursuing planned race slavery.' (p. 163) Pecora draws the larger inference: 'If the specific and terrifying suffering endured by the victims of Nazi persecution is not mobilised to remind the West of the barbarity folded into even its most admirable traditions, but instead serves to obscure it, then that suffering will end up serving barbaric purposes all over again.'

15 Abdulrazak Gurnah, *Guardian Weekly*, 2 February 1997, p. 29.

16 Examples, unhappily, abound. One notes the irony by which the massacre of nearly one and a half million Armenians by Turks between 1915–1923 has come to be known as the 'Armenian Holocaust', so being named for events which post-dated it by twenty-five years.

17 Gitta Sereny, *Albert Speer: His Battle with Truth*, Macmillan, London, 1995, p. 15.

18 Friedländer, 'The "Final Solution" ', p. 32.

19 Peter Haidu, 'The Dialectics of Unspeakability: Language, Silence, and the Narratives of Desubjectification', in *Probing the Limits of Representation*, pp. 277-99, p. 295.

20 Fonseca, *Bury Me Standing*, p. 254.

21 Elie Wiesel, 'Trivializing Memory', and 'Testimony at the Barbie Trial', in his *From the Kingdom of Memory*, p. 166, p. 187. The difficulties attending the use of volunteer witnesses in a court striving to operate under legal restraints are insightfully discussed by Arendt, *Eichmann in Jerusalem*, p. 290, pp. 223-31.

22 Filip Müller, quoted Ota Kraus and Erich Kulka, *The Death Factory: Document on Auschwitz*, trans. Stephen Jolly, Pergamon Press, London, 1966, p. 156.

23 For an enthralling account of the delayed impact of a single diary on a vast popular audience and its later transformation into drama and film, see Alvin H. Rosenfield, 'Popularization and Memory: The Case of Anne Frank', in Peter Hayes, *Lessons and Legacies*, pp. 243-78. Hannah Arendt's electrifying reflections on the 1961 Eichmann trial, *Eichmann in Jerusalem*, had appeared in 1963.

24 Professor Yehuda Bauer, foreword to Filip Müller, *Auschwitz Inferno: The Testimony of a Sonderkommando*, with literary collaboration by Helmut Freitag, ed. and trans. Susanne Flatauer, Routledge and Kegan

Paul, London and Henley, 1979. [American title: *Eyewitness Auschwitz: Three Years in the Gas Chambers*], xi–xii. For an Auschwitz *Sonderkommando* account translated and published after the Müller story, see Rebecca Camhi Fromer, *The Holocaust Odysseys of Daniel Bennahmias, Sonderkommando*, with an introduction by Steven B. Bowman, University of Alabama Press, Tucaloosa and London, 1993.

25 Müller, *Auschwitz Inferno*, esp. pp. 69–71, pp. 161–2. For his suicide attempt, see pp. 113–19; for the dancer, pp. 87–9. Bruno Bettelheim took the dancer story to be true, making it a key narrative for his *The Informed Heart: Autonomy in a Mass Age*, New York, The Free Press of Glencoe, 1960, pp. 264–5. The variations on the dancer theme are handily gathered together in the editors' afterword, Sara Nomberg-Przytyk, *Auschwitz: True Tales from a Grotesque Land*, eds. Eli Pfefferkorn and David H. Hirsch, University of North Carolina Press, Chapel Hill and London, 1985, pp. 175–81.

26 Philip Roth, *Operation Shylock: A Confession*, Jonathan Cape, London, 1993, pp. 290–5.

27 István Deák: 'The truth is that not all survivors were heroes; nor do they all know how to write a book. An accurate record of the Holocaust has been endangered, in my opinion, by the uncritical endorsement, often by well-known Jewish writers or public figures, of virtually any survivor's account or related writings'. *New York Review of Books*, 26 June 1997, p. 38.

28 Primo Levi, *The Drowned and the Saved*, trans. Raymond Rosenthal, Michael Joseph, London, 1988 [first pub. 1986], p. 56. For the numbers of inmates in Auschwitz I, which was also the administrative centre, the Birkenau complex, which contained the Women's Camp and the crematoria, and the work camp 'Monowitz', that lay seven kilometres from Auschwitz I, see Raul Hilberg, *The Destruction of the European Jews*, Quadrangle Books, Chicago, 1961, n. 30, p. 580.

29 Salmen Lewenthal, member of the Auschwitz *Sonderkommando*, from 'The Manuscript of Salmen Lewenthal', quoted Lawrence Langer, *Versions of Survival: The Holocaust and the Human Spirit*, State University of New York Press, Albany, 1982, p. 96.

30 Hermann Langbein, quoted Langer, *Versions of Survival*, p. 6. Langbein, (a German from the Fatherland) had been assigned a post in the administration. He acknowledges his Auschwitz was much less terrible than the great majority of prisoners.

31 See Cohen, *Human Behaviour in the Concentration Camp*; Kraus and Kulka, *The Death Factory*; Eugen Kogon, *The Theory and Practice of Hell (Der SS Staat)* [on Buchenwald], trans. Heinz Norden, Farrar,

Straus and Co., 1950. Hermann Langbein's *Menschen in Auschwitz*, Europaverlag, Vienna, 1972, is regrettably not yet in English.

WITNESSING

1 For a brilliant critique and evaluation of audiovisual testimonies see Lawrence Langer, *Holocaust Testimonies: The Ruins of Memory*, Yale University Press, New Haven and London, 1991.
2 See Langer, *Versions of Survival*.
3 For a few pages of prose that read like poetry, see Wiesel, 'Why I Write', in *From the Kingdom of Memory*, pp. 13–21.
4 Scarlett Freund, letter to author, August 1997.
5 Charlotte Delbo, *Days and Memory*, trans. Rosette C. Lamont, The Marlboro Press, Marlboro, Vermont, 1990, p. 2.
6 Elizabeth Bowen, 'The Demon Lover', in *The Mulberry Tree: Writings of Elizabeth Bowen*, Harcourt, Brace Jovanovich, San Diego, New York and London, 1986, pp. 95–7.
7 Italo Calvino, *Times Literary Supplement*, 14–20 July 1989. For a shining example from Primo Levi, see *The Truce*, pp. 217–18.
8 Václav Havel, *New York Review of Books*, 31 May, 1990, p. 43.
9 Primo Levi, *If This Is a Man and The Truce*, trans. Stuart Wolf, introduced by Paul Bailey, with an 'Afterword: The Author Answers His Readers' Questions', Abacus, London, 1987, p. 381. The Afterword, written for this double-volume publication which first appeared in 1979, is undated, but internal evidence establishes it as having been revised during 1985 or 1986. Primo Levi died by suicide in April 1987.
10 Primo Levi, 'Chromium', *The Periodic Table*, [1975] trans. Raymond Rosenthal, Abacus, London, 1985, p. 150. *The Periodic Table* won the Premio Prato in 1975. Only in that year did Levi retire from the practice of chemistry.
11 Levi, 'Chromium', *The Periodic Table*, p. 151.
12 Jerome Bruner, *Acts of Meaning*, Harvard University Press, Cambridge, Mass., 1990, p. 33.
13 Levi, *If This Is a Man*, p. 139.
14 Levi, *If This Is a Man*, p. 55.
15 In 1989 the Fortunoff Video Archive for Holocaust Testimonies at Yale University held more than 14,000 filmed testimonies, some from relatives and contemporaries, but the great majority from survivors of the camps. Langer, *Holocaust Testimonies*, p. xvii.
16 Langer, *Holocaust Testimonies*, p. 117. It is possible that the witness was

agitated, which might make the intervention protective, but the recorded words do not suggest that. Langer, clearly a man of courage, nonetheless buries the cannibalism episode pretty much in the middle of a dense book, and refers only in a footnote to an abundance of other examples, including an eyewitness report from Bergen-Belsen testifying to between 200 and 300 cases of cannibalism in the weeks before the camp's liberation. Langer, *Ibid.*, n. 28, p. 213. Given the strength of the European taboo against the eating of human flesh, these breaches are good evidence of the extremity of the prisoners' situation.

17 Marek Edelman of Adina Sczwajger, quoted in Hanna Krall, *Shielding the Flame: An Intimate Conversation with Dr Marek Edelman, the Last Surviving Leader of the Warsaw Ghetto Uprising*, trans. Joanna Stasinska and Lawrence Weschler, Holt, New York, 1986, p. 9.

18 Olga Lengyel, *Five Chimneys*, Panther, New York, 1959 [first published 1947], p. 22.

19 Langer, *Versions of Survival*, p. ix.

20 Levi, *If This Is a Man*, p. 129. See 'Argon', in *The Periodic Table*, where the idiosyncrasies of the Piedmont-Jewish dialect are identified and anatomised.

21 Levi, *The Drowned and the Saved*, p. 71. Levi had been forewarned by his first meeting with the Nazis in Italy. For his vivid record of that initial experience, see Levi, *The Drowned and the Saved*, pp. 70–4. See also Kraus and Kulka, *The Death Factory, passim*.

22 The language/experience gap between survivors and other citizens of Israel has become an enduring theme in Israeli literature: see Sidra Dekoven Ezrahi, 'Revisioning the Past: The Changing Legacy of the Holocaust in Hebrew Literature', *Salmagundi*, no. 68–69, Fall 1985–Winter 1986, pp. 245–70.

23 Levi, *If This Is a Man*, pp. 77, 85.

24 Müller, *Auschwitz Inferno*, p. 154. The *Sonderkommando* comprised those prisoners, many of them Jewish, selected to provide the labour to run the crematoria and execution pits, and to dispose of the corpses.

25 Levi, *If This Is a Man*, pp. 101–4, p. 109, p. 151. For another product of the Lager, see the twelve-year-old Kleine Kiepura, 'The Main Camp', in *The Truce*, pp. 200–2.

26 Levi, *If This Is a Man*, p. 35.

27 Anton Chekhov, Letter to Maria Kiseleva, 14 January 1887, Moscow, in *The Selected Letters of Anton Chekhov*, ed. and with an introduction by Lillian Hellman, Picador Classics, London, 1984, p. 20.

28 Levi, *The Periodic Table*, p. 153.

29 Levi, *The Drowned and the Saved*, pp. 113–14.

30 Levi, *If This Is a Man*, pp. 111–12. For Levi memories of the camp neither thinned with the years nor blurred into conventional story, but 'became enriched with details I thought were forgotten, which sometimes acquire meaning in the light of other people's memories . . . ' Primo Levi, 'Last Christmas of the War', *Moments of Reprieve*, [1979], Viking Penguin Inc., New York, 1987.

31 The bonded pair appears to have been the most 'natural' and durable of concentration camp relationships, and was usually swiftly remade when broken – as, of course, it usually was. See Elmer Luchterhand, 'Social Behavior in Concentration Camp Prisoners: Continuities and Discontinuities with Pre- and Postcamp Life', in *Survivors, Victims and Perpetrators: Essays on the Holocaust*, ed. Joel E. Dimsdale, M.D., Taylor and Francis, Washington, 1980, pp. 259–82, esp. pp. 267–8.

32 For an article which sheds surprising light on the evolution of Wiesel's *Night*, see Naomi Seidman, 'Elie Wiesel and the Scandal of Jewish Rage', *Jewish Social Studies*, vol. 3, no. 1, Fall 1996, pp. 1–19.

33 Levi, quoted Ferdinando Camon, *Conversations with Primo Levi*, trans. John Shepley, The Marlboro Press, Marlboro, Vermont, 1989, p. 68.

34 Levi, *If This Is a Man*, Afterword, p. 382.

35 Levi, *If This Is a Man*, pp. 46, 63, 127–8.

36 Levi, *If This Is a Man*, Afterword, p. 389.

37 Levi, *The Drowned and the Saved*, p. 120.

38 Levi, *The Drowned and the Saved*, p. 75. Levi later claimed that German-speaking Jews of central Europe were ten times more likely to survive the camps than non-German speakers, which is remarkable given that the former would typically have endured longer periods of incarceration. Camon, *Conversations with Primo Levi*, p. 48.

39 Levi, *If This Is a Man*, Afterword, p. 381.

40 The precise number of those who died in that last exodus cannot be established. Langbein gives an overall figure of 60,000 survivors from Auschwitz, distributed between various camps as the Russians approached. Hermann Langbein, quoted Langer, *Versions of Survival*, p. 94.

41 Levi, *If This Is a Man*, pp. 26, 171, 179. As I write, the former Nazi SS officer Erich Priebke, one-time deputy to the head of the Rome SS, has been freed by an Italian military court for his role in a massacre. He had organised, supervised and participated in the slaughter of 335 Italian civilians, seventy-five of them Jews, slaughtered in the Ardeatine caves in 1944 in retaliation for a Resistance ambush killing of thirty-three German soldiers. The court ruled that Priebke had not acted with cruelty or premeditation.

42 When the slightly built Levi unwisely (and atypically) dared a small defensive gesture when being roughed up by the monstrous dwarf Elias, he found himself on the ground and strangled to the point of unconsciousness, until Elias chose to let go. Levi, *The Drowned and the Saved*, p. 116.

43 See e.g. Levi, 'The Survivor', printed as preface to *The Truce*. It seems time does not erode that guilt. Jenny Diski introduces us to Pearl, now nearly seventy, who punctuated their conversation with the question 'Why do I deserve to be alive?' Pearl had lost every member of her family, 'all of them: uncles, aunts and cousins, her parents, her eight brothers and sisters, her favourite sister's five children of whom the oldest was six', to the Nazis. Jenny Diski, *London Review of Books*, 19 October 1995.

44 Levi, *The Drowned and the Saved*, p. 62.

45 Levi, *The Drowned and the Saved*, pp. 63–4.

46 Anne Frank, *The Diary of a Young Girl*, Otto Frank and Mirjam Pressler (eds.), trans. Susan Masotty, Viking Penguin, New York, 1996.

47 Levi, 'Vanadium', *The Periodic Table*, p. 213. He had earlier claimed that 'of my two years of life outside the law I have not forgotten a single thing. Without any deliberate effort, memory continues to restore to me events, faces, words, sensations, as if at that time my mind had gone through a period of exalted receptivity, during which not a detail was lost.' Levi, Preface, *Moments of Reprieve*, pp. 10–11.

48 Quoted Camon, *Conversations with Primo Levi*, p. 21.

49 Levi, *The Truce*, pp. 207–12.

50 This biographical information comes from Lawrence Langer's introduction to Charlotte Delbo, *Auschwitz and After*, trans. Rosette C. Lamont, Yale University Press, New Haven and London, 1995, pp. ix–xviii. I first became aware of Delbo's writings by way of Langer's work, most especially his superb *Holocaust Testimonies*.

51 Of the trilogy for which Charlotte Delbo is best known, *Auschwitz et après, None of Us Will Return*, written in 1945, was published 1965, *Useless Knowledge*, partly written in 1946–7, in 1970, and *The Measure of Our Days* in 1971. Her final work, *La mémoire et les jours*, English translation, *Days and Memory*, appeared in 1986, the year of her death. Only recently did the trilogy appear in English, published by Yale University Press and titled *Auschwitz and After*.

52 See especially Delbo, 'The Measure of Our Days', *Auschwitz and After*.

53 Levi, 'Chromium', *The Periodic Table*.

54 Levi, *If This Is a Man*, p. 108.

55 Levi, *The Truce*, pp. 379–80. See also his dream inside Auschwitz of trying to tell his sister and a cluster of friends what 'life' was like in the camp – and being ignored. Levi, *If This Is a Man*, p. 66.
56 Delbo, *Days and Memory*, p. 2.
57 Delbo, *Auschwitz and After*, 'The Measure of Our Days', esp. 'The Return'.
58 Levi, 'Lorenzo's Return', *Moments of Reprieve*.
59 Delbo, *Auschwitz and After*, p. 254.
60 Jean Améry, quoted Levi, *The Drowned and the Saved*, p. 12.
61 Charlotte Delbo, *Auschwitz and After*, p. 86.
62 Michael Wood, *London Review of Books*, 5 September 1996, p. 15.

RESISTING

1 Levi's most explicit and succinct answer to such questioners is in the 1985 revision to his Afterword in the Abascus edition of *If This Is a Man* and *The Truce*, pp. 387–8. See also 'Stereotypes' in *The Drowned and the Saved*, chapter 7. For a harsh assessment of Jewish failure to resist before being sent to the camps, see Hilberg, *The Destruction of the European Jews*, pp. 662–69: 'For the first time in the history of Western civilization the perpetrators had overcome all administrative and moral obstacles to a killing operation. For the first time, also, the Jewish victims – caught in the strait jacket of their history – plunged themselves physically and psychologically into catastrophe.'
2 Bruno Bettelheim, Foreword, Miklos Nyiszli, *Auschwitz: An Eyewitness Account of Mengele's Infamous Death Camp*, trans. Tibere Kremer and Richard Seaver, Seaver Books, New York, 1960, pp. vi–vii. For Bettelheim's naive use of the dancer myth, see his *The Informed Heart*, p. 259.
3 Bruno Bettelheim, quoted Langer, *Versions of Survival*, 1982, pp. 44, 46. For an evaluation of the alarmingly influential writings of Viktor Frankel and Bruno Bettelheim, see Langer, *ibid*. The recent fine biography by Nina Sutton, *Bettelheim: A Life and a Legacy*, trans. David Sharp, Basic Books/HarperCollins, 1995, does much to reveal the inner dynamics of Bettelheim's public writings on the camp experience. For a corrective to the view that Jews habitually 'went quietly', see Christopher R. Browning, *Ordinary Men: Reserve Police Battalion 101 and the Final Solution in Poland*, Aaron Asher Books, HarperCollins, New York, 1992, Chapter 4.
4 For a formidable attack on the persistent questioners at the Eichmann trial, see Arendt, *Eichmann in Jerusalem*, pp. 11–12.

5 Lengyel, *Five Chimneys*, p. 162. For a scholarly elaboration of this position, see Yehuda Bauer, *The Jewish Emergence from Powerlessness*, University of Toronto Press, Buffalo, 1978.

6 Debórah Dwork and Robert Jan van Pelt, 'Reclaiming Auschwitz', in Hartman, *Holocaust Remembrance*, pp. 232–51.

7 For a fine discussion of ambiguities see Michael R. Marrus, *The Holocaust in History*, University Press of New England, Hanover and London, 1987, Chapter 7; for an overview of events in the ghettos, with the focus on Warsaw and Lodz, see Hilberg, *The Destruction of the European Jews*, pp. 317–29. See also Simha Rotem, ('Kazik') *Memoirs of a Warsaw Ghetto Fighter: The Past Within Me*, trans. Barbara Harshav, Yale University Press, New Haven and London, 1994, and Emmanuel Ringelblum, *Notes from the Warsaw Ghetto*, Schocken, New York, 1958.

8 The most accessible account of Treblinka is Gitta Sereny's extraordinary examination of the mind of Camp Commander Franz Stangl in her *Into That Darkness: An Examination of Conscience*, McGraw-Hill, New York, 1974, and Richard Glazar, *Trap with a Green Fence: Survival in Treblinka*, trans. Roslyn Theobald, Foreword by Wolfgang Benz, Northwestern University Press, 1995. For Sobibor see Thomas Toivi Blatt, *From the Ashes of Sobibor: A Story of Survival*, Foreword by Christopher Browning, Northeastern University Press, Evanston, Illinois, 1997. For the recollections of another Sobibor survivor, a boy goldsmith, preserved for his skills, see Sereny, *Into That Darkness*, pp. 121–31. Many concentration camps supported crematoria to deal with deaths from 'natural' causes: starvation, disease and exhaustion.

9 Glazar, quoted Sereny, *Into That Darkness*, p. 246, and Glazar, *Trap with a Green Fence*, pp. 137–46.

10 Blatt, *From the Ashes of Sobibor*, pp. 145–53, 232–33.

11 Wieslaw Kielar, *Anus Mundi: Five Years in Auschwitz*, [1972] trans. Susanne Flatauer, Penguin Books, Harmondsworth, 1981. For the remarkable story of a Jew who contrived to distinguish himself in the Polish Resistance while posing as a Christian Pole, see Arthur Spindler, *Outwitting Hitler, Surviving Stalin*, University of New South Wales Press, Sydney, 1997.

12 For this and for the following quotation, and for Lengyel's account of her work, see Lengyel, *Five Chimmneys*, esp. chapter 10, pp. 164–65.

13 Hermann Langbein, *Against All Hope: Resistance in the Nazi Concentration Camps 1938–1945*, Constable, London, 1994.

14 See, for example, almost any of Bruno Bettelheim's writings. For a more recent attempt to map the moral fields of victims, see Tzvetan Todorov, *Facing the Extreme: Moral Life in the Concentration Camp* (1992),

trans. Arthur Denner and Abigail Pollak, Metropolitan Books, Henry Holt and Co., New York, 1996. Todorov's arguments are appealing, but in my view he is far too selective, and too little attentive to context. For resistance to Hitler within Germany and the 'Generals' Plot' of 20 July 1944, see Joachim Fest, *Plotting Hitler's Death: The Story of the German Resistance*, trans. Bruce Little, Metropolitan Books, Henry Holt, New York, 1996. The generals had their best chance in September 1938, when what Thomas Powers calls a 'realistic and well-organized attempt to mount a military coup' was thwarted 'by the abject surrender of the British Prime Minister Neville Chamberlain to Hitler's demands for the dismemberment of Czechoslovakia'. Powers also reminds us that 'virtually nothing the resistance attempted either stopped or hindered Hitler in anything he wanted to do, from making war in the first place to killing the Jews'. Thomas Powers, *New York Review of Books*, 9 January 1997, p. 49.

INSIDE THE GREY ZONE

1 Filip Müller, in Kraus and Kulka, *The Death Factory*, pp. 157, 160.
2 Daniel Jonah Goldhagen, *Hitler's Willing Executioners: Ordinary Germans and the Holocaust*, Little, Brown & Co., London, 1996, p. 165.
3 Hilberg, *The Destruction of the European Jews*, 1, p. 269 and 3, p. 1212. For a tragic 'insider' account of Lódz ghetto, the longest surviving closed ghetto because it was the most profitable to the Nazis, see *The Diary of Dawid Sierakowiak: Five Notebooks from the Lódz Ghetto*, ed. Alan Adelson, trans. Kamil Turowski, Oxford University Press, Oxford, 1996. See also Raul Hilberg, Stanislaw Staron, and Joseph Kermisz (eds.) *The Warsaw Diary of Adam Czerniakow: Prelude to Doom*, Schocken, New York, 1979; Emmanuel Ringelblum, *Notes from the Warsaw Ghetto*, Schocken New York, 1958, and for an overview of the ghettos of Lódz and Warsaw, Christopher Browning, 'Nazi Ghettoization Policy in Poland, 1939–1941', in his *The Path to Genocide: Essays in the Launching of the Final Solution*, Cambridge University Press, Cambridge and New York, 1992, pp. 28–56.
4 *The Diary of Dawid Sierakowiak*, and Calel Perechodnik, *Am I a Murderer? Testament of a Jewish Ghetto Policeman*, ed. and trans. Frank Fox, Westview Press, Boulder, Colo., 1996.
5 Müller, *Auschwitz Inferno*, pp. 54–5.
6 Levi, *If This Is a Man*, p. 97. The point is further elaborated in 'The Grey Zone', the third chapter of Levi's last book, *The Drowned and the Saved*.
7 Levi, *The Drowned and the Saved*, p. 35.

8 Levi, *The Drowned and the Saved*, esp. pp. 34, 36, 37, 42.

9 Quoted Langer, *Versions of Survival*, pp. 96–7.

10 W. T. Bartoszewski, Introduction to Samuel Willenberg, *Surviving Treblinka*, Basil Blackwell in association, with the Institute for Polish-Jewish Studies, Oxford, 1989, p. 2; Langer, *Versions of Survival*, note. 7, p. 255.

11 Simon Srebnik, quoted Lanzmann, *Shoah: An Oral History of the Holocaust*, pp. 102–3.

12 Müller, *Auschwitz Inferno*, p. 13.

13 Friedländer appears to be moving further towards psychological explanations not only for the phenomena of the Holocaust, but to explain the hesitations, gaps and stases in the analyses offered by scholars. Saul Friedländer, 'Trauma, Memory, and Transference', in Hartman, *Holocaust Remembrance*, pp. 252–63.

14 Robert Jay Lifton, *The Nazi Doctors: A Study in the Psychology of Evil*, Macmillan, London, 1986, p. 171. Dr Miklos Nyszli estimated that there were about 120 SS and 860 prisoners assigned to the *Sonderkommando* by May 1944. Nyiszli, *Auschwitz: An Eyewitness Account*, p. 38.

15 Nyiszli, *Auschwitz: An Eyewitness Account*, pp. 44–5. From Müller's account it seems the Auschwitz *Sonderkommando* did not take part in the physical coercion of the gas-chamber victims, the whips and sticks being wielded by the SS. Compare with Treblinka, where the SS and the Ukrainian guards flogged their naked victims through the narrow passage from the undressing barracks to the gas chambers.

16 By mid-May 1944, as the escalation was beginning, Müller reports a *Sonderkommando* comprising '450 Hungarians, 200 Poles, 180 Greeks, 3 Slovak and 5 German Jews, as well as 19 Russian prisoners of war, 5 Polish prisoners in 'preventative custody' and one *Reichsdeutscher Kapo*'. Müller, *Auschwitz Inferno*, pp. 132–3. Some of the teams were sorted into national groups: e.g. the Salonika Greeks, so successful in the work camps, were isolated in the *Sonderkommando* by their lack of language, and were routinely allocated the dirtiest and most dangerous jobs, such as the 'treading' of the ash pits.

17 Müller, *Auschwitz Inferno*, pp. 58–9. A small, teasing puzzle: in Auschwitz I this *Kapo* Mietek had been a conspicuous dandy, wearing 'a clean made-to-measure uniform and a clean shirt daily' (p. 43), yet in Birkenau he was the only one of the *Kapos* to choose to wear 'official' striped prison garb (p. 59). Why?

18 Müller, *Auschwitz Inferno*, pp. 64–5.

19 Nyiszli, *Auschwitz: An Eyewitness Account*, pp. 40–1, pp. 58–9. A Greek survivor dictating his recollections to a sympathetic listener thirty years after the events recalls the only *Sonderkommando* privilege to be a

double ration of bread, supplemented by the occasional crust filched from a corpse. His account must be suspect, at least on this issue. See Fromer, *The Holocaust Odyssey of Daniel Bennahmias, Sonderkommando*.

20 Müller, *Auschwitz Inferno*, pp. 61–2, 82. See p. 62 for bribery of SS officers to gain access to the women's camp. Dr Nyiszli confirms the ubiquity of exchange, but has the trade going the other way, with the SS taking cigarettes and alcohol in exchange for fresh food from the possessions of the murdered. Nyiszli claims that 'the SS received only two cigarettes a day and no alcohol at all. Yet . . . both were indispensable here'. Nyiszli, *Auschwitz: An Eyewitness Account*, pp. 61–2. For similar exchange relations at Treblinka, mainly with the Ukrainian guards, see Sereny, *Into That Darkness*, p. 191, and Richard Glazar, *Trap with a Green Fence*.

21 Nyiszli, *Auschwitz: An Eyewitness Account*, pp. 47–8.

22 Müller, *Auschwitz Inferno*, pp. 99–100, 138.

23 Nyiszli, *Auschwitz: An Eyewitness Account*, pp. 57–8.

24 Primo Levi, *The Drowned and the Saved*, p. 38.

25 Nyiszli claims that every four months or so the SS would machine gun the whole squad, the incoming squad's first task being the stripping and burning of their predecessors' bodies. Nyiszli, *Auschwitz: An Eyewitness Account*, p. 60. Müller gives a more tempered and psychologically more plausible account, pivoting on the usual SS game of deception: the call for 'volunteers' for some pretended new project with better conditions. Only if there were too few volunteers would there be overt 'selection'. His own survival through five selections suggests he was a particularly valued member of the team.

26 Müller, *Auschwitz Inferno*, pp. 167–9.

27 Müller, *Auschwitz Inferno*, pp. 125–9. As might be expected, discrepancies between the few accounts from *Sonderkommando* men cluster most thickly about the events of the famous 'uprising' of October '44, a highly secret and complicated plot which appears to have gone badly awry. See n. 34, below.

28 Müller, *Auschwitz Inferno*, p. 142.

29 Nyiszli, *Auschwitz: An Eyewitness Account*, p. 71.

30 Müller, *Auschwitz Inferno*, pp. 124–6.

31 For a recent overview of this confused affair, see Steven B. Bowman, Introduction, in Fromer, *The Holocaust Odyssey of Daniel Bennahmias*. Bowman acknowledges the difficulty in unravelling what actually happened, especially as the 'revolt' 'has developed its own mythologies among the different ethnic groups that survived Auschwitz'. Bowman,

Introduction, p. xxiv. Filip Müller obliquely confirms the main aspects of the Bowman account.

32 Glazar, *Trap with a Green Fence*, pp. 17, 18, 25, 27, 59–60.

33 Glazar, *Trap with a Green Fence*, pp. 61, 92–3, 96–8, 103–5.

34 Glazar, *Trap with a Green Fence*, pp. 81, 92–3, 95–6.

35 Glazar, *Trap with a Green Fence*, pp. 51–2.

36 Glazar, quoted Sereny, *Into That Darkness*, pp. 178–79. For a terrifying personal 'kindness' from Commandant Stangl, see pp. 207–9.

LEADERS

1 Quoted Lanzmann, *Shoah: An Oral History of the Holocaust*, p. 240.

2 Aharon Appelfeld, quoted Roth, *Operation Shylock: A Confession*, Vintage Books, London, 1993, p. 84.

3 Levi, Afterword, *If This Is a Man* and *The Truce*, p. 382; Camon, *Conversations with Primo Levi*, p. 13.

4 For example, his little story about 'one human German' encountered in the laboratory is cancelled by his oblique but deliberate attempt, by way of a shared, possibly infected pipette, on the life of young Fräulein Drechsel. Levi, *Moments of Reprieve*, pp. 90–2, 113.

5 Contrast this with Levi's transparent delight in Russian anarchistic exuberance and conviviality – even though Russian casualness cost him weeks and months of lost time in getting home to Turin. Levi, *The Truce*.

6 Levi, *If This Is a Man*, esp. pp. 46, 36, 147, 153–54. Late in his life Levi was to mute some of these claims, and to acknowledge two Germans who overcame his mistrust to become valued friends. Levi, *The Drowned and the Saved*, Chapter 8. See also Levi, Camon, *Conversations with Primo Levi*.

7 Levi, *If This Is a Man*, pp. 127–28.

8 Primo Levi, Afterword, *If This Is a Man* and *The Truce*, p. 395.

9 Hilberg, Introduction, *The Destruction of the European Jews*. Another remarkable book, *The Anatomy of the SS State*, published a few years later, contains essays prepared by expert historians for the instruction of the court preliminary to the Frankfurt trials. See Krausnick, Buchheim, Broszat and Jacobsen, *Anatomy of the SS State* [1965], Walker & Co., New York, 1968.

10 Browning, *Ordinary Men*.

11 It was only after writing these paragraphs that I happened on a footnote in Goldhagen's *Hitler's Willing Executioners*, note 51, p. 482, which says much the same thing. It is reassuring to have an outsider's impression confirmed by an insider.

12 Bruno Bettelheim, *The Empty Fortress: Infantile Autism and the Birth of the Self*, The Free Press, New York, 1965. For analysis of an adjacent English case, see Francis Spufford, *I May Be Some Time: Ice and the English Imagination*, Faber, London, 1996.

13 Saul Friedländer, 'The "Final Solution": On the Unease in Historical Interpretation', in *Lessons and Legacies: The Meaning of the Holocaust in a Changing World*, ed. Peter Hayes, Northwestern University Press, Evanston, Ill., 1991, pp. 23-35, p. 25.

14 Himmler, quoted Friedländer, 'The "Final Solution" ', in *Lessons and Legacies*, p. 25.

15 Friedländer, 'The "Final Solution" ', in *Lessons and Legacies*, p. 26.

16 Arendt, *Eichmann in Jerusalem*, pp. 85-6.

17 Omer Bartov's recent study demonstrates how little separated the murderous actions of the German army in Poland and Russia from those of the official killing squads, the SS *Einsatzgruppen*. Omer Bartov, *Hitler's Army: Soldiers, Nazis and War in the Third Reich*, Oxford University Press, Oxford, 1996.

18 Friedländer, 'The "Final Solution" ', in *Lessons and Legacies*, pp. 26, 32.

19 Friedländer, 'The "Final Solution" ', in *Lessons and Legacies*, p. 27.

20 Friedländer, 'The "Final Solution" ', in *Lessons and Legacies*, p. 27.

21 Friedländer, 'The "Final Solution" ', in *Lessons and Legacies*, p. 32.

22 Friedländer, 'The "Final Solution" ', in *Lessons and Legacies*, p. 31.

23 Friedländer, 'The "Final Solution" ', in *Lessons and Legacies*, p. 30.

24 Friedländer, 'The "Final Solution" ', pp. 31-2, 34. He extends the incapacity to include those with very little moral sensitivity: 'Actually, even the "interpreters" belonging to the neo-Nazi lunatic fringe do not try to justify the "Final Solution"; they deny its very existence'.

25 Friedländer, 'The "Final Solution" ', in *Lessons and Legacies*, p. 32.

26 Levi, Afterword, *If This Is a Man* and *The Truce*, p. 395.

27 Jerry Fodor, *London Review of Books*, 28 November 1996, p. 22.

28 For more on Landa and on the springs of missionary violence in Mexico, see Inga Clendinnen, *Ambivalent Conquests: Maya and Spaniard in Yucatan, 1517-1570*, Cambridge University Press, 1987, and 'Disciplining the Indians: Franciscan Ideology and Violence in Sixteenth-Century Yucatan', *Past and Present*, Vol. 94, February 1982, pp. 27-48.

29 Himmler, quoted Buchheim, 'Command and Compliance', in *Anatomy of the SS State*, pp. 303-96, p. 335.

30 See Albert Speer's musings on the 'romantic mysticism' of Himmler in Sereny, *Albert Speer: His Battle with Truth*, Macmillan, London, 1995, pp. 323-4 – and, indeed, throughout that remarkable book, as an intel-

ligent and conscientiously 'rational' man considers his less-than-rational past.

31 Kenneth Burke, 'The Rhetoric of Hitler's Battle', in his *The Philosophy of Literary Form: Studies in Symbolic Action*, Louisiana State University Press, Baton Rouge, 1941, pp. 191–220, p. 210 note.

32 Sereny, *Albert Speer*, p. 388.

33 Speer insisted that he had not been present at Himmler's address to the Nazi Party's regional heads on 6 October and that he remained ignorant of the systematic murder of the Jews until after the war, when he heard the evidence at the Nuremberg Trials. After an exemplary examination of the evidence Gitta Sereny decides that Speer had indeed been present, and had contrived to 'misremember'. Sereny, *Albert Speer*, pp. 324, 392–401.

34 Perhaps such analyses already exist. The best I have seen is Peter Haidu's brief but illuminating discussion. See Haidu, 'The Dialectics of Unspeakability', in Friedländer, *Probing the Limits of Representation*, p. 289. It is Haidu who drew my attention to the Burke essay (*supra.*). Haidu, p. 395, note 28.

35 Bormann, quoted Sereny, *Albert Speer*, p. 310. I have heard Bormann Jnr. repeat the same story on television.

36 Saul Friedländer, *Nazi Germany and the Jews: Volume One: The Years of Persecution*; Christopher Browning, *The Path to Genocide: Essays in the Launching of the Final Solution*, Cambridge University Press, Cambridge and New York, 1992. Browning is not only concerned with the policy-making leadership, but with the institutional and administrative inventions of the lower- and middle-echelon personnel who implemented those decisions: with bureaucrats, administrators, and some of the hands-on killers. His second essay, on the working of Nazi policy in the Lódz ghetto, tackles the functionalist-intentionalist debate directly.

37 Browning, *The Path to Genocide*, p. 7.

38 Browning, *The Path to Genocide*, p. 143. For the process in action see the response of German doctors to the risks to public health posed by the prevalence of disease inside the ghettos of late 1941. Browning, *Ibid.*, pp. 143–68.

39 Peter Pulzer, *The Rise of Political Anti-Semitism in Germany and Austria*, Wiley, New York, 1964; *Jews and the German State: the Political History of a Minority*, Blackwell, Oxford, 1992.

40 For details of the program see Henry Friedländer, *Origins of Nazi Genocide: From Euthanasia to the Final Solution*, University of North Carolina Press, Chapel Hill, 1995.

41 Gitta Sereny, *Into That Darkness*, pp. 485–86.

42 Arthur Miller, *Australian's Review of Books* 12 February 1997, pp. 22–3.

43 For a study which forcefully reanimates the thesis of radical anti-Semitism but which systematically overstates its case see Daniel Goldhagen, *Hitler's Willing Executioners*.

44 Speer, quoted Sereny, *Albert Speer*, pp. 82–3.

45 Hilberg, *The Destruction of the European Jews*; Hugh Trevor-Roper, *The Last Days of Hitler*, Macmillan, London, 1947; Brigitte Hamann, *Hitlers Wien*, Piper, Munich, 1996. For the disturbing argument that Hitler's coming to power was largely the result of a series of chance occurrences, see Henry Ashby Turner Jnr, *Hitler's Thirty Days to Power: January 1933*, Addison-Wesley, Reading, Mass., 1996. For an overview John Lukacs, *The Hitler of History*, Knopf, N.Y., 1998.

46 Arendt, *Eichmann in Jerusalem*, p. 252.

47 See *Eichmann Interrogated: Transcripts from the Archives of the Israeli Police*, Jochen von Lang and Claus Sibyll (eds.), trans. Ralph Manheim, Introduction by Avner W. Less, Bodley Head, London, 1983, esp. pp. 94–102, 203–6.

48 Arendt, *Eichmann in Jerusalem*, pp. 24–5.

49 Rudolph Hoess, *Commandant of Auschwitz: The Autobiography of Rudolph Hoess*, trans. Constantine FitzGibbon, Weidenfeld and Nicolson, London, 1959, p. 181.

50 For the transformation Hoess wrought in Auschwitz, a shabby military camp left over from WWI, see Debórah Dwork and Robert Jan van Pelt, *Auschwitz: 1270 to the Present*, Yale University Press, New Haven, 1996.

51 Hoess, *Commandant of Auschwitz*, pp. 129, 154. Hannah Arendt would argue that Hoess was following a practised SS psychological manoeuvre devised by Himmler: turning any impulse of compassion for one's victim towards oneself. Arendt, *Eichmann in Jerusalem*, p. 106.

52 Hoess, *Commandant of Auschwitz*, p. 128, for the Jews see pp. 128–36, for the Gypsies see pp. 124–9. See also Robert Jay Lifton, *The Nazi Doctors: A Study in the Psychology of Evil*, esp. pp. 173, 425–6, 461.

53 Hoess, *Commandant of Auschwitz*, pp. 178–79.

54 Hoess, *Commandant of Auschwitz*, p. 29.

55 Sereny, *Into That Darkness*, p. 76. Sereny demonstrates the continuity in techniques and personnel between the euthanasia program and the destruction of political enemies, 'social criminals' and 'racial undesirables' in the death camps of Poland, with men selected for the second task because of their proven efficiency at the first. See Sereny, *Into That Darkness*, pp. 53–4, 79–86, 225–26.

56 Sereny, *Into That Darkness*, pp. 49–51, 55–6, 60–90, 76–7. For child euthanasia, effected by injection, and begun earlier and practised longer, see pp. 54–5. For Sereny's (careful and informed) opinion on the connection between euthanasia personnel and the extermination camps, see esp. pp. 86–8. For an angry letter of protest from an ardent Nazi supporter, see Buchheim, 'Command and Compliance', pp. 369–71.

57 Sereny, *Into That Darkness*, p. 170.

58 Sereny, *Into That Darkness*, esp. pp. 272–79, 289.

59 Sereny, *Into That Darkness*, p. 254. Sereny gives an account of her own life, and sheds light on her relationship with Stangl and Speer in her 'My Journey to Speer', *Granta* 51, pp. 48–72.

60 Even Gustave Münzberger, the Sudeten German who had flogged naked Jews into Treblinka's gas chambers, who had served six years in jail, and who, when Sereny found him, was living with his wife, son and his son's family in a charming Bavarian village, ceases to be a faceless monster when we meet him in the ageing, flaccid, tearful flesh. We also encounter the anguished loyalty of his son, who had known nothing of the nature of his father's war service until he read the trial indictment. Sereny, *Into That Darkness*, pp. 221–25.

61 Sereny gives the last word on the number of people who died in Treblinka to the Pole who had the job of traffic supervisor of Treblinka Station. He was also a member of the Polish underground, and from the first day counted the sealed railway cars and recorded the mysterious numbers (at first he had not known what the cargo was) chalked on the sides. He told Sereny, when she tracked him down and persuaded him to come to Treblinka with her, that 'the number of people killed in Treblinka was 1,200,000, and there's no doubt about it whatever'. Sereny, *Into That Darkness*, p. 250.

62 Sereny, *Into That Darkness*, p. 164.

63 Sereny, *Into That Darkness*, p. 255. Janet Malcolm, who has cast a very cold eye on the complexities of the relationship between interviewer and interviewee, biographer and subject, would identify these priorities as uncommon. See Janet Malcolm, *The Journalist and the Murderer*, Knopf, New York, 1990; *The Silent Woman: Sylvia Plath and Ted Hughes*, Knopf, New York, 1994.

64 Sereny, *Into That Darkness*, p. 366.

65 Sereny, *Into That Darkness*, p. 23.

66 See Lifton's enthralling analysis of the responses of Nazi doctors inside Auschwitz: 'The "Auschwitz Self" did continuous psychological work to maintain that internal sense of numbed habituation in order to fend off potentially overwhelming images of its relationship to guilt, death and

murder'. Lifton, *The Nazi Doctors: A Study in the Psychology of Evil*, p. 446. The 'Auschwitz Self' was achieved by the psychological process Lifton dubs 'doubling'. Lifton's analysis of Dr Josef Mengele is unsurpassed, see *The Nazi Doctors*, Chapter 17, pp. 337–83.

67 Friedländer, 'The "Final Solution" ', pp. 26–30. This manoeuvre of invoking a hidden psychological state as operating across a collective is similar to Robert Lifton's notion of 'the Auschwitz self' cited above.

68 Trevor-Roper, *The Last Days of Hitler*.

69 Arendt, *Eichmann in Jerusalem*, pp. 46–7.

70 Browning, 'One Day in Józefów', *Paths to Genocide*, p. 169.

71 Levi, Afterword, *If This Is a Man* and *The Truce*, p. 396.

THE MEN IN THE GREEN TUNICS

1 Goldhagen, *Hitler's Willing Executioners*.

2 As, for example, the 'harvest festival' of November 1943, during which Jewish men, conserved until that time for their labour, were stripped, led to a mass grave, forced to lie down (neatly, to conserve space) on the bodies of their dead and dying comrades, and machine-gunned. Browning, *Ordinary Men*, p. 139.

3 For an overview of the process by a major scholar in the field, see Raul Hilberg, 'The Nature of the Process', in Dimsdale, *Survivors, Victims and Perpetrators*, p. 16. The rest of this absorbing volume comprises a sometimes awkward but always serious effort to see how far the discipline of psychology can illuminate the actions and reactions of both the perpetrators and the victims of the Holocaust.

4 Goldhagen, *Hitler's Willing Executioners*, Part IV, 'Jewish "Work" is Annihilation'.

5 Friedländer, *Nazi Germany and the Jews*, p. 4. See also Pulzer, *The Rise of Political Anti-Semitism in Germany and Austria*, and his *Jews and the German State: The Political History of a Minority*.

6 Goldhagen, *Hitler's Willing Executioners*, Introduction and Part I, and especially pp. 7, 21, 28–30.

7 Clifford Geertz, 'Thick Description: Towards an Interpretive Theory of Culture', in his *The Interpretation of Cultures: Selected Essays*, Basic Books, New York, 1973, pp. 3–30, and esp. pp. 5, 27. For a superb worked example, see the final essay in the collection: 'Deep Play: Notes on the Balinese Cockfight', pp. 412–53.

8 Goldhagen, *Hitler's Willing Executioners*, p. 6.

9 Goldhagen describes the Order Police of 1942 as 'an inauspicious lot', haphazardly selected, without any ideological screening. Goldhagen, *Hit-*

ler's Willing Executioners, p. 183. For the stages of the incorporation of the civilian police into the SS state, see Buchheim, 'The SS – Instrument of Domination', in Krausnick, Buchheim, Broszat and Jacobsen, *Anatomy of the SS State*, pp. 127–301, esp. pp. 143–247.

10 Goldhagen, *Hitler's Willing Executioners*, p. 187–202.

11 Browning, *Ordinary Men*, note 26 p. 199, and e.g. note 9, p. 20. Browning gives a fine, terse overview of the methodological and moral difficulties of 'perpetrator' history in Browning, 'German Memory, Judicial Interrogation, Historical Reconstruction', in Friedländer, *Probing the Limits of Representation*, pp. 22–36. I first discovered both the Józefów event, Christopher Browning, and curiosity about both through Browning's exemplary narrative, analysis and interpretation of the action in his 'One Day in Józefów: Initiation to Mass Murder', in Hayes, *Lessons and Legacies*, pp. 196–209, or in his *The Path to Genocide*, pp. 169–83.

12 Goldhagen, *Hitler's Willing Executioners*, p. 228.

13 Goldhagen, *Hitler's Willing Executioners*, p. 56.

14 Goldhagen, *Hitler's Willing Executioners*, p. 213.

15 For Goldhagen's main strictures against Browning's interpretation, see Goldhagen, *Hitler's Willing Executioners*, note 22, p. 580. See also note 68, pp. 540–41, and note 98, pp. 543–44.

16 Ervin Staub, quoted Browning, *Ordinary Men*, note 14, pp. 216–17. No further details are available. Staub knew the story through personal communication from the man who had interviewed the veteran. See Ervin Staub, *The Roots of Evil: The Origins of Genocide and Other Group Violence*, Cambridge University Press, Cambridge, 1989, p. 134. For an Auschwitz example of habituation, see Linton, *The Nazi Doctors*, esp. pp. 196–7.

17 M. S. Peck, *People of the Lie: The Hope of Healing Human Evil*, Simon and Schuster, New York, 1983, p. 214; Robert Jay Lifton, 'The Concept of the Survivor', in Dimsdale, *Survivors, Victims and Perpetrators*, pp. 113–26, p. 214.

18 For a study of the psychological cost to warrior-survivors of battleground horrors, and the changing labels and etiologies devised to account for their postwar condition, see Allan Young, *The Harmony of Illusions: Inventing Post-Traumatic Stress Disorder*, Princeton University Press, Princeton, 1996. For the war in the Pacific, John W. Dower, *War without Mercy: Race and Power in the Pacific War*, Faber, London, 1986.

19 See Philip Roth's extraordinary evocation of the ecstasy of 'Ivan the Terrible' clubbing Jews through the 'Tube' at Treblinka. Philip Roth, *Operation Shylock*, pp. 60–1.

20 Stanley Milgram, *Obedience to Authority: An Experimental View*, Tavistock, London, 1974; Craig Haney, Curtis Banks, and Philip Zimbardo, 'Interpersonal Dynamics in a Simulated Prison', *International Journal of Criminology and Penology*, Vol. 1, 1983, pp. 69–97; Browning, *Ordinary Men*, pp. 167–68, 171–73; Goldhagen, *Hitler's Willing Executioners*, p. 383, note 19, p. 580. For an accessible discussion of the Milgram experiment and its implications regarding the Nazis, see John P. Sabini and Maury Silver, 'Destroying the Innocent with a Clear Conscience: A Sociopsychology of the Holocaust', in Dimsdale, *Survivors, Victims and Perpetrators*, pp. 329–58.

21 Staub, *The Roots of Evil*, p. 151. Staub has a number of other useful things to say, albeit in the strangely flat tones of the professional psychologist.

22 David Grossman, *On Killing: The Psychological Cost of Learning to Kill in War and Society*, Little, Brown & Co., New York, 1995, p. 13.

23 Michelle Rosaldo, *Knowledge and Passion: Ilongot Notions of Self and Social Life*, Cambridge University Press, Cambridge, 1980.

24 Goldhagen, *Hitler's Willing Executioners*, pp. 184–5. Goldhagen, *Hitler's Willing Executioners*, pp. 182–4, 210–11 and note 13, p. 528.

25 Goldhagen, *Hitler's Willing Executioners*, p. 184.

26 For insight into the German army and the swift erosion of its protocols in Poland and Russia, see Omer Bartov, *Hitler's Army: Soldiers, Nazis and War in the Third Reich*, Oxford University Press, Oxford, 1991, esp. Chapter 4, 'The Distortion of Reality', which is based on soldiers' letters from the Eastern Front. Many of the letters come from a collection officially approved by Goebbels (Bartov, note 145, p. 212), but Bartov judges them to be indicative of general attitudes.

27 Goldhagen, *Hitler's Willing Executioners*, pp. 245, 260; Browning, *Ordinary Men*, p. 88.

28 Compare with Goldhagen: 'Anti-Semitism tells us nothing about Jews, but much about anti-Semites and the culture that breeds them'. Goldhagen, *Hitler's Willing Executioners*, p. 39.

29 Browning, *Ordinary Men*, pp. 153–4.

30 For Goldhagen's analyses of photographs and their meanings, see Goldhagen, *Hitler's Willing Executioners*, pp. 246–7 and 256–61.

31 Browning, *Ordinary Men*, p. 112.

32 See Goldhagen, *Hitler's Willing Executioners*, pp. 191, 256. See also Sereny, *Albert Speer: His Battle with Truth*, pp. 255–57. Sereny usefully charts the escalation of anti-Jewish actions inside Germany (and incorporates recently uncovered material) in Chapter 10 of her pursuit of Speer.

33 For the battalion's leisure activities, see Goldhagen, *Hitler's Willing Executioners*, pp. 264–8.

34 Goldhagen, *Hitler's Willing Executioners*, pp. 241–3. Goldhagen diagnoses the disapproval as indicating a 'sense of chivalry and propriety', and alarm regarding 'possible damage to her sensibilities and person', p. 242.

35 Browning, *Ordinary Men*, p. 127; Goldhagen, *Hitler's Willing Executioners*, p. 244.

36 For the theory behind this indispensable notion, see Goffman, *The Presentation of Self in Everyday Life*.

37 Friedländer, 'The "Final Solution" ', in Hayes, *Lessons and Legacies*, pp. 23–35, p. 30.

38 Browning, *Ordinary Men*, p. xx.

THE AUSCHWITZ SS

1 Quoted Kraus and Kulka, *The Death Factory*, p. 216.

2 Quoted Gordon Williamson, *The SS: Hitler's Instrument of Terror*, Macmillan, London, 1994, p. 37.

3 For an exegesis of why he believes the camp to be 'the paradigmatic institution of [Nazi] destruction and genocide', see Goldhagen, *Hitler's Willing Executioners*, pp. 176–78. For Eicke's regulations of October 1933 for his guards at Dachau (which became the model for other camps) see Martin Broszat, 'The Concentration Camps 1933–45', in Krausnick, Buchheim, Broszat and Jacobsen, *Anatomy of the SS State*, pp. 399–504, pp. 432–34.

4 Hoess, *Commandant of Auschwitz*, pp. 35–8, 46, 59, 48.

5 For the fascinating detail of SS structure and practices, see Buchheim, 'Command and Compliance', in Krausnick et al., pp. 303–96.

6 Cohen, *Human Behaviour in the Concentration Camp*, p. 209. For similar views from the women's camp, where there was little work 'outside', and largely maintenance or make-work within, see Lengyel, *Five Chimneys*, esp. pp. 125–27.

7 Levi, *If This Is a Man* and *The Truce*, pp. 154, p. 57; *The Drowned and the Saved*, pp. 92, 100.

8 Clendinnen, *Aztecs*, esp. Chapter 10, 'Ritual'.

9 For an expanded discussion, see Bruce Kapferer, 'Performance and the Structure of Meaning and Experience', in Victor W. Turner and Edward M. Bruner (eds.), *The Anthropology of Experience*, University of Illinois Press, Urbana and Chicago, 1986, pp. 188–203. The incomparably fertile Victor Turner is obligatory reading, most especially his *From Ritual to*

Theatre: The Human Seriousness of Play, Performing Arts Journal Press Inc., New York, 1982.

10 For an illuminating diagnosis of Mengele from someone who worked with him in Auschwitz, see Sereny, *Albert Speer*, pp. 465-8. See also Lifton, *The Nazi Doctors*, esp. chapter 17.

11 On these and related issues see Staub's analysis, *The Roots of Evil*, esp. chapter 10. For Saul Friedländer's suggestion of the development of an automatic state to explain what he sees as a ' "mechanical," non-human aspect of their actions', see Friedländer, 'The "Final Solution" ', in Hayes, *Lessons and Legacies*, pp. 23-35, p. 30.

12 Robert Lifton explores what may have lain behind some of those stony faces in his *The Nazi Doctors*.

13 Levi, *If This Is a Man*, pp. 25-6.

14 Levi, *The Drowned and the Saved*, p. 14.

15 For 'the business of the caps' see also Müller, *Auschwitz Inferno*, p. 1.

16 Kraus and Kulka, *The Death Factory*, p. 162.

17 Lifton, *The Nazi Doctors*, p. 447. Lifton recognised that 'Auschwitz epitomised the overall Nazi preoccupation with ritual, much of it having to do with healing and killing. The regime drew much of its power from its ritualisation of existence, so that every act it called forth could be seen as having profound mythic significance for the "Third Reich" and the "Aryan race" '. Lifton, *The Nazi Doctors*, p. 432.

18 Müller, *Auschwitz Inferno*, p. 52.

19 Goldhagen, *Hitler's Willing Executioners*, esp. chapters 10 and 11. For what may be the most extreme example of Nazi 'symbolic expression', see Goldhagen, pp. 308-9. While the beatings of Jews were far more savage than those inflicted on non-Jewish prisoners, all prisoners were subjected to the exercises.

20 Müller, *Auschwitz Inferno*, pp. 1-5. It is a stunning opening, which presumably owes something to Müller's 'literary collaborator'. There is certainly nothing like it in Müller's 1946 evidence as given to Kulka and Kraus. Müller's spoken testimony for Claude Lanzmann's *Shoah* closely follows his written account, as does the testimony of Rudolph Vrba, who also had a written account to draw on. The congruence is unsurprising, and throws no light on the question of the reliability of the accounts.

21 Burkhardt, quoted Buchheim, 'Command and Compliance', *Anatomy of the SS State*, pp. 303-96, pp. 340-1. Buchheim identifies this as a 'degenerate form of militarism', p. 341.

22 Nyiszli, *Auschwitz: An Eyewitness Account*, pp. 96-7.

23 Müller, *Auschwitz Inferno*, pp. 36-9. For another example, this time manipulating the coercive potential of extreme thirst, p. 135.

24 Levi, *The Drowned and the Saved*, p. 101.

25 Müller, *Auschwitz Inferno*, pp. 150–1.

26 For the affability of *Kommandoführer* Johann Gorges, especially when drunk (as he often was), and a description of a *Sonderkommando* SS 'party', see Müller, *Auschwitz Inferno*, pp. 3–4.

27 Müller, *Auschwitz Inferno*, esp. pp. 60–87.

28 Müller, *Auschwitz Inferno*, pp. 137–8, 140.

29 For Treblinka see Sereny, *Into That Darkness*, pp. 199, 219, 239; Glazar, *Trap with a Green Fence*, esp. 'Masquerade', pp. 117–25. Christopher Browning tells us that Ukrainian, Lithuanian and Latvian recruits from prisoner of war camps outnumbered the German staff at the death camps of Operation Reinhard by 4:1. Browning, 'One Day in Józefów', *The Path to Genocide*, p. 197. That was certainly the Treblinka ratio.

30 Glazar, *Trap with a Green Fence*, pp. 40–41.

31 For Levi's first experience of the SS style, see Levi, *The Drowned and the Saved*, pp. 70–71.

32 Nyiszli, *Auschwitz: An Eyewitness Account*, pp. 118–25.

33 Müller, *Auschwitz Inferno*, p. 141.

34 See e.g. Lengyel, *Five Chimneys*, pp. 193, and Delbo, *Auschwitz and After*, p. 85.

35 The paradigm performance remains Clifford Geertz's 'Deep Play: Notes on the Balinese Cockfight', in his *The Interpretations of Cultures*, pp. 412–53. These luminous essays were published close to a quarter-century ago, but too few historians seem to have internalised them. Anthropologists have done better: see Michelle Rosaldo, *Knowledge and Passion: Ilongot Notions of Self and Social Life*, Cambridge University Press, Cambridge, 1980, and Suzette Heald, 'The Ritual Use of Violence: Circumcision Rituals among the Gisu of Uganda', in David Riches (ed.), *The Anthropology of Violence*, Basil Blackwell, Oxford, 1986, pp. 70–83. For some high-flying but illuminating theory perilously connecting physical expressions to a repertoire of human emotions, see Richard Schechner, 'Magnitudes of Performance', in *The Anthropology of Experience*, Victor W. Turner and Edward M. Bruner (eds.), University of Illinois Press, Urbana and Chicago, 1986, pp. 344–69; *Essays on Performance Theory*, Drama Book Specialists, New York, 1977, and his *Between Theater and Anthropology*, University of Pennsylvania Press, Philadelphia, 1985.

36 Lengyel, *Five Chimneys*, pp. 150–1.

37 See e.g. Isaac Babel's brilliant elaboration of an actual event in his short story, 'The Life Story of Pavlichenko Matvey Rodionych', *Collected Stories*, trans. David McDuff, Penguin, 1995. Compare Babel's diary entry

for the same event: Isaac Babel, *1920 Diary*, ed. with introduction and notes Carol J. Avins, trans. H. T. Willetts, Yale University Press, New Haven and London, 1995, entry for 9 August 1920, pp. 60–61, and Alberto Manguel's exploration into the mind of an Argentinian torturer in his novel *News from a Foreign Country Came*. Babel's diary appears to provide an abundance of evidence for my final conclusion.

38 Some believe so. See the disquieting letter by Michael Moorcock, *London Review of Books*, 20 February 1997, p. 4. There has been altogether too much evidence of the ease of transition from neighbour to murderer or torturer over the last decade.

REPRESENTING THE HOLOCAUST

1 Richard Rorty, *Contingency, Irony, and Solidarity*, Cambridge University Press, Cambridge and New York, 1989, pp. xiii–xvi.

2 In a response to my 'Fellow-Sufferers' essay (see Bibliography) Professor Rorty declared that the insulting omission was unintended; that he had simply forgotten to put history in. Rorty, private communication 20 November 1996. I remain unappeased.

3 For a ferocious repudiation of aesthetic representations of the Holocaust, see Elie Wiesel, 'Trivializing Memory', in his *From the Kingdom of Memory*, pp. 165–72.

4 Sylvia Plath, *Ariel: Poems by Sylvia Plath*, Faber, London, 1968, p. 54.

5 For criticism from a fellow poet, see Seamus Heaney, *The Government of the Tongue*, Faber, London, 1988. For an exploration of Plath's usages, see James E. Young, 'The Holocaust Confessions of Sylvia Plath', in his *Writing and Rewriting the Holocaust: Narrative and the Consequences of Interpretation*, Indiana University Press, Bloomington, 1988, pp. 117–33. Jacqueline Rose discovers justifications in her *The Haunting of Sylvia Plath*, Harvard University Press, Cambridge, Mass., 1991, esp. chapter 6. For a bibliography of the discussion arising from the borrowing, see Young, *Writing and Rewriting the Holocaust*, pp. 53–7.

6 D. M. Thomas, *The White Hotel*, Victor Gollancz, London, 1981.

7 See e.g. Aharon Appelfeld, *The Retreat, Badenheim 1939, Tzili: A Story of a Life*, and, most perfectly, *To The Land of the Cattails*. For some comments of his own, see Appelfeld as quoted in Roth, *Operation Shylock*, pp. 83–6.

8 Dan Pagis, quoted Sidra DeKoven Ezrahi, "The Grave in the Air": Unbound Metaphors in Post-Holocaust Poetry', in Friedländer, *Probing the Limits of Representation*, pp. 259–76. Unlike Appelfeld's Toni or Lotte, Pagis's female victim is prescient – but silenced before she can speak her

numinous words. Could they exist: the Pagis poem is a written message complete in its space, so the putative message has no possible locus for existence.

9 Contrast this with the choices of his compatriots Appelfeld and Pagis, who emigrated to Israel and wrote their European past in their new country's renovated Hebrew.

10 Celan, 'Todesfuge'. For the poem in the original German and in John Felstiner's translation, see Felstiner, 'Translating Paul Celan's *"Todesfuge"* ' in Friedländer, *Probing the Limits of Representation*, pp. 240–58, or in Felstiner, *Paul Celan: Poet, Survivor, Jew*, Yale University Press, New Haven, Conn., 1996, pp. 31–2. In an act of ritual exorcism and as a sign of penitence, the Celan poem was appropriated by postwar Germany and set as a text in schools.

11 Tadeusz Borowski, *This Way for the Gas, Ladies and Gentlemen*, first published in Polish in 1948, Viking, 1967. For a fine discussion of Borowski's fiction, of the world of moral cannibalism he described and survived and of his struggle to come to terms with his world after his release, see Langer, *Versions of Survival*, esp. pp. 103–24. Borowski killed himself by gas in Warsaw in 1951, at twenty-nine.

12 Gustave Flaubert, quoted Victor Brombert, *The Hidden Reader*, Harvard University Press, Cambridge, Mass., 1988, p. 151.

13 Vladimir Nabokov, 'Signs and Symbols', *The Stories of Vladimir Nabokov*, Vintage International, 1997. See also the even more oblique and marginally less telling 'Conversation Piece', 1945, in the same volume. For a different and equally moving backward glance, see Cynthia Ozick, *The Shawl*, Alfred A. Knopf, New York, 1988.

14 Theo Richmond, *Konin: A Quest*, Vintage, London, 1996, p. 335. If you prefer the French style, 'a photograph is wholly ballasted by the contingency of which it is the weightless, transparent envelope'. Roland Barthes, *Camera Lucida: Reflections on Photography*, trans. Richard Howard, Hill and Wang, New York, 1981, p. 5.

15 Or, as Barthes later puts it, 'The thing of the past, by its immediate radiations (its luminances), has really touched the surface which in turn my gaze will touch'. Barthes, *Camera Lucida*, p. 81. Obviously, photographs can be faked – objects superimposed or excised, airbrushes put to work – but at some time those actual objects were before the lens, which is Barthes's point. For some sophisticated philosophising on photography beguilingly confected into a short story, see Italo Calvino's 'The Adventure of a Photographer', in his *Difficult Loves*, Minerva Press, London, 1993.

16 See note on Illustrations, Hoess, *Commandant of Auschwitz*.

17 Gitta Sereny, *Into That Darkness*, pp. 158–9.

18 Elie Wiesel, 'Trivializing Memory', p. 167.

19 Young, *Writing and Rewriting the Holocaust*, p. 162. Young is always illuminating, but I especially recommend his third section, 'Texts of the Holocaust: A Narrative Critique'. *Breaking the Silence* is Eva Fogelman's film about the children of the survivors, who have inherited a coherent understanding of events very different from the verbal accounts given them by their parents. The alternative account had been expressed and communicated through a thousand non-verbal signs.

20 Young, *Writing and Rewriting the Holocaust*, p. 161.

21 Lanzmann shot 350 hours of film. Clearly, there could have been multiple *Shoahs*. He freely acknowledges that the film is 'his': 'The film is made around my own obsessions; it wouldn't have been possible otherwise.' Quoted Young, *Writing and Rewriting the Holocaust*, p. 157.

22 Compare Pauline Kael, prestigious film critic of the *New York Times*, who found *Shoah* 'logy [sic.] and exhausting right from the start', and summed the whole up as 'a long moan'. She opines that 'a moan is not an appropriate response to the history of the Jews'. Pauline Kael, *Hooked*, Dutton, New York, 1989, p. 88. Unaware of their literary pasts, Kael is charmed by the fluency and the 'simple, unforced dramatic power' of a Filip Müller or a Rudolph Vrba. She is merely bored by 'the silences, the hesitancies, the breakdowns'. p. 84.

23 Hayden White, 'Historical Employment and the Problem of Truth', in Friedländer, *Probing the Limits of Representation*, pp. 37–53.

24 Lanzmann, *Shoah: An Oral History of the Holocaust*, p. 287. It is possible that those cheerful Poles may have innocently misrepresented themselves because of their ignorance both the medium and of Lanzmann's ferocious intentions.

25 David Ben-Gurion, quoted Arendt, *Eichmann in Jerusalem*, p. 10.

26 Friedländer, 'Trauma, Memory, and Transference', in Hartman, *Holocaust Remembrance*, pp. 252–63, esp. pp. 254–5, 261.

27 Milan Kundera, *The Book of Laughter and Forgetting*, p. 3.

28 Wislawa Szymborska, 'Could Have', in *View with a Grain of Sand: Selected Poems*, trans. Stanislaw Baranczak and Clare Cavanagh, Harcourt Brace & Company, New York, 1996, pp. 65–6.

SELECT BIBLIOGRAPHY

The Holocaust literature available in English is vast, and this bibliography is therefore highly selective. Scholars might well find it arbitrary, and every reader will discover puzzling absences. I can only say that these are the books which have most instructed me.

Were I to recommend one book on the Holocaust for readers unused to reading history it would be Gitta Sereny's *Albert Speer: His Struggle with Truth,* because Sereny gives us an individual life story to follow from the early 1930s through to the triumph and destruction of the Thousand Year Reich, because Speer was an intimate associate of Hitler up to Hitler's suicide, because Sereny's serene moral presence inhabits every page. For those accustomed to reading history the single book would be Christopher R. Browning's *The Path to Genocide: Essays on Launching the Final Solution,* because his essays deal cogently with the stages and process of the decision to kill Europe's Jews and with the beginnings of its implementation. For the years of gathering menace in Germany – perhaps the period most important to us if we are to understand the how of this moral and political disaster – I would recommend Saul Friedländer's *Nazi Germany and the Jews: The Years of Persecution.* For readers wanting an overview of recent historiography, the book would be Charles S. Maier's *The Unmasterable Past: History, Holocaust, and German National Identity,* or Michael Marrus, *The Holocaust in History.* For those wanting to trace a community's experience of the Holocaust I suggest Theo Konin's *Konin: A Quest,* and for the experience of an individual, Primo Levi's *If This Is a Man.* For a humane, moving response to the denial of the Holocaust I recommend Pierre Vidal-Naquet, *Assassins of Memory.*

GENERAL REFERENCES

Gilbert, Martin, *Atlas of the Holocaust,* Joseph, London, 1982.
The Encyclopedia of the Holocaust, 4 vols., editor-in-chief Israel Gutman, Macmillan, New York, 1990.

Gilbert, Martin, *The Holocaust: The Jewish Tragedy,* Collins, London, 1986.
'This book is an attempt to draw on the nearest of the witnesses, those closest to the destruction, and through their testimony to tell something of the suffering of those who perished, and are forever silent.'
Hilberg, Raul, *The Destruction of the European Jews,* Quadrangle Books, Chicago, 1961.
'[This] book is not about the Jews. It is a book about the people who destroyed the Jews ... The following chapters will describe the vast organization of the Nazi machinery of destruction and the men who performed important functions in this machine.'

BIBLIOGRAPHY

Améry, Jean (Hans Mayer), *At the Mind's Limits: Contemplation by a Survivor on Auschwitz and its Realities* [1966], trans. Sydney Rosenfeld and Stella P. Rosenfeld, Schocken Books, New York, 1990. The original German publication was reissued with a new author's preface in 1977, a year before Améry's suicide.
Appelfeld, Aharon, *Badenheim 1939,* David R. Godiene, Boston, 1980.
Appelfeld, Aharon, *Tzili: The Story of a Life,* E. P. Dutton, New York, 1983.
Appelfeld, Aharon, *To the Land of the Cattails,* Weidenfeld and Nicolson, London, 1986.
Appelfeld, Aharon, *The Retreat,* Quartet, London, 1991.
Appelfeld, Aharon, *The Age of Wonders,* Quartet, London, 1993.
Appelfeld, Aharon, *The Immortal Bartfuss,* Quartet, London, 1995.
Arendt, Hannah, *Eichmann in Jerusalem: A Report on the Banality of Evil,* [1963], Viking Press, New York, 1965.
Babel, Isaac, 'The Life Story of Pavlichenko Matvey Rodionych', *Collected Stories,* trans. David McDuff, Penguin, Harmondsworth, England, 1995.
Babel, Isaac, *1920 Diary,* ed. and with an introduction and notes by Carol J. Avins, trans. H. T. Willetts, Yale University Press, New Haven and London, 1995.
Barthes, Roland, *Camera Lucida: Reflections on Photography,* trans. Richard Howard, Hill and Wang, New York, 1981.

Bartov, Omer, *Hitler's Army: Soldiers, Nazis and War in the Third Reich*, Oxford University Press, Oxford, 1991.

Bartov, Omer, *Murder in Our Midst: The Holocaust, Industrial Killing, and Representation*, Oxford University Press, Oxford, 1996. (Note the fine backnote commentaries and the evocation of modern Israel.)

Bauer, Yehuda, *The Jewish Emergence from Powerlessness*, University of Toronto Press, Buffalo, 1978.

Bettelheim, Bruno, *The Informed Heart: Autonomy in a Mass Age*, The Free Press of Glencoe, New York, 1960.

Bettelheim, Bruno, *The Empty Fortress: Infantile Autism and the Birth of the Self*, The Free Press, New York, 1965.

Blatt, Thomas Toivi, *From the Ashes of Sobibor: A Story of Survival*, foreword by Christopher Browning, Northeastern University Press, Evanston, Illinois, 1997.

Borowski, Tadeusz, *This Way for the Gas, Ladies and Gentlemen*, [1947] Viking, New York, 1967.

Bowen, Elizabeth, *The Mulberry Tree: Writings of Elizabeth Bowen*, Harcourt, Brace Jovanovich, San Diego, New York and London, 1986.

Browning, Christopher R., *Fateful Months: Essays on the Emergence of the Final Solution*, Holmes and Meier, New York and London, 1985.

Browning, Christopher R. 'German Memory, Judicial Interrogation, and Historical Reconstruction: Writing Perpetrator History from Postwar Testimony', in Friedländer, *Probing the Limits of Representation*, 1992.

Browning, Christopher R., *Ordinary Men: Reserve Police Battalion 101 and the Final Solution in Poland*, HarperCollins, New York, 1992.

Browning, Christopher R., *The Path to Genocide: Essays in the Launching of the Final Solution*, Cambridge University Press, Cambridge and New York, 1992.

Browning, Christopher R., 'One Day in Józefów: Initiation to Mass Murder', in his *The Path to Genocide*.

Browning, Christopher 'Nazi Ghettoization Policy in Poland, 1939–1941', in his *The Path to Genocide*.

Bruner, Jerome, *Acts of Meaning*, Harvard University Press, Cambridge, Mass., 1990.

Burke, Kenneth, 'The Rhetoric of Hitler's Battle', in his *The Philosophy of Literary Form: Studies in Symbolic Action*, Louisiana State University Press, Baton Rouge, 1941.

Calvino, Italo, 'The Adventure of a Photographer', in his *Difficult Loves*, Minerva Press, London, 1993.

Camon, Ferdinando, *Conversations with Primo Levi*, trans. John Shepley, The Marlboro Press, Marlboro, Vermont, 1989.

Clendinnen, Inga, *Ambivalent Conquests: Spaniard and Maya in Yucatan, 1517–1577*, Cambridge University Press, Cambridge and New York, 1987.

Clendinnen, Inga, *Aztecs: An Interpretation*, Cambridge University Press, Cambridge and New York, 1991.

Clendinnen, Inga, 'Disciplining the Indians: Franciscan Ideology and Violence in Sixteenth-Century Yucatan', *Past and Present*, No. 94, February 1982.

Clendinnen, Inga, 'Fellow-Sufferers: History and the Imagination', *Australian Humanities Review*, September 1996: Internet: http://www.lib.latrobe.edu.au/AHR, September 1996

Cohen, Elie A., *The Abyss: A Confession*, Norton, New York, 1973.

Cohen, Elie A., *Human Behaviour in the Concentration Camp*, [1954] trans. by the author, Free Association Books, London, 1988.

Delbo, Charlotte, *Auschwitz and After*, Yale University Press, New Haven, Conn., 1995.

Delbo, Charlotte, *Days and Memory* [1985], trans. and with a preface by Rosette Lamont, The Marlboro Press, Vermont, 1990.

Dimsdale, Joel E. ed., *Survivors, Victims and Perpetrators: Essays on the Holocaust*, Taylor and Francis, Washington, 1980.

Dower, John W., *War without Mercy: Race and Power in the Pacific War*, Faber, London, 1986.

Dwork, Debórah and Robert Jan van Pelt, 'Reclaiming Auschwitz', in Hartman, *Holocaust Remembrance*.

Dwork, Debórah and Robert Jan van Pelt, *Auschwitz: 1270 to the Present*, Yale University Press, New Haven, Conn., 1996.

Ezrahi, Sidra DeKoven, 'Revisioning the Past: The Changing Legacy of the Holocaust in Hebrew Literature', *Salmagundi*, no. 68–69, Fall 1985-Winter 1986.

Ezrahi, Sidra DeKoven, 'The Grave in the Air: Unbound Metaphors in Post-Holocaust Poetry', in Friedländer, *Probing the Limits of Representation*.

Eichmann Interrogated: Transcripts from the Archives of the Israeli Police, Jochen von Lang and Claus Sibyll (eds.), trans. Ralph Manheim, introduction by Avner W. Less, Bodley Head, London, 1983.

Feldman, Yael S., 'Whose Story Is It, Anyway? Ideology and Psychology in the Representation of the Shoah in Israeli Literature', in Friedländer, *Probing the Limits of Representation*.

Felstiner, John, 'Translating Paul Celan's "Todesfuge" ', in Friedländer, *Probing the Limits of Representation*.

Felstiner, John, *Paul Celan: Poet, Survivor, Jew*, Yale University Press, New Haven, Conn., 1996.

Fest, Joachim, *Plotting Hitler's Death: The Story of the German Resistance*, trans. Bruce Little, Metropolitan Books/Henry Holt, New York, 1996.

Fonseca, Isabel, *Bury Me Standing: The Gypsies and Their Journey*, Chatto and Windus, London, 1995.

Frank, Anne, *The Diary of a Young Girl*, Otto Frank and Mirjam Pressler (eds.), trans. Susan Masotty, Viking, London, 1996.

Friedländer, Henry, *Origins of Nazi Genocide: From Euthanasia to the Final Solution*, University of North Carolina Press, Chapel Hill, 1995.

Friedländer, Saul ed., *Probing the Limits of Representation: Nazism and the "Final Solution"*, Harvard University Press, Cambridge, Mass., 1992.

Friedländer, Saul, 'The "Final Solution": On the Unease in Historical Interpretation', in Hayes, *Lessons and Legacies*.

Friedländer, Saul, 'Trauma, Memory, and Transference', in Hartmann, *Holocaust Remembrance*.

Friedländer, Saul, *When Memory Comes*, trans. Helen R. Lane, Farrar Straus & Giroux, New York, 1979.

Friedländer, Saul, *Nazi Germany and the Jews: Volume One: The Years of Persecution*, HarperCollins, London, 1997.

Fromer, Rebecca Camhi, *The Holocaust Odyssey of Daniel Bennahmias, Sonderkommando*, introduction by Steven B. Bowman, University of Alabama Press, Tuscaloosa and London, 1993.

Fussell, Paul, *The Great War and Modern Memory*, Oxford University Press, New York and London, 1975.

Geertz, Clifford, 'Thick Description: Towards an Interpretive Theory of Culture', in his *The Interpretation of Cultures: Selected Essays*, Basic Books, New York, 1973. See also his 'Deep Play: Notes on the Balinese Cockfight' in the same volume.

Glazar, Richard, *Trap with a Green Fence: Survival in Treblinka*, trans. Roslyn Theobald, foreword by Wolfgang Benz, Northwestern University Press, Evanston, Ill., 1995.

Goffman, Erving, *Asylums: Essays on the Social Situation of Mental Patients and Other Inmates*, Penguin Books, Harmondsworth, England, 1961.

Goffman, Erving, *The Presentation of Self in Everyday Life* [1959], Penguin Books, Harmondsworth, England, 1990.

Goldhagen, Daniel Jonah, *Hitler's Willing Executioners: Ordinary Germans and the Holocaust*, Little Brown, London, 1996.

Haidu, Peter, 'The Dialectics of Unspeakability: Language, Silence, and the Narratives of Desubjectification', in Friedländer, *Probing the Limits of Representation*.

Habermas, Jürgen, 'Historical Consciousness and Post-Traditional Identity: The Federal Republic's Orientation to the West', in his *The New Con-*

servatism: *Cultural Criticism and the Historians' Debate*, ed. and trans. Shierry Weber, Nicholsen, Polity Press, 1989.

Hamann, Brigitte, *Hitlers Wien*, Piper, Munich, 1996.

Hart, Kitty, *Return to Auschwitz*, Panther, Granada Publishing Ltd., London 1983. An earlier 1961 printing titled *I Am Alive*, lacks the prefatory chapter on Hart's experiences in postwar England.

Hartman, Geoffrey H. ed., *Holocaust Remembrance: The Shapes of Memory*, Basil Blackwell, Oxford and Cambridge, 1994. The backnotes of the Hartman volume have some fine bibliographies e.g. on the art of the Holocaust.

Hartman, Geoffrey H., *The Longest Shadow: In the Aftermath of the Holocaust*, Indiana University Press, Bloomington, 1996.

Hayes, Peter ed., *Lessons and Legacies: The Meaning of the Holocaust in a Changing World*, Northwestern University Press, Evanston, Ill., 1991.

Heald, Suzette, 'The Ritual Use of Violence: Circumcision Rituals among the Gisu of Uganda', in *The Anthropology of Violence*, David Riches ed., Basil Blackwell, Oxford, 1986.

Hilberg, Raul, *The Destruction of the European Jews*, Quadrangle Books, Chicago, 1961. See also the revised edition, Hilberg, *The Destruction of the European Jews*, rev. ed., New York, 1985.

Hilberg, Raul, Stanislaw Staron, and Joseph Kermisz (eds.), *The Warsaw Diary of Adam Czerniakow: Prelude to Doom*, Schocken, New York, 1979.

Hilberg, Raul, 'The Nature of the Process', in *Survivors, Victims and Perpetrators: Essays on the Holocaust*, ed. Joel E. Dimsdale, M.D., Taylor and Francis, Washington, 1980.

Hilberg, Raul, 'The Goldhagen Phenomenon', in *Critical Inquiry*, vol. 23, Summer 1997.

Hoess, Rudolph, *Commandant of Auschwitz: The Autobiography of Rudolph Hoess*, trans. Constantine FitzGibbon, Weidenfeld and Nicolson, London, 1959.

Höhne, Heinz, *The Order of the Death's Head*, trans. Richard Barry, Coward-McCann, New York, 1970.

Joyce, James, *A Portrait of the Artist as a Young Man*, Jonathan Cape, London, 1953.

Kapferer, Bruce, 'Performance and the Structure of Meaning and Experience', in *The Anthropology of Experience*, Victor W. Turner and Edward M. Bruner (eds.), University of Illinois Press, Urbana and Chicago, 1986.

Keegan, John, *The Face of Battle*, Cape, London, 1976.

Kielar, Wieslaw, *Anus Mundi: Five Years in Auschwitz*, [1972] trans. Susanne Flatauer, Penguin Books, Harmondsworth, England, 1981.

Klee, Ernst, Willi Dressen, and Volker Riess (eds.), '*The Good Old Days*': *The Holocaust as Seen by Its Perpetrators and Bystanders*, Free Press, New York, 1988.

Kogon, Eugen, *The Theory and Practice of Hell, (Der SS Staat)* (on Buchenwald), trans. Heinz Norden, Farrar, Straus and Co., New York, 1950.

Krall, Hanna, *Shielding the Flame: An Intimate Conversation with Dr Marek Edelman, the Last Surviving Leader of the Warsaw Ghetto Uprising*, trans. Joanna Stasinska and Lawrence Weschler, Holt, New York, 1986.

Kraus, Ota and Erich Kulka, *The Death Factory: Document on Auschwitz*, [1946] trans. Stephen Jolly, Pergamon Press, London, 1966.

Krausnick, Helmut, Hans Buchheim, Martin Broszat, and Hans-Adolf Jacobsen, *Anatomy of the SS State*, [1965], Walker and Company, New York, 1968.

LaCapra, Dominick, 'Representing the Holocaust: Reflections on the Historians' Debate', in Friedländer, *Probing the Limits of Representation*.

Langbein, Hermann, *Against All Hope: Resistance in the German Concentration Camps 1938–45*, Constable, London, 1994.

Langer, Lawrence, 'The Americanization of the Holocaust on Stage and Screen', in *From Hester Street to Hollywood*, ed. Sarah Blacher Cohen, Indiana University Press, Bloomington, Indiana, 1983.

Langer, Lawrence, *Versions of Survival: The Holocaust and the Human Spirit*, State University of New York Press, Albany, 1982.

Langer, Lawrence, *Holocaust Testimonies: The Ruins of Memory*, Yale University Press, New Haven and London, 1991.

Langer, Lawrence, 'Redefining Heroic Behavior: The Impromptu Self and the Holocaust Experience', in Hayes, *Lessons and Legacies*.

Langer, Lawrence, *Admitting the Holocaust: Collected Essays*, Oxford University Press, Oxford and New York, 1995.

Lanzmann, Claude, *Shoah: An Oral History of the Holocaust*, Pantheon Books, New York, 1985.

Lengyel, Olga, *Five Chimneys* [1947], Panther, New York 1959. (English ed. Avon Books titled *Hitler's Ovens*.)

Levi, Primo, *If This Is a Man* [1947] (also published as *Survival in Auschwitz*), and *The Truce* [1963], (also published as *The Reawakening*), trans. Stuart Wolf, introduction Paul Bailey, with an afterword by the author, Abacus, London, 1987.

Levi, Primo, *The Periodic Table* [1975], trans. Raymond Rosenthal, Schocken Books, New York, 1984.

Levi, Primo, *The Wrench* [1978], trans. William Weaver, Michael Joseph, London, 1988.

Levi, Primo, *Moments of Reprieve: A Memoir of Auschwitz* [1979], trans. Ruth Feldman, Penguin, Harmondsworth, England, 1987.

Levi, Primo, *The Drowned and the Saved* [1986], trans. Raymond Rosenthal, Michael Joseph, London, 1988.

Lifton, Robert Jay, *The Nazi Doctors: A Study in the Psychology of Evil*, Macmillan, London, 1986.

Lukacs, John, *The Hitler of History*, Knopf, New York, 1998.

Maier, Charles S., *The Unmasterable Past: History, Holocaust, and German National Identity*, Harvard University Press, Cambridge, Mass., 1988.

Manguel, Alberto, *News from a Foreign Country Came*, HarperCollins, London, 1991.

Markus, Hazel and Paula Nurius, 'Possible Selves', in *American Psychologist*, no. 41, 1986.

Marrus, Michael R., 'The Use and Misuse of the Holocaust', in Hayes, *Lessons and Legacies*.

Marrus, Michael R., *The Holocaust in History*, University Press of New England, Hanover and London, 1987.

Milgram, Stanley, *Obedience to Authority: An Experimental View*, Tavistock, London, 1974.

Müller, Filip, *Auschwitz Inferno: The Testimony of a Sonderkommando*, with literary collaboration by Helmut Freitag, ed. and trans. Susanne Flatauer, Routledge and Kegan Paul, London and Henley, 1979. (American title: *Eyewitness Auschwitz: Three Years in the Gas Chambers*)

Nabokov, Vladimir, *Bend Sinister* [1947] Weidenfeld and Nicolson, London, 1960.

Nabokov, Vladimir 'Signs and Symbols' and 'Conversation Piece, 1945' in his *The Stories of Vladimir Nabokov*, Vintage International, London, 1997.

Nomberg-Przytyk, Sara, *Auschwitz: True Tales from a Grotesque Land*, Eli Pfefferkorn and David H. Hirsch (eds.), University of North Carolina Press, Chapel Hill and London, 1985.

Nyiszli, Miklos Dr, *Auschwitz: An Eyewitness Account of Mengele's Infamous Death Camp*, trans. Tibere Kremer and Richard Seaver, with a foreword by Bruno Bettelheim, Seaver Books, New York, 1960.

Ozick, Cynthia, *The Shawl*, Alfred A. Knopf, New York, 1988.

Pagis, Dan, *Points of Departure*, trans. Stephen Mitchell, introduction Robert Alter, Jewish Publication Society, Philadelphia, 1981.

Peck, M. S., *People of the Lie: The Hope of Healing Human Evil*, Simon and Schuster, New York, 1983.

Pecora, Vincent P., 'Habermas, Enlightenment, and Anti-Semitism', in Friedländer, *Probing the Limits of Representation*.

Perechodnik, Calel, *Am I a Murderer? Testament of a Jewish Ghetto Policeman*, ed. and trans. Frank Fox, Westview Press, Boulder, Colo., 1996.

Pulzer, Peter, *The Rise of Political Anti-Semitism in Germany and Austria*, Wiley, New York, 1964.

Pulzer, Peter, *Jews and the German State: The Political History of a Minority*, Blackwell, Oxford, 1992.

Richmond, Theo, *Konin: A Quest*, Vintage Books, London, 1996.

Ringelblum, Emmanuel, *Notes from the Warsaw Ghetto*, Schocken, New York, 1958.

Robinson, Jacob, *Psychoanalysis in a Vacuum: Bruno Bettelheim and the Holocaust*, Yad Vashem-YIVO Documentary Projects, New York, 1970.

Rorty, Richard, *Contingency, Irony, and Solidarity*, Cambridge University Press, Cambridge and New York, 1989.

Rosaldo, Michelle, *Knowledge and Passion: Ilongot Notions of Self and Social Life*, Cambridge University Press, Cambridge, 1980.

Rosenbaum Alan S. ed., *Is the Holocaust Unique? Perspectives on Comparative Genocide*, foreword by Israel Charny, Westview Press, Boulder, Colo., 1996.

Rosenfield, Alvin H. and Irving Greenberg (eds.), *Confronting the Holocaust: The Impact of Elie Wiesel*, Indiana University Press, Bloomington and London, 1978.

Rosenfield, Alvin H., 'Popularization and Memory: The Case of Anne Frank', in Hayes, *Lessons and Legacies*.

Rotem, Simha ('Kazik'), *Memoirs of a Warsaw Ghetto Fighter: The Past Within Me*, trans. Barbara Harshav, Yale University Press, New Haven and London, 1994.

Roth, Philip, *Operation Shylock: A Confession*, Vintage Books, London, 1993.

Schechner, Richard, 'Magnitudes of Performance', in *The Anthropology of Experience*, Turner and Bruner (eds.).

Schechner, Richard, *Essays on Performance Theory*, Drama Book Specialists, New York, 1977.

Schechner, Richard, *Between Theater and Anthropology*, University of Pennsylvania Press, Philadelphia, 1985.

Sereny, Gitta, *Into That Darkness: An Examination of Conscience*, McGraw Hill, New York, 1974.

Sereny, Gitta, *Albert Speer: His Battle with Truth*, Macmillan, London, 1995.

Sereny, Gitta, 'My Journey to Speer', in *Granta* 51, August 1995.

Seidman, Naomi, 'Elie Wiesel and the Scandal of Jewish Rage', *Jewish Social Studies*, vol. 3 no. 1, Fall 1996.

The Diary of Dawid Sierakowiak: Five Notebooks from the Lódz Ghetto, ed. Alan Adelson, trans. Kamil Turowski, Oxford University Press, Oxford, 1996.

Sofsky, Wolfgang, *The Order of Terror: The Concentration Camp*, translated by William Templer, Princeton University Press, Princeton, New Jersey, 1997.

Spindler, Arthur, *Outwitting Hitler, Surviving Stalin*, University of New South Wales, Sydney, 1997.

Staub, Ervin, *The Roots of Evil: The Origins of Genocide and Other Group Violence*, Cambridge University Press, Cambridge, 1989.

Sutton, Nina, *Bettelheim: A Life and a Legacy*, trans. David Sharp, Basic Books/HarperCollins, New York, 1995.

Szymborska, Wislawa, *View with a Grain of Sand: Selected Poems*, trans. Stanislaw Baranczak and Clare Cavanagh, Harcourt Brace & Company, New York, 1996.

Thomas, D. M., *The White Hotel*, Victor Gollancz, London, 1981.

Todorov, Tzvetan, *Facing the Extreme: Moral Life in the Concentration Camp*, [1992] trans. Arthur Denner and Abigail Pollak, Metropolitan Books, Henry Holt and Co., New York, 1996.

Trevor-Roper, Hugh, *The Last Days of Hitler*, Macmillan, London [1947] 1987.

Turner, Henry Ashby Jnr., *Hitler's Thirty Days to Power: January 1933*, Addison-Wesley, Reading, Mass., 1996.

Turner, Victor, *From Ritual to Theatre: The Human Seriousness of Play*, Performing Arts Journal Press Inc., New York, 1982.

Turner, Victor W. and Edward M. Bruner (eds.), *The Anthropology of Experience*, University of Illinois Press, Urbana and Chicago, 1986.

Vidal-Naquet, Pierre, *Assassins of Memory: Essays on the Denial of the Holocaust*, trans. and foreword Jeffrey Mehlman, Columbia University Press, New York, 1992.

Vidal-Naquet, Pierre, *The Jews: History, Memory and the Present* [1991], ed. and trans. David Ames Curtis, Columbia University Press, New York, 1996.

Vrba, Rudolph and Alan Bestic, *I Cannot Forgive*, Sidgwick and Jackson, London, 1963.

White, Hayden, 'Historical Emplotment and the Problem of Truth', in Friedländer, *Probing the Limits of Representation*.

Wiesel, Elie, *Night*, trans. Stella Rodway, Macgibbon and Kee, 1960. (originally published as *La Nuit*, Paris, 1958.)

Wiesel, Elie, *From the Kingdom of Memory: Reminiscences*, Simon and Schuster, New York, 1990.

Willenberg, Samuel, *Surviving Treblinka*, Basil Blackwell, Oxford, 1989.

Young, James E., *Writing and Rewriting the Holocaust: Narrative and the Consequences of Interpretation*, Indiana University Press, Bloomington, Indiana, 1988.

Zimbardo, Philip, 'Interpersonal Dynamics in a Simulated Prison', *International Journal of Criminology and Penology*, vol. 1, 1983.

INDEX